Quaker Process

for Friends on the Benches

Mathilda Navias

Quaker Process for Friends on the Benches

Cover design by Barbara Benton. Book design by Alla Podolsky.
Published by Friends Publishing Corporation, Philadelphia, Pennsylvania.

For information, please contact Friends Publishing Corporation, publishers of *Friends Journal*, 1216 Arch Street, Suite 2A, Philadelphia, PA 19107 or email *info@friendsjournal.org*.

ISBN: 978-0-9779511-4-7

Acknowledgments

This whole writing project began when my friend Olwen Pritchard needed help when she was clerking Lake Erie Yearly Meeting's Nominating Committee. Early encouragement, advice, and practical help came from Deborah Fisch, who has mentored me through so much in the Quaker world. Hugh Barbour, long-time friend and Quaker historian, vetted the glossary and then demanded to read and comment on the entire manuscript.

A group of seasoned Friends, many unknown to me, agreed to read and comment on an early draft and provide advice and seasoning. Many thanks go to them: Zach Alexander, Micah Bales, Dick Bellin, Rosemary Coffey, Marty Grundy, Jan Hoffman, Zachary Moon, Beckey Phipps, Sally Rickerman, Trudy Rogers, Susan Smith, Ken Stockbridge, and Virginia Wood. Later comments came from Thomas Taylor. I have ignored some of their advice but taken more, and the book is much better for it.

The Friends I worship with weekly in Bluffton, Ohio, have provided much support and encouragement over the four years the book has been in process. Broadmead Meeting has provided help with clearness, an anchoring committee, and a lively discussion group. I am grateful to the editors and staff at *Friends Journal* for believing that the book is worth sharing with Friends widely, and working to bring that about.

As always, I have benefitted from my husband, Dan Bell, both for his love and support and for his depth of Quaker understanding. When he answers one of my innumerable questions about Quakerism as he understands it, he often comments, "I didn't know that I knew that until you asked."

Contents

Often, the best way to learn a new task is to see how someone else has done the job. In writing this book, it seemed that, in addition to the descriptions in the text, sample minutes and letters would be useful to Friends, particularly those doing them for the first time. Over 35 sample forms, letters, minutes, and reports are available on the web as PDF files. These can be printed and downloaded. In using these materials, Friends are urged to adapt them to their own circumstances and purposes. To edit them, you can copy the text and paste it into a word processing program.

Contents include:

- Best practices for non-face-to-face committee meetings
- Finance: A bequest to be included in a will; year-end receipt and request for information
- First-day school registration form
- Healthcare and final affairs, including sample memorial minutes
- Marriage: Letters; queries for couples; clearness committee report; marriage certificate; more
- Meeting for business; sample guidelines
- Membership: Membership records; letters; report of clearness committee; membership transfers; more
- A minutes for recording a minister
- Nominating slates
- Travel minutes and letters of introduction
- Worship groups and meetings: Establishing and changing status

Introduction

Quaker process is much more than what goes on during business meeting. It encompasses how we interact with one another. It includes how the different pieces of our local meetings—officers, committees, business meeting, individuals, sometimes a pastor—interact. It includes how we deal with leadings, concerns, and discernment, both as individuals and as corporate bodies. It includes how the larger organizations—regional meetings, yearly meetings, and umbrella organizations—interact.

It is my experience that good Quaker process helps us unite in finding God's path forward and in building community, while poor process or misuse can tear us apart. The most painful schisms in Quaker history—the Hicksite-Orthodox split and the Gurneyite-Wilburite split—were marked by blatant misuse of Quaker process and unloving treatment of some Friends by other Friends.

In earlier times, Quaker culture and processes were learned by children and new attenders by observation, osmosis, and mentoring. In meetings where many members come to Quakerism as adults, some sort of conscious guidance would be helpful, but few meetings offer instruction or have written down their practices or developed guidelines or explanations of the week-to-week workings of the monthly and yearly meeting. As a result many Friends and meetings do not understand the practices that have come down to us, how to use them, or the spiritual reasons for them.

I have found among many Friends, both unprogrammed and pastoral, a need for understanding the processes that lead up to and come after a meeting for business as well as what happens during a meeting for business. I have found a lack of understanding of our organizational structures, about the variety of beliefs and practices among Friends, and of established processes for handling various situations.

This book attempts to fill some of those gaps by documenting processes that little has been written about, like threshing sessions and how to prepare for meeting for business; by describing how individuals and worshiping communities can interact with the Spirit in identifying, testing, and supporting leadings; by raising up emerging understandings of eldering and faithful living among Friends; and by addressing new questions that have arisen about the use of technology—websites, e-mail communication, phone, and video conferencing.

Much has been written about Quaker decision making, and some good pamphlets and guides are available about conducting business meetings and on the jobs of the clerk and the recording clerk, so I have touched on these subjects lightly. A list of existing resources may be found in the Reference section.

Just as Friends periodically revise books of discipline—Faith and Practice—we need to periodically evaluate and revise our processes. This book describes ways Friends in both the unprogrammed and pastoral traditions currently operate. Some of these ways of operating date back to early Friends, while others are still new and not quite completely formed. As new conditions arise, new processes may be needed. I think it is useful at times to tell the story of how a process developed as an aid in looking at how processes may develop in the future.

Our task is ongoing: to identify and understand existing Quaker processes; to use them; and to evaluate what is and isn't working well. When a traditional practice isn't working well, we need to discern whether the fault lies in the process or in how we are using it. When a process no longer serves us, we need to look for divine guidance* to help us develop and use processes that fit our current conditions.

This book describes and prescribes how to do Quaker process. It would be incomplete without acknowledging the things that make doing Quaker process possible. First and foremost is mutual submission to God's will. We gather to listen for the

---

* For a discussion of the use of different terms for God and the Divine in this book and among Friends, see the sections on "Speaking of God, Christ, and the Divine" and "Speaking of God, Christ, and the Divine" beginning on page 90.

still, small voice that leads to greater wisdom, better decisions, and loving relationships. As we do this, we come to know one another "in that which is eternal"**—at the deepest level of our being. We listen for the Spirit in worship, in meeting for business, and in one another. It is this seeking together for guidance that lays the foundation for our communal life. It is what makes us distinctively Quaker.

Over the last 40 or so years as a member and active participant in a number of monthly meetings, worship groups, and yearly meetings, I have learned much about ways of doing things that don't work well—through being part of the groups that did it that way—as well as ways of doing things that do work well—through being part of groups that did it another way. It is my hope that this book will provide very practical insight on how to do the work that God calls us to do.

Unlike a book of Faith and Practice, which embodies the practices and discernment of a particular yearly meeting, this book has no claim to authority. This is not a rule book, but a collection of common practices and variations used by contemporary Friends, with guidance from the experience of this author on what has worked particularly well or posed problems. It provides step-by-step instructions on how to use different processes in order to flesh out the bare bones. It can provide a starting place or provide some new ideas for Friends as we discern how God is calling us to be today. I sincerely hope that it is not used as a stick to hit other Friends over the head with ("This is how the book says to do it!"), but as a walking stick to shore up faltering footsteps.

Quakerism can't be done well by following a recipe. Motivations, inspirations, even emotions play a role in doing Quaker process well. The only way to really understand Quaker process is by doing it. The best learning ground is participating in Quaker

** "Friends, meet together and know one another in that which is eternal, which was before the world was." George Fox, Epistle 149 (1657)

process when it is done well.

Ultimately, the goal of this book is to help Friends find and use processes that work well—that bring everyone in the process into unity and loving concern for one another, and that resonate with the greater truths, where ensuing actions are undergirded by the power of the Spirit.

Mathilda Navias
August 2011

Section I: History, Organization, and Relationships

Chapter 1. A Brief History of Quaker Process and Organization

Beginnings

In the 1650s, George Fox along with others in England started what they hoped would be a revival of authentic Christianity. They taught people to "hearken to the voice of God in their own hearts, who was now come to teach His people Himself"[1]—no priest, church building, ritual, or outward authority was necessary. Instead, those who waited patiently in expectation of divine communication would encounter the Present Christ, who would give guidance and power to those who opened their hearts to him. Their core beliefs included the ministry of all believers, a rejection of creeds, an emphasis on inward sacraments over ritual, spiritual equality, and a deep and practical commitment to integrity and pacifism.[2]

This experiential Christianity was found convincing to many, and the movement spread. George Fox's conversion of Margaret Fell, who managed a sizeable estate, gave the movement a headquarters and an able administrator. While many flocked to the new movement, others, particularly church and civic leaders, took exception to it, and large numbers of "Friends of Truth" were imprisoned, fined, or otherwise persecuted.

---

1 George Fox, *Autobiography*

2 *Faith and Practice*, Freedom Friends Church, p. 13

Basic Organization

To care for the needs of individual Friends and maintain order, George Fox and Margaret Fell set up the basic organization that remains to this day. Local worshiping communities usually met twice each week, on Sunday and midweek. Monthly meetings conducted business and made decisions on a local level using group discernment. Quarterly meetings conferred on a regional level, and a yearly meeting brought all the preachers and leaders in a larger area together. This tiered organizational structure has been the glue that has held Quakers together over the years.

Lewis Benson wrote:

> It seemed clear to Fox that Christians had erected ecclesiastical structures that were actually preventing the church from being taught by Christ. From the beginning, Fox was seeking for the true order of God's people in the new covenant. If the Gospel is the good news that Christ is alive and present in the midst of his people as their Teacher, then the Gospel fellowship must be ordered in such a way that the voice of this living teacher can be heard by God's people.
>
> (Lewis Benson, "The Gospel Generates Moral and Fellowship Forming Power")

George Fox affirmed that those gathered in any meeting for business could be guided directly by Christ, but he made local meetings subservient to larger area meetings. Overall responsibility lay with the leaders of the yearly meeting. To early Friends, this structure reflected "Gospel order," which was "an integral part of the revelation received from their Living Teacher. Friends understood that individuals could misinterpret leadings, fall into pride or self-will, run off into notions. The discernment of the broader community was a surer guide to Truth. Fox even put his own leadings under the discipline of the corporate body."[3]

All of this was tied together by the sending of copious letters, and by leaders who traveled both to preach and to visit one

---

[3] Elizabeth Cazden, *Fellowships, Conferences, and Associations: The Limits of the Liberal Quaker Reinvention of Meeting Polity*, pp. 4-5

another. Quaker preachers, called "ministers," often traveled in pairs. A committee in London called Meeting for Sufferings was set up to organize help for the large number of Quakers who were imprisoned or had their possessions taken, and also to look after their families.

Quietism

Quaker historian Tom Hamm writes of the 1690s, "With the passing of the first two generations of Quaker ministers and leaders, Friends settled into an age of what historians have labeled Quietism. They became more inward looking, more focused on the maintenance of good internal order."[4] Over time, rules became even stricter. "After 1740, a new generation of young Quaker leaders emerged. . . . These Friends saw reform, a tightening of discipline and further protections from the blandishments of an enticing world, as required."[5] "The reformers . . . tightened the discipline, the body of Quaker rules and regulations for corporate and personal conduct: giving more attention to plain dress and speech, moving against those who attended services of other denominations, and especially dropping from membership, or 'disowning,' Friends who married 'out of meeting.'"[6] The role of elders was developed: "Friends who were charged with nurturing ministers and silencing those whose speaking in meeting was not edifying."[7] Quietism prevailed both in England and in North America.

Migration

Under Quietism, Quakers were a clannish lot. Tom Hamm describes the patterns of migration and establishing new meetings in the U.S. "The Quaker impulse toward separation from the world and the need for oversight of members encouraged Friends to cluster in certain neighborhoods. . . . Even when they spread

---

4 Thomas D. Hamm, *The Quakers in America*, p. 29
5 Ibid., pp. 31-32
6 Ibid., p. 32
7 Ibid., p. 30

west, they continued to settle near each other in a few places."[8]

When members of a meeting moved to a new part of the country, new meetings they formed were established under the care of the members' original meeting. When a new yearly meeting was established, it was done by the parent yearly meeting. It was as if the parent meeting was a plant that sent out runners under the ground, and the new meetings popped up out of the ground at a distance, but remained vitally connected to the parent.

Schisms and Branches

Quakers have not always followed our own carefully worked out business processes. Beginning in the 1820s, Quakers in the U.S. underwent a series of schisms that resulted in separate, competing yearly meetings, each claiming to be the only authentic Quaker body in its area.[9] The first major schism, called "The Great Separation" or "the Hicksite-Orthodox Separation," began in Philadelphia Yearly Meeting in 1827. A struggle was going on between proponents of the traditional Quaker emphasis on an Inner Light as a direct, unmediated experience of the Divine and Orthodox Friends who had taken up evangelical beliefs about the Bible and atonement that were current in sophisticated society. Relations between Friends became ugly when Orthodox Friends tried to silence Elias Hicks, a Long Island Friends minister who traveled and preached widely among Friends. In the ensuing schism, rural Friends largely sided with Hicks. A contributing factor in polarizing Friends were the autocratic actions of Philadelphia Yearly Meeting's presiding clerk, who took it upon himself to pronounce what he felt to be the will of God in the face of vociferous opposition from many in the meeting.[10] Philadelphia Hicksites were also outraged by the Orthodox body's use of ecclesiastical machinery to try to enforce

---

8 Thomas D. Hamm, *The Quakers in America*, p. 38

9 Drawing adapted from Quaker Tree by Ed Nicholson, found in Wilmer A. Cooper, *A Living Faith*, p. 165

10 Thomas D. Hamm, *The Quakers in America*, p. 98

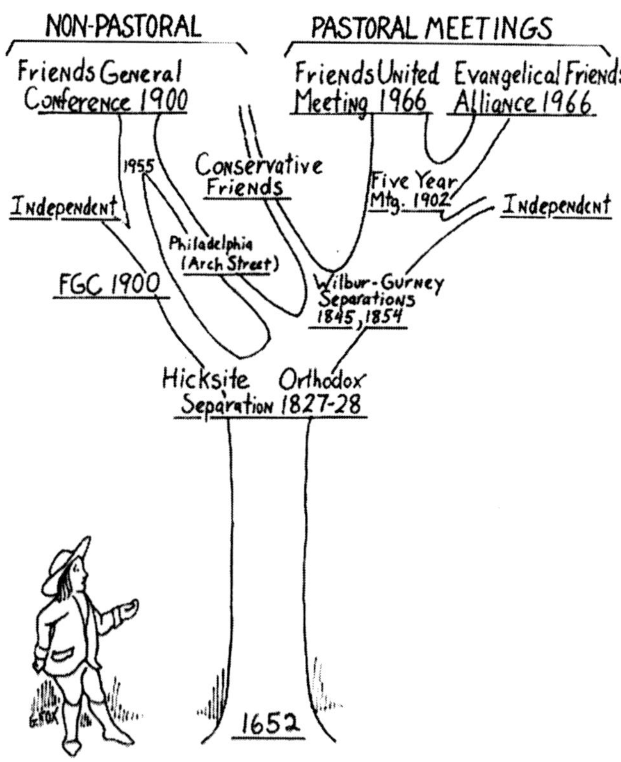

doctrinal uniformity.[11] The split among Philadelphia Friends spread to other yearly meetings.

In the early 1840s, the Orthodox branch split between evangelicals who stood with Joseph John Gurney, a Quaker evangelist from England, and those who stood with John Wilbur of Rhode Island, who wanted to maintain quietist Quakerism. Gurney emphasized Scriptural authority and favored working closely with other Christian groups. Wilbur and other Friends defended the authority of the Holy Spirit as primary, and worked to prevent the dilution of Friends' tradition of Spirit-led ministry. New England Friends dissolved Wilbur's monthly meeting and then disowned him. Outraged by this blatant misuse of power, in 1845 Wilbur's supporters left, taking about ten percent of

[11] Elizabeth Cazden, *Fellowships, Conferences, and Associations*, p. 10

New England Yearly Meeting with them.[12] Over the next several decades, a number of Wilburite-Gurneyite separations occurred.

A branch of Quakers independent from any existing body was unintentionally started by Quaker ministers Joel and Hannah Bean in San Jose, California, in the 1880s. The Beans had moved from Iowa to San Jose, where they established a Friends worship group. Tensions between the Beans and Orthodox Friends in Iowa ultimately led to Iowa Yearly Meeting disowning the Beans and rescinding their recording as ministers. The Beans did something new: the meeting they had started, called the College Park Association, went ahead without permission from any larger body, incorporated, built a meetinghouse, and behaved in many ways like a monthly meeting. Friends associated with the College Park Association went on to found three independent yearly meetings in the western United States: Pacific, North Pacific, and Intermountain.

A separate independent meeting movement arose in the early 1900s due mainly to increased geographic mobility among Friends. Quaker teachers or students transplanted to a college town with no unprogrammed meeting nearby often looked for other Quakers interested in holding a silent meeting for worship. A cluster of a few families or committed individuals would start a worship group, which might blossom into an established meeting. From Cambridge, Massachusetts, to Ann Arbor, Michigan, and in dozens of smaller communities in between, college meetings took firm root in the 1930s.[13] They were often joined by "participants in Civilian Public Service Camps and American Friends Service Committee work camps, seekers who had read Rufus Jones and were looking for a group that embodied his vision, and a high proportion of college professors."[14] Retirees and other Quaker migrants in some of the southern states played a similar role in seeding new meetings. These meetings do not trace their

[12] Thomas D. Hamm, *The Quakers in America*, pp. 48-49

[13] Deborah Haines, "FGC Friends: Growing and Changing"

[14] Elizabeth Cazden, *Fellowships, Conferences, and Associations: The Limits of the Liberal Quaker Reinvention of Meeting Polity*, p. 11

beginnings to one of the 19th century Quaker branches; they are neither Hicksite, Orthodox, Gurneyite, or Wilburite. Virtually all practice unprogrammed worship. Rather than following the traditional model of new meetings being established by parent meetings, these groups were more like mushrooms that pop up on the lawn under the right conditions, seeded there by spores carried on the wind.

In the 1860s and '70s, an interdenominational Wesleyan holiness movement swept the U.S.[15] The holiness movement had a wide influence among western Quakers, especially among California, Oregon, Kansas, Iowa, and Indiana Evangelical Friends. In the east, it also influenced Friends in New York and North Carolina. A young Quaker minister, David B. Updegraff, wrote, I "joined with others in imploring that . . . we might unite in preaching the Gospel and in getting converts to Jesus. In the providence of God such counsel prevailed,"and Friends in Ohio and Indiana began holding Wesleyan-style revival meetings.[16] With the influx of huge numbers of converts, these Gurneyite Friends found that they needed to provide pastoral care and teach converts about Quakerism and Christian life. At first, this need was met by volunteers, but soon meetings began "releasing" ministers from their need to earn a living in order to serve full-time. Unintentionally, a pastoral ministry became established among Gurneyite Friends.

Most historians identify four current branches of Quakerism: Conservative, Liberal, Pastoral, and Evangelical. There is a great deal of variation, especially within Liberal and Pastoral Friends, and there are individuals and meetings that qualify for more than one category. Assigning Quakers to categories is useful only for broad generalizations.

The features that distinguish the branches include:

- *Manner of worship.* Is worship largely unprogrammed and

---

[15] Holiness Christians do not consider a person fully saved without an experience of "Second Blessing" or perfect holiness, separate from and following conversion, a sudden infusion of love.

[16] Thomas D. Hamm, *The Quakers in America*, p. 51

organized on the basis of inward listening to God's direct and unmediated leading, or is worship led by a pastor and at least partly planned?

- *Theology.* Is mainstream or evangelical Christian theology central to the worshiping community or is a range of theology welcome?
- *Where authority lies.* Do Friends place a strong emphasis on the authority of Scripture, on the Inward Light, and/or on Quaker tradition and the discernment of the meeting community? Are smaller bodies subordinate to larger bodies?
- *Evangelism.* Do Friends see converting others to Christ as an important part of their mission?
- *Affiliation.* Do Friends affiliate with the Evangelical Friends Church International, Friends United Meeting, Friends General Conference, none of the above, or more than one of the above?

Arguments over which of the branches is most authentically "Quaker" sometimes arise, with the different branches pointing to different aspects of early Quakerism as the roots for their own faith and practice. The truth is that all contemporary Quaker branches have moved away from early Quakerism in significant areas.

Conservative Friends

These are Friends who wish to "conserve" the traditional faith and practice of Friends. There are Conservative yearly meetings in Iowa, Ohio, and North Carolina. They practice "waiting worship" (worship based on silence) and are pacifist. They acknowledge the authority of Christ within, of Scripture, and of Friends tradition and the discernment of the meeting community.

They maintained the traditional Quaker distinctives of plain dress and language much longer than other branches of Friends, and a few still do. Conservative Friends do not have an affiliating organization. Interested Conservative Friends gather every other year for sharing under the initiative of Ohio Yearly Meeting (Conservative) at Barnesville, Ohio. Other Conservative gatherings take place from time to time in various locations.

Ohio Yearly Meeting is uniformly Christ-centered, while North Carolina Yearly Meeting accepts some theological diversity, and Iowa Yearly Meeting includes universalists. The smallest branch, Conservative Friends constitute about .003 percent of Friends worldwide.[17]

Liberal Friends

Liberal Friends come out of a tradition of liberal theology, which accepts both direct experience and reason informed by learning as authoritative. They practice worship based on silence and traditionally emphasize the authority of the Inward Light. They also see the discernment of the meeting community as important. They include members with a wide range of theology, including universalists and non-theists. They are usually socially progressive, and are often active in working for social justice and peace. Currently, a majority of members join Friends as adults.

Unprogrammed Friends, except those in the Conservative tradition, constitute the Liberal branch of Friends. This branch of Friends is also referred to as "liberal unprogrammed," "unprogrammed," "non-pastoral" (by pastoral Friends) and in North America "FGC," even though not all are affiliated with Friends General Conference, a service organization based in Philadelphia. Worldwide, there are Liberal Friends in Europe, Russia, Australia, New Zealand, South Africa, Mexico, Central America, Egypt, Hong Kong, Japan, Korea, Lebanon, Palestine, Canada, and the U.S. Liberal Friends constitute about 11 percent of Friends worldwide. [18]

Pastoral Friends

Pastoral Friends hold programmed or semi-programmed worship led by a pastor. Traditionally, the service includes a time of "open worship" (worship based in silence). The degree of programming varies widely. Almost all are explicitly Christian.

---

[17] Figures from Friends World Committee for Consultation, 2005

[18] Figures from FWCC, 2005

They are active in service and missionary work. This branch of Friends is also called "programmed" (by non-programmed Friends) or "FUM" (Friends United Meeting) for the international Quaker organization based in Richmond, Indiana, with which they are affiliated. Begun in 1902 as Five Years Meeting, throughout its history FUM has experienced internal conflict and the breaking away of various yearly meetings that see the core group as either too liberal or too evangelical in theology. It contains the widest spectrum of theology of any of the branches, as it includes evangelicals, fundamentalists, orthodox Christians, and some Unitarian-leaning members. Several mostly Liberal yearly meetings affiliate with both FGC and FUM, thereby bringing the whole range of FGC theology into play as well.

Pastoral Friends have supported missionary work around the globe. Currently, there are Pastoral Friends in Kenya, Uganda, Tanzania, India, Sri Lanka, Belize, Cuba, El Salvador, Jamaica, Mexico, and the U.S. They make up about 49 percent of Friends worldwide,[19] and continue to grow in east Africa and other mission fields.

Evangelical Friends

Most Friends worldwide are evangelical in the sense that they seek to spread the Christian Gospel. Evangelical Friends as a branch of Quakerism began around 1926 when several yearly meetings pulled out of FUM. An umbrella organization was later organized, currently known as Evangelical Friends Church International (EFCI).

Evangelical Friends are similar to other evangelical Christian bodies, with a strong emphasis on atonement and the authority of Scripture. Worship is programmed and under the direction of a pastor, and revivals are held on a regular basis. Most refer to their organization as the Friends Church rather than the Religious Society of Friends, and refer to themselves as Friends rather than Quakers. They are sometimes fundamentalist, not always pacifist, usually socially conservative, and strongly mis-

[19] Figures from FWCC, 2005

sion focused.[20] Members of EFCI make up about 40 percent of Friends worldwide.[21] EFCI today includes churches in 24 countries, including parts of Africa, India, Asia, Europe, Mexico, and Central and South America.

Reunification, Cooperation, and Convergence

In the mid-1900s, several yearly meetings that had gone their separate ways in the Great Separation came back together to form what are called united yearly meetings: Baltimore, Canadian, New England, and New York. Most of these now include a few pastoral meetings alongside the unprogrammed ones.

Friends World Committee for Consultation (FWCC) is an international organization that encourages consultation among all the branches of Friends. It was organized in 1937 to draw Friends from all branches into a worldwide fellowship, "to act in a consultative capacity to promote better understanding among Friends the world over, particularly by the encouragement of joint conferences and intervisitation, the collection and circulation of information about Quaker literature and other activities directed towards that end."[22] It hosts international conferences and encourages visitation and discussion among the different kinds of Friends. It sponsors service projects around the world and supports Quaker United Nations Offices (QUNO) in New York City and Geneva, Switzerland. Its central offices are in London.

Outside of FWCC there are various ongoing interactions between Friends from different branches. Earlham School of Religion in Richmond, Indiana, a Quaker seminary founded in 1960, encourages students from all branches of Friends to apply. Its alumni can be found in positions of leadership in EFCI, FUM, and FGC.[23]

---

[20] *Faith and Practice*, Freedom Friends Church, p. 14

[21] Figures from FWCC, 2005

[22] Quoted in *Meeting the Spirit: An Introduction to Quaker Beliefs and Practices* by Hans Weening, p. 22

[23] Thomas D. Hamm, *The Quakers in America*, p. 150

For almost three decades, under the leadership of Peggy Senger Parsons and Margery Post Abbot, there have been periodic gatherings of Friends from North Pacific Yearly Meeting, one of the most liberal in North America, and its Evangelical neighbor, Northwest Yearly Meeting. They have succeeded in overcoming some deep-seated hostility and suspicion.[24] In 2005, a World Gathering of Young Friends was held in Lancaster, England. Largely energized by that experience, several smaller conferences for young adult Friends of all branches have been held in the U.S.

In the U.S. and Canada, a phenomenon called "Convergent Friends" has arisen recently. The name alludes to an affinity for both Conservative Friends and the Emergent Church. The Emergent Church is "a conversation" currently taking place particularly among young Christian leaders which looks beyond denominational boundaries. Convergent Friends are interested in and willing to enter into shared experiences with Friends from across the spectrum.

Organization, Authority, and Business Process Today Across the Branches

Organization and Authority of Meetings

The basic organization established by early Quakers consisting of local worshiping communities and monthly, regional, and yearly meetings for business remain today among all Friends, with a few modifications. While the terms for local worshiping groups vary in different parts of the world, and traditional quarterly meetings have given way to a variety of "half-yearly" or simply "area" meetings or have been phased out, the basic organization of monthly and yearly meetings remains in use throughout the Quaker world today.

The amount of authority assigned to larger bodies varies. Tom Hamm notes, "The Quaker structure that emerged in the 1660s was essentially presbyterian, with monthly meetings subordinate to quarterly meetings and quarterly meetings in turn subordinate

---

[24] Thomas D. Hamm, *The Quakers in America*, p. 150

to the yearly meeting. Yearly meetings in the Orthodox tradition [Pastoral Friends, Evangelicals, and Conservatives] continue this structure."[25] In the 1900s, Liberal yearly meetings largely chose to renounce power of one tier over another. Instead, monthly meetings were viewed as autonomous, while regional and yearly meetings were considered useful groupings for common work and fellowship. Friends United Meeting used to claim some authority over its member yearly meetings, but no longer does, while Friends General Conference never has.

Authority of Monthly Meetings over Their Members

Among Pastoral, Evangelical, and Conservative Friends, oversight of individual members within a monthly meeting is seen as a necessary function. Traditionally, this was the role of overseers and, to some extent, elders. Many Pastoral and Conservative meetings still appoint elders, overseers, or a combined committee and assign them some measure of authority over individual members. The following statement is typical:

> Elders of the meeting shall . . . deal lovingly and firmly with Friends whose life and witness may hinder the fellowship of the meeting.
>
> (Wilmington Yearly Meeting *Faith and Practice*, p. 61)

Liberal Friends in the last half of the 1900s tended to resist anything that hinted at authority by the group over the individual. What had been committees of "Ministry and Counsel" or "Ministry and Oversight" have been renamed "Ministry and Nurture" or "Worship and Care." In *Fellowships, Conferences, and Associations: The Limits of the Liberal Quaker Reinvention of Meeting Polity*, Betsy Cazden gives a historical perspective:

> After 1827 the Philadelphia Hicksites reacted against the Orthodox body's use of ecclesiastical machinery to enforce doctrinal uniformity, and tried to build a structure that would support individual spiritual growth and encourage participation of "all who felt the spirit of God within them." They envisioned a loosely-knit structure with weak central organization, diffused power with frequent rotation of

[25] Thomas D. Hamm, *The Quakers in America*, p. 136

> officers, and authority centered in the general membership rather than an elite class of ministers and elders. . . .
>
> With these changes came a shift in the relationship of individuals to their monthly meetings. As Philip Benjamin has remarked, religious liberty took on such importance for Philadelphia Hicksite Friends that they "even went so far as to try to practice it themselves," embracing theological diversity, firmly resisting anything that was viewed as an attempt to force one person's views upon others, and trusting tolerance and charity to smooth over any resulting conflicts.
>
> (Elizabeth Cazden, *Fellowships, Conferences, and Associations*, p. 10)

This has led to problems, however. There is movement among Liberal Friends to return to some measure of authority of monthly meetings over members and attenders, though not of regional or yearly meetings over monthly meetings. This has been partly fueled by some meetings' struggles to come to terms with having a child molester in their midst and the need to exert some control over the situation.

There is also a strong movement in some quarters for a renewed emphasis on mutual accountability, the recognition and exercise of spiritual gifts, and of more deliberate mentoring and building up of members' spiritual lives. These can be seen in the development of spiritual formation programs in several Liberal yearly meetings and in renewed interest in elders and traveling ministers. Some of this energy is coming from young adult Friends, especially as they have gathered with their peers from the different branches of Quakers.

Business Process

The basic Quaker processes for conducting business appear to remain very similar across the spectrum of Quakerism today. Tom Hamm comments,

> If Friends have taken traditional ideas of worship and ministry in radically different directions in the last century, they have shown considerably more unity in holding to old ways of decision making. A Quaker business meeting, what previously would have been

> called a meeting for discipline, is much the same among pastoral and unprogrammed, Evangelical and Liberal Friends, albeit . . . with some regional variations. . . .
>
> Friends of all persuasions still generally try to adhere to the traditional Quaker method of not voting or submitting to the decisions of a leader but instead seeking unity through discussion, prayer, and waiting.
>
> (Thomas D. Hamm, *The Quakers in America*, p. 95 and p. 119)

The business processes described in this book, especially in the chapter on meeting for business, are found in use by Friends worldwide.

Chapter 2: Officers and Committees

> The essential purpose of religious organization is to foster and encourage the spiritual life and to bring the human spirit into intimate relation with the Divine Spirit.
>
> (Ohio Valley Yearly Meeting *Faith and Practice*, p. 14)

Quaker process happens within the framework of our organization. The particular organization we use is informed just as much by God's guidance as the processes we employ. In setting up monthly, regional, and yearly meetings—in establishing clerks, committees, and various decision making bodies—Friends throughout our history have aimed for Gospel order—a right ordering of our meetings in ways informed by and compatible with divine order.

Officers and Other Appointees

Overview of the Roles of Officers

Officers are servants of the meeting. Each monthly meeting appoints a clerk, a treasurer, and whatever other officers it finds useful. These usually include a recording clerk and a recorder (called in some branches a statistician). Among Conservative Friends, where the clerk writes the minutes, there is usually an assistant clerk instead of a recording clerk. Some meetings have co-clerks or have other shared positions, either on an ongoing basis or from time to time. The clerk is sometimes called the "presiding" clerk to make it clear which clerk is being referred to.

Appointments are made through a nominating process (see Chapter 9: *The Nominating Process*). The following descriptions of the roles of officers are overviews. For more details on conducting business, see the sections on "The Recording Clerk and Minutes" on page 215179 and "The Role of the Recording Clerk" on page 183.

The Clerk

The clerk:

- Prepares the agenda and presides at business meetings.
- Is responsible for seeing that any follow-up action is carried out and reported back to the meeting.
- Is responsible for seeing that a full and correct record of all proceedings is kept.
- Signs all official papers and minutes; if there are both a clerk and an assistant or recording clerk, both usually sign the minutes.
- Writes minutes for sojourning members, travel minutes, and letters of introduction, as well as endorsing minutes or letters of visiting Friends (see the Glossary for brief descriptions of these terms or see "Sojourning Membership" on page 260 and "Travel Minutes, Minutes of Religious Service, and Letters of Introduction" on "Worship Sharing" on page 79156).
- Serves as the liaison with the regional and yearly meeting.
- Speaks on behalf of the meeting when a spokesperson is required.

In addition to responsibilities for the business meeting, the clerk usually handles the meeting mail. The clerk often acts as a representative of the meeting in arranging for such things as bank accounts and answering questions about the meeting from outside groups. If the meeting does not have trustees, the clerk may serve as the meeting's legal representative. Other members of the meeting may take on any or all of these tasks as asked by the meeting.

The role of the clerk does not include responsibility for any other functions. While many meetings have a tradition of the clerk being responsible for such things as setting up the room for worship, closing the worship, making announcements, or welcoming new people, these are functions that may be undertaken by other members of the meeting. The clerk's job is plenty big enough; it is good for others to share in the work and responsibility for the meeting.

Speaking for the meeting

> Your office [of clerk] gives you some authority to act or speak for the meeting. Beware of exceeding your authority. Use discretion and consult Friends of experience in deciding which matters may conveniently be handled by yourself and which need reference to the meeting.
>
> (Baltimore Yearly Meeting *Faith and Practice*, p. 74)

One of the roles of a meeting clerk is to speak on behalf of the meeting when needed. There needs to be a very clear distinction made between acting in an approved capacity and acting on one's own initiative. For instance, if the clerk of a monthly meeting writes a letter to the editor of a newspaper, unless the meeting has approved the letter, the clerk should sign it with his or her own name with no reference to the meeting. If, on the other hand, a meeting writes and approves a letter to the editor, it should go out over the clerk's name and the designation, "Clerk, such-and-such Quaker meeting of the Religious Society of Friends" or "on behalf of such-and-such Quaker meeting."

Qualifications for a clerk

The clerk should be a member of the meeting who has the confidence of its membership and who, in turn, has a real respect and warm regard for its individual members and attenders. The clerk should faithfully attend meeting for worship.

> A clerk must be experienced and comfortable with the process of knowing and trusting God's faithfulness—that's the most important qualification. . . .
>
> Clerks serve best if they have a disposition that feels comfortable with ambiguity and process. It will help greatly if they can avoid feeling they have to fix or save situations. They must have the capacity to deal with dissent without getting emotionally caught up in it.
>
> (Lon Fendall, Jan Wood, and Bruce Bishop, *Practicing Discernment Together*, pp. 85-86)

The clerk should be spiritually sensitive so that the meeting for business may be helped to come under the guidance of the Spirit. An understanding of Quaker business process is essential.

The clerk should be able to comprehend, evaluate, and state clearly and concisely an item of business or concern. In order to gather the sense of the meeting, the clerk needs to be able to listen receptively to what is said.

The Recording Clerk

In most meetings a recording clerk takes the minutes for business meetings. In some meetings the presiding clerk takes the minutes. The latter is the practice in Conservative yearly meetings as well as in Britain Yearly Meeting.

For more information, see "The Role of the Recording Clerk" on page 183.

The Treasurer, the Finance Committee, and Meeting Finances

See also "Tips on how to Give a Financial Report without Having Friends' Eyes Glaze Over" on page 195.

The treasurer is responsible for:

- Receiving and disbursing funds as directed by the meeting.
- Maintaining accurate financial records.
- Making deposits in a timely fashion.
- Reporting to the meeting as requested.

In some meetings, a routine financial report is requested for each monthly business meeting; some ask for a report every quarter. Once a year, a complete written report including both income and expenses and a balance sheet showing assets and liabilities should be presented. The treasurer is a servant of the meeting, advising and carrying out the decisions made by the meeting but leaving decisions to the meeting itself. It is good practice for a meeting to plan ahead for the timely release of its treasurer, possibly appointing an assistant who can work with the current treasurer to learn the task.

The treasurer is an ex officio[26] member of the Finance Com-

---

[26] Ex officio is Latin for "by virtue of official position." Being an ex officio member means that whoever is treasurer is a member of the committee.

mittee and works closely with the committee. The Finance Committee is responsible for raising funds and preparing an annual budget for the consideration of the meeting. In setting up a checking account, it is wise to have more than one person who can sign checks. Finance Committees are often asked to recommend where to put any funds that the meeting expects to hold for a while or to research and bring recommendations on other financial matters. The Finance Committee should arrange for an audit or review of the accounts every year.

Members of the meeting are expected to contribute as they are able to meet the financial obligations agreed on by the group. This is voluntary and usually the amount of individual contributions is not publicized. In many meetings, the treasurer or the Finance Committee sends out an annual letter to members and attenders giving them details on the budget and asking for contributions. The letter may also list the amount of the household's contributions in the previous year. This serves as a reminder and helps Friends decide how much to contribute.

Most unprogrammed meetings do not publicize how to make contributions except in such an annual letter and occasionally at a business meeting. Some have a "Donation Box" in a public area. Some routinely announce after worship how to make donations.

Qualifications for a treasurer

The treasurer should be a member of the meeting. He or she should be comfortable working with numbers, but neither accounting skills nor a computer are necessary for most monthly meeting finances. The treasurer should be able to work in a timely fashion, be honest, and be willing to act as directed by the meeting.

The Recorder or Statistician

The recorder, called by some meetings a statistician, keeps a record of memberships and transfers of membership, births, deaths, and marriages. If a meeting hasn't recorded divorces in the past, it might start doing so. It is good practice for the recorder to report to the meeting once a year. The recorder also sends an annual report to the yearly meeting. A copy of this should go into the monthly meeting's minutes.

Generally, these records are kept on paper rather than in a computer. Acid-free paper is widely available, is more fail-safe than electronic records, does not expose Friends' personal information to possible public exposure, is more portable, and can be archived. The recorder may keep a duplicate set of records in a second location or a fire-safe place to protect them against possible loss.

Other Positions

In addition to officers, the meeting may have a newsletter editor, a web master, or other positions that serve the needs of the meeting. There is no general term for these positions.

Paid Staff

Most unprogrammed meetings have no paid staff, but some large meetings hire a secretary or youth worker. Most pastoral meetings pay their pastor, but there are a few that function with volunteer pastors. Pastoral meetings which can afford it sometimes hire, in addition to a pastor, youth leaders, an organist, a choir director, a religious education supervisor, or other staff. See "Testing a Leading or Concern in Community" on page 140.

Committees

> Perhaps we view our participation in Quaker committees the way many of us view housework: it is not particularly fun, but it has to be done. And yet—what potential our committee hours together hold! We can get to know each other and each other's families much better than we can at meeting on Sunday; we can be more relaxed and informal. In committee meetings, there is time to make jokes and laugh, time to share. We can give and receive nurture and appreciation, and can inspire each other to develop a grand vision together. It is in committees that we do the actual creative work of shaping the building blocks of our meeting community, laying them in place, anchoring them together. What satisfaction

to see the results of our work together and know that what we have created is very good!

(Marty Walton, *The Meeting Experience: Practicing Quakerism in Community*, p. 25)

What They Are

Quakers appoint committees to perform functions more easily carried out by a small group than the entire body. This can be either hands-on tasks or research, reflection, and discernment—"seasoning." Meetings set up, change, and lay down committees according to the meeting's needs and concerns. It is a rare meeting outside the pastoral tradition that has any paid staff. Instead, the bulk of the work is done by committees.

Meetings appoint committees to concentrate on tasks they want done. Committees:

- Perform specific tasks.
- Think through issues.
- Come up with options or recommendations to present to the full meeting for consideration and decision making.

Among Pastoral Friends, while a certain amount of work and particular responsibilities are given to the pastor and any other paid staff, typically more of the congregation actively participate in the ongoing work of the church through serving on committees and participating in business meeting than in other Protestant denominations.

What a committee is called, how it is organized, and what responsibilities it has need to be defined by the meeting as a whole. In addition to whatever ongoing responsibilities a committee has, the meeting may from time to time ask a committee to take on a particular short-term task.

While a committee exists to perform particular tasks, committee work also offers the opportunity for its members to get to know one another and to learn Quaker process through participating in it. Friends have found that incorporating fellowship, personal sharing, and explicit discussion of Quaker process helps the members of a committee work together and also builds up the life of the meeting as a whole.

It is helpful to remember that a committee serves best by looking constantly for divine guidance in all that it is does.

> So many of us sit on secular committees which have an outward resemblance to those of Friends, that it becomes very easy to transfer their methods, attitudes and goals to Friends' committees.... Friends [are] at risk of eroding their life as Friends by assimilating to the secular values of efficiency, decisiveness, effectiveness, and dispatch.
>
> (Patricia Loring, *Spiritual Responsibility in the Meeting for Business*)

Core Committees

Some yearly meetings require monthly meetings to have certain core committees and have descriptions of these in their Discipline or Book of Procedure. For instance, Baltimore Yearly Meeting requires meetings to have a Nominating Committee, Ministry and Counsel, and Overseers. In Western Yearly Meeting, each monthly meeting is expected to appoint a corresponding set of boards and committees to the ones the yearly meeting has.[27] Other yearly meetings, such as North Pacific, leave it up to each monthly meeting.[28]

Descriptions of Some Common Committees

Quaker committees fall into two general types: functional and concerns. Functional committees are entities like Buildings and Grounds, Ministry and Counsel, Finances, and Pastoral Care. They help the group function. Concerns are things like Peace and Social Justice, Race Relations, and Earthcare. They deal with concerns that the group as a whole wishes to address.

Ministry and Counsel

Other names used: Ministry and Nurture, Ministry and Oversight, Care and Visitation, Worship and Pastoral Care, Ministry and Worship, Clearness and Care. In the cause of simplicity, this

---

[27] Western Yearly Meeting *Faith and Practice*, Part III, Committees and Boards, Monthly Meeting Boards

[28] North Pacific Yearly Meeting *Faith and Practice*, p. 63

text uses "Ministry and Counsel."

This committee has two areas of responsibility: one for fostering the quality of worship, vocal ministry,[29] and the spiritual life of the meeting; and the other for pastoral care of members. Some meetings have two separate committees, one traditionally called Ministry and Counsel and the other Overseers.

Advancement and Outreach

Other names used: Membership and Outreach, Mission (among Pastoral meetings).

"Advancement" refers to nurturing existing meeting members; "outreach" refers to anything that gives the meeting visibility in the community or carries the message of Quakerism to those in the community and invites them to worship with Friends.

Religious Education

Other names used: First-day school, Adult Religious Education, Christian Education.

This can be a committee with oversight solely of children's programs (First-day school), of both children's and adult programs, or (in a meeting without children) solely of adult programs. Larger meetings may have separate committees for children's and adult programs.

Adult programs often consist of discussion groups, but can encompass a great variety of activities, including worship sharing, outdoor activities, Bible study, small group sharing, fellowship in members' homes, and lectures.

Children's programs in unprogrammed meetings are usually held during part or all of meeting for worship, and vary widely depending on the number and ages of children, whether they come to meeting regularly or sporadically, the physical spaces available, and adults' interest and willingness to spend time with children rather than participate in worship. Some meetings have teen groups and intergenerational activities. In Pastoral meetings, children's programs are generally held after worship.

---

[29] Spoken messages given during worship

Peace and Social Concerns

Other names used: Community Relations, Social Action, Witness in the World, Peace and Social Action, Peace and Social Justice.

Friends are sometimes confused about the role of this committee. Is the committee's task to "do" social justice in whatever ways the individual members are able? Is the committee's task to serve as a think tank for the larger group? To collect and disseminate information and ideas? To bring political petitions to business meeting for endorsement? What is it that the meeting wants the committee to do on its behalf?

While members of Peace and Social Concerns committees are often activists, actions taken by individuals on their own initiative are not a part of committee work. Friend Fry may lead workshops on nonviolence in prisons, Friend Cadbury may work on issues of slavery in the manufacture of chocolate, and Friend Janeway may have concerns about pollution by a local manufacturer. None of these are committee concerns unless or until the committee as a whole agrees to take them up or the meeting directs the committee to work on these issues. Until then, discussion of these activities during committee meetings can serve to support and nurture the individuals' work, but does not constitute committee work.

Generally, the work of a committee of concern is to seek divine guidance and, when led, to provide information to the meeting and ask if the body as a whole is led to engage with a concern. The committee might invite everyone in the meeting to participate in a monthly letter-writing campaign based on Friends Committee on National Legislation recommendations. The committee might bring in a speaker to present a program to the meeting on slavery among cocoa workers in Northern Africa and ask Friends to consider not buying chocolate tied to such slavery. It might research and bring to the meeting a recommendation to change how the meetinghouse is heated to be more energy efficient.

Trustees

Any meeting that accepts substantial funds for investment or holds real property (buildings or grounds) should look into incorporating and appointing trustees. If the meeting does not incorporate, it will still need to appoint trustees to hold title and execute legal business pertaining to property or securities held by the meeting. Trustees should be appointed in accordance with applicable state laws and for specified terms.

The trustees, like other committees of the meeting, are selected by the meeting and are expected to act for the whole meeting in carrying out their responsibilities under the law. Thus, while trustees must be conscious of their obligation to preserve the assets of the meeting, they must also be continuously sensitive to the spirit of the meeting and its wish to fulfill the social testimonies of Friends. The meeting, in turn, should be sensitive to the legal responsibilities of trustees which can, in certain circumstances, make them personally liable for actions taken in the name of the meeting. For instance, some meetings and Quaker organizations have found themselves in legal trouble when they have failed to withhold the portion of an employee's federal taxes that would pay for war.

Trustees holding gifts in trust must see that these are used as designated by the donors. If, however, these purposes become obsolete, the trustees may seek advice from the meeting. Baltimore Yearly Meeting has a set of specific advices to meetings and those proposing to leave property to meetings in their wills.

No meeting property may be distributed among individual members. If the meeting ceases to exist, its property passes to the regional or yearly meeting in most cases.

Other Committees

Other committees often encountered include: Building and Grounds, Nominating, Hospitality, and Library. Finance Committees work closely with the treasurer. In recent years, many meetings have added a committee to concentrate on environmental concerns, often called Earthcare. Meetings can set up other committees, either for a temporary project or for long-standing work. Additional committees are created when a meeting finds a need.

Is Membership Required to Serve on a Committee?

Membership in a meeting brings with it the responsibility to serve on committees as one is able. In many Liberal monthly meetings, other individuals who participate regularly in the life of the meeting, but have not yet committed to membership (usually referred to as "active attenders") also serve on some committees.

Monthly and yearly meetings vary on whether membership is a requirement for certain positions. In Ohio Yearly Meeting (Conservative), only members participate in business meeting, so all positions require membership (attenders may sit in on business meetings to observe). Some, like North Pacific Yearly Meeting, recommend membership for key positions but do not require it:

> Meetings customarily appoint experienced and capable members of the Society of Friends to the Committee on Worship and Ministry, the Committee on Oversight, the Nominating Committee, and as clerks of most committees. The purpose is to assign those responsibilities to persons of spiritual depth who are familiar with Friends' faith and ways of organizing and conducting meeting work. When meetings identify such persons, even though they may not be members, they may choose to invest them with those responsibilities.
>
> (North Pacific Yearly Meeting *Faith and Practice*, p. 63)

A middle ground is taken by New York Yearly Meeting and Evangelical Friends Church Southwest. NYYM specifies that service on overseers, ministry and counsel, nominating, finance, and advancement committees require membership,[30] while EFCS requires that Friends in "positions of leadership" such as pastoral staff, Elders/Ministry and Counsel, Nominating Committee, officers, Trustees/Finance and chairpersons of committees be members.[31]

---

[30] New York Yearly Meeting *Faith and Practice*, p. 99

[31] Evangelical Friends Church Southwest *Faith and Practice*, p. 69

The positions of clerk, treasurer, trustee, and members of clearness committees for membership and marriage are often reserved for members. In some meetings, these must be members of the meeting; in others, they may be members of any Quaker meeting.

Membership requirements do not need to be all or nothing. Some meetings have found that some committees in which a certain portion must be members work well.

How Duties are Established

The duties of a committee should be clearly defined and minuted by the meeting when it is created and if its role changes. The written description can be used to review and revise the committee's purpose as appropriate. A purpose can be nebulous, such as "pursue issues of social justice as appropriate to Friends" or explicit, such as "plan a second-hour program on Earthcare," or some of both, such as "work to deepen the spiritual life of the meeting, and submit an article to each edition of the newsletter."

It is important for a committee to understand what lies within its scope—what the committee may decide on its own and simply report to the meeting—and what matters are outside the committee's charge. For instance, in an unprogrammed meeting it is usually within a First-day school Committee's scope to decide on a set of materials to use with the children, but a decision about what part of worship the children attend would usually be decided by the meeting as a whole. Usually, the scope is not written down anywhere, as it is a matter of judgment and tradition. Sometimes a committee will feel led to a particular action outside its scope; these leadings should to be taken to the larger group for consideration.

Size and Terms of Service

Through the years Friends have found that groups of three to eight people work together best. If more person-power is needed, it works well to divide into sub-committees to work on specific tasks so that the basic working unit remains eight people or less. Generally, the more complex the task, the more people it may take to complete the work. When deciding on the size of a committee, it is good to allow room for less experienced Friends as well as seasoned Friends.

Where terms of service are set, they are typically anywhere between one year and three years. These terms are often renewable, but many yearly meetings and other large Quaker bodies limit the number of consecutive terms on a committee. Shorter terms generally work fine at the local level; longer terms are useful for regional or larger bodies to give committee members time to learn their job. It is good practice to stagger the start and end of individuals' terms so that there are always experienced members on the committee. In the case of one-year terms, this can be accomplished by re-appointing useful members of the committee.

Organization

Committees need someone to:

- Convene meetings—schedule meetings as needed at a time and place that works for all committee members.
- Maintain records—take minutes or notes, distribute them to committee members as appropriate, and keep a permanent record as appropriate.
- Report to the larger body.
- Keep committee meetings on task.
- See that the work is carried out.

Committee meetings work better and take less time if an agenda has been prepared and someone monitors the meeting to be sure that all items on the agenda are addressed as appropriate. Traditionally, these roles have been taken on by a committee clerk, sometimes with the help of someone who takes minutes. Sometimes these roles are shared by co-clerks. Some Friends prefer to designate a "convener" of a committee rather than a "clerk." For the sake of simplicity, this text uses "clerk" to refer to whoever performs these tasks.

In some cases, committee clerks are named by the meeting; in others, they are selected by the committee from among its members. In the latter case, the first gathering of the committee is traditionally convened by the person named first in the nominating committee's report.

All of the members of a committee are responsible for seeing that the committee's tasks are completed, whether by individuals, small groups, or by the committee as a whole. Committee members should expect to work both during committee meetings and in between meetings. Committee members should expect to attend all committee meetings and if unable to attend to send regrets and an update on that part of the group's work they have done since the last meeting, if appropriate.

In "A Practical Mystic's Guide to Committee Clerking," Deborah Haines describes the committee clerk's role, like a meeting clerk's role, as the servant of the group:

> A committee clerk is responsible for exercising a certain amount of leadership. Setting agendas, establishing guidelines for the conduct of committee business, holding the mission of the committee in the Light, trying to discern how individual leadings are woven into the whole, offering encouragement and counsel. . . . But the clerk should never seek to dominate. The committee is not a tool for implementing the clerk's ideas about what ought to be done. It is an organic entity, with a life and spirit of its own. Clerking thus requires flexibility, openness, and a large dose of humility. The clerk is the servant of the committee, as it offers itself in service to God.
>
> (Deborah Haines, "A Practical Mystic's Guide to Committee Clerking")

Record Keeping

The more details the committee work involves and the longer-term a project, the more important it is to keep a paper record. This may be in the form of informal notes, more formal written summaries, or minutes. For instance, the Planning Committee for the annual Friends General Conference Gathering, a week-long conference for over a thousand Friends, needs to keep detailed notes of all its decisions and plans. For a committee planning a Christmas party for the meeting, notes that indicate who is to follow up with the various tasks may be important to write down, but there may or may not be a reason to preserve any of the plans after the party is held. It is a good idea for committees that meet less frequently than monthly to keep written notes or minutes and distribute them to the committee members as a reminder.

When writing formal minutes, it is usual to begin with the following information:

- The name of the committee.
- Date/s of the meeting.
- Place of the meeting.

Some committees also record:

- A list of committee members present.
- A list of committee members not present who sent regrets.
- Absent members (those who did not send regrets; this is optional).
- The names of any visitors.

If some members or visitors were present only part of the time, this can be noted.

Reporting

A committee reports to the larger body as requested. A report might include telling the group of its activities and challenges, asking for support, or asking for guidance and discernment. In some small meetings, all committees report at every monthly meeting. In other meetings, committees do not report at all, but are heard from only when they bring items for decision to the business meeting. The meeting clerk may let committees know how often and what kind of report is appropriate. It is good practice for committees to report at least once a year. See "Presenting a Report" on page 194 for some suggestions.

Committee recommendations should be well seasoned before coming to meeting for business. The committee must be in unity with a recommendation. Just like minutes written during business meeting, writing a committee recommendation down and reading it aloud or having committee members read it helps ensure that there is agreement. Either the committee clerk or any member of the committee may give a report or present a recommendation. It is good for most or all the members of the committee to be present at the business meeting. See "Presenting an Item for Decision" on page 196 for more on bringing a recommendation to the business meeting.

Serving on a Committee

Accepting Service on a Committee

In *The Meeting Experience: Practicing Quakerism in Community*, Marty Walton addresses the responsibility of Friends not to overcommit:

> Sometimes we do not treat committee work with respect. . . . We may have not done what we promised we would do. It hurts other people who are counting on us. . . . We break the covenant with ourselves, each other, and God when we do not do what we say we will do; and we break the covenant again when we do not let others know how that affects us.
>
> To the extent that none of us directly addresses this problem, little resentments and mistrusts build up. Our commitment to the meeting is to help make it a place where God is visible through our actions. We are accountable to each other. . . . We need to listen to that person and see if, together, we cannot find . . . some way we can help each other take on only those responsibilities that we will fulfill.
>
> (Marty Walton, *The Meeting Experience: Practicing Quakerism in Community*, p. 26)

The point is not that Friends should follow through on their commitments as much as that Friends should be careful what commitments they make in the first place.

Role of Committee Members

At a minimum, committee members should plan on attending all committee meetings. It is helpful if individuals consider whether or not they are going to be able to attend committee meetings and do the work before they accept appointment to a committee. It is also helpful to the clerk if a committee member who cannot attend sends regrets.

The clerk can draw upon committee members when preparing an agenda. It is helpful to all if members of a committee are prepared to work on committee business between meetings. It is the committee as a whole, not just the clerk, that is responsible for seeing that the committee functions.

It is also the responsibility of committee members to make sure that the committee clerk is enabled to do his/her job and to make sure that the clerk is not doing an unreasonable share of the work. Not all will contribute the same skills or number of hours of work, but it is important to support those in leadership positions and make sure they are not carrying too heavy a load.

A committee is given certain tasks. Sometimes, however, that does not mean that only committee members can help with those tasks. Except for issues involving sensitive personal information such as a Ministry and Counsel Committee often handles, it is appropriate to seek out other Friends with particular skills or gifts to help with the work. These individuals can be consulted as needed or co-opted, which means that they function as a member of the committee for a period of time. Again, it is the committee's responsibility to see that the task gets done, and sometimes the best way to do that is to involve people outside the committee.

Suggestions for Committee Meetings

Committee clerks are often tempted (or pressured) to focus on products. There are decisions that need to be made, and tasks that need to be done. It may seem necessary to hurry the process along, or to strong-arm Friends to take on jobs no one seems led to do. Resist that urge! Focus on keeping the process grounded. Remind yourself that a good tree will inevitably bear good fruit, in its own time. If the committee cannot reach unity on a particular matter, even after extended worship, the matter needs to be set aside. If there are no volunteers to take on particular tasks, even after centered worship, those tasks need to be set aside. You may have to bring the problem to the monthly meeting (or larger organization) to ask for guidance, or for additional volunteers. You should also keep in mind the possibility that those particular decisions and tasks are simply not what the committee is meant to take on, however logical or necessary they may seem. The process of attending to God and each other is always more important than the product.

(Deborah Haines, "A Practical Mystic's Guide to Committee Clerking")

The following practices have been found helpful:

- Start with worship. Not just silence, but worship. This is as important for a Finance Committee as for a Ministry and Counsel Committee. We are all to do the tasks laid before us as led by the Spirit.
- Do a brief "check in" where members share what is going on in their personal lives. This can help members set aside preoccupations as they prepare to focus on the work of the group.
- Before beginning the business, it is useful for the clerk to read the items on the agenda and solicit any additions from those present. Knowing the full scope of the agenda helps keep everyone on track.
- Be explicit about what tasks need to be done between meetings and who will do them.
- End the meeting with worship.

Interest and Support Groups

In some meetings, groups of Friends meet to share a common interest or support one another. This may be a group of people who want to share information and ideas with one another or a group that gathers to share what each individual member is doing. While these can be very useful, they are something different than a committee. A committee exists to perform a function that the meeting has identified as being needed. Committees have something they are supposed to accomplish, often within a given time frame.

Sometimes a named committee functions instead as an interest or support group. Confusion about the role of a committee particularly tends to be a problem with committees for peace, earthcare, and social action. When setting up such a committee, the establishing body needs to be very clear about what work it wants the committee to do on its behalf, and the members of the committee need to be clear that they are to do such work as furthers all Friends' understanding and involvement. A committee is not a support group for activists who each do their own thing. A group that wants to get together for mutual support and sharing around an issue can be called an "interest group" rather than a committee, so everyone is clear about the group's function.

When Officers or Committees Don't Function

What does a meeting do if it becomes apparent that an officer or committee isn't fulfilling the assigned duties? The worst thing to do is nothing. The situation needs to be addressed for the ongoing health of the meeting. An important thing to keep in mind is that what is important is that the duties be carried out, not who carries them out. Guilt and blame are not helpful. Depending on the situation, practical help in carrying out the duties may be needed, persons may need to be replaced, or Friends may simply need to be reminded of commitments.

Chapter 3: Meetings

Monthly Meetings

Gathering monthly to conduct business was one of the first organizing principles used in the early Quaker movement. In most countries, the body of Friends that meet monthly for business is the same body that worships together weekly. However, in some places, particularly in Britain and Kenya, a more common pattern is to set up small groups that meet weekly for worship, and that then join with one or more other worshiping groups in the area for business. In Britain the worshiping groups were originally called "preparative" meetings, as they "prepared" business to go to the monthly meeting; in Kenya they are called "village meetings."

In 2007, Britain Yearly Meeting changed the designations, and groups that meet weekly for worship are now called "local" meetings and what were monthly meetings are now called "area" meetings. "The change was made to give more emphasis to the area meeting as a spiritual community rather than a regular event, and in the interests of accuracy because many monthly meetings no longer met monthly."[32] For simplicity's sake, British area meetings and the rest of the world's monthly meetings will be referred to in this text as monthly meetings.

Typically, each local meeting gathers for worship weekly on Sunday morning. This may be preceded or followed by fellowship, religious education, a planned discussion, singing, and/or food. In an unprogrammed meeting, children typically join the worship for 15-20 minutes either at the beginning or at the end of the hour and spend the rest of the time in First-day school (Sunday School) or with a babysitter. Some unprogrammed meetings, especially in the Conservative tradition, have their children join them for all of meeting for worship, and First-day school for both adults and children is held either before or after

[32] Britain Yearly Meeting *Faith and Practice*, 4.01

meeting. In meetings with pastors and programmed worship, as with other Protestant services, Sunday School may be held either before or after worship. Some meetings also hold a midweek meeting for worship.

The monthly meeting is the body in which membership resides, to which most matters affecting the life of the Religious Society are referred, and from which flow many of the initiatives for action among Friends. The monthly meeting takes responsibility for its own affairs, including accepting people into membership, overseeing marriages, holding property, hiring staff, and managing finances. For the care of such matters a meeting for business consisting of the whole membership convenes each month. Some meetings do not conduct business in the summer, or hold business meetings less frequently than once a month, but almost all meet at least four times a year.

Members of a monthly meeting are also members of the regional and yearly meeting the monthly meeting belongs to. They are also members of the Religious Society of Friends or, among Evangelical Friends, the Friends Church. Officially, a monthly meeting consists of all persons recorded on its list of members. Many Liberal Friends meetings, however, make little or no functional distinction between members and active attenders. (See "The History and Meaning of Membership" on page 242.)

The monthly meeting:

- Fosters the spiritual life of members and attenders.
- Extends spiritual care and, if needed, material aid to its members.
- Appoints members and committees for service.
- Receives and transfers people into membership and discontinues membership.
- Oversees marriages.
- Oversees funerals and memorial meetings and approves memorial minutes when appropriate.

It may also:

- Collect and dispense funds to carry on its work.
- Hold title to property and see to the suitable administration of trust funds.

- Set up or lay down preparative meetings or worship groups and provide spiritual and practical guidance to them.
- Issue travel minutes.
- Appoint representatives to attend regional and yearly meeting sessions and receive their reports.
- Appoint or recommend members to yearly meeting committees as requested.
- Prepare and dispatch reports requested by the regional or yearly meeting.
- Interact with its regional and yearly meeting, with other bodies of Friends, and with other organizations.

Unaffiliated monthly meetings sometimes arise when Friends from various branches of Quakers come together to form a meeting. Such a monthly meeting may have a choice of yearly meetings to affiliate with.

How Large Should a Monthly Meeting Be?

When establishing a new monthly meeting, it is important to consider if there are enough active participants who are likely to remain in the area over the years to sustain the meeting. Given this practical minimum, is there an ideal size for a meeting? There are functioning monthly meetings with fewer than 10 members and with over 500. In Britain, there is a tradition of keeping the geographic area of a local worshiping community small, and of several of these local meetings joining together to conduct business. In the U.S. and Canada, Friends tend to pull from a wide enough area so that each worshiping community is also a monthly meeting. Large cities tend to have one large meeting with sometimes one or two much smaller ones. In most of North America, Quakers are thin on the ground, and in a few cases one monthly meeting pulls from a geographic area of 100 miles or more. More usually, Friends do not travel more than an hour one way to reach a meeting. Among unprogrammed Friends, worship groups fill in some of the geographic gaps between monthly meetings.

Unprogrammed meetings, especially those that do not own a building, have significantly fewer expenses than Pastoral meetings, and more flexibility in deciding where and when to meet. For a Pastoral meeting, the economics of paying a pastor and maintaining a building often dictate a minimum size for the congregation in order to be viable economically.

Friends in small meetings often assume that any problems they experience are due to their small size. Small meetings can find it difficult to raise enough money to maintain property or pay a pastor and may also face challenges in nurturing children and teens. Other problems, however, are seldom directly related to the small size of the meeting. Small meetings with financial difficulties can consider divesting themselves of their property or finding a part-time pastor. On the upside, small meetings are often friendly and sociable, may have a rich sense of community, may experience deep and centered worship, and may achieve unity in decision making on a regular basis.

Large meetings have different advantages and disadvantages. Large meetings may be able to divide the First-day school into age groups, hold different meetings for worship in different styles, and sponsor a number of small groups. On the downside, large meetings may face difficulties providing appropriate pastoral care, achieving a sense of community, may suffer from "popcorn meetings,"[33] and may find real unity in decision making elusive. Setting up a variety of small groups within the meeting can help.

In *Fostering Vital Friends Meetings*, Jan Greene and Marty Walton pull together the collective experience and wisdom of a number of Friends employed in one way or another as field workers among unprogrammed Friends. They offer the following advice:

> Meetings need to consider Friends' earlier advice that big is not necessarily best when it comes to meeting size. Although many meetings resist it, by the time a meeting community gets to be about thirty families, it may be time to split into two groups.
>
> (Jan Greene and Marty Walton, *Fostering Vital Friends Meetings*, p. 92)

---

[33] A meeting for worship in which many people pop up and speak, one after another, leaving insufficient time to consider what has been said.

Laying Down a Monthly Meeting

A monthly meeting that feels unable to continue the administrative work of a monthly meeting or that has so little business that it is unable to hold business meetings at least four times a year should consider laying itself down or reverting to a worship group. The meeting can consult with appropriate officers of the regional or yearly meeting to assist in discerning whether it should change its status. All members of the meeting should be notified that the meeting is considering laying itself down and be invited to participate in the discernment process and the meeting for business at which the decision will be made. If a meeting becomes entirely inactive without changing its status, the regional or yearly meeting can initiate steps to lay the meeting down.

Issues to be addressed in such a change include transferring any real property (buildings and land), which usually goes to the regional or yearly meeting; and transferring capital or trust funds, which should be turned over to the regional or yearly meeting for appropriate administration. Friends who hold membership in a meeting being laid down should be encouraged to transfer their membership to another meeting.

Preparative Meetings

There are two kinds of preparative meetings. A group of preparative meetings can form a larger monthly meeting and as such do not expect to change their status; they *prepare* business for submission to the monthly meeting. North Carolina Yearly Meeting (FUM) has some preparative meetings of this kind:

> If two or more congregations are associated in one monthly meeting, each congregation may have a local or preparative business meeting, subordinate to the monthly meeting and limited in its authority to purely local matters.
>
> (North Carolina Yearly Meetin (FUM) *Faith and Practice*, p. 61)

"Preparative meeting" is also used in a different sense to refer to a newly formed group that will eventually become a monthly meeting when its stability seems assured; it is *preparing* to become a monthly meeting and is under the care of a monthly meeting.

This is how the term is usually used in the U.S. and Canada.

Worship Groups

When a group of people get together regularly to worship after the manner of Friends but not to conduct business, it is called a *worship group*. Historically, such a group was always under the care of a monthly meeting and was called an "allowed" or "indulged" meeting.

Some yearly meetings still use the terms "allowed" or "indulged" to refer to a regular meeting for worship sponsored by a monthly meeting but held at a different time or place than the meeting's regular worship, but in the U.S. and Canada any group that meets regularly for worship and fellowship tends to be referred to simply as a worship group. Usually, a person or couple takes responsibility for convening the group and communicating with other Friends bodies. They are called conveners rather than clerks.

Looking For a Meeting

A worship group with no formal ties to any Quaker body may look for a monthly meeting to take it under its care. This is usually a monthly meeting where some of the people in the worship group hold membership or have been active in the past, or a meeting with compatible theology and practices that is reasonably close geographically. Sometimes there is no obvious monthly meeting to turn to. In this case, the worship group may try contacting the yearly meeting(s) whose geographic region they are in to ask for guidance.

Sometimes there are several meetings from which to choose. In this case, the worship group has to decide not only whether to seek to come under a meeting's care, but which meeting. Some visits and dialog with people in the various meetings are in order. Contacting the regional or yearly meeting for advice may also be helpful.

Things to look for in a monthly meeting include:

- Is the worship in the monthly meeting deep and Spirit-led?
- Do Friends in the meeting know and care for one another?
- During meetings for business, do Friends seek fresh inspiration?

- Is the monthly meeting well established or is it struggling?
- Is the monthly meeting as a whole interested in taking the worship group under its care? Sometimes some individuals are enthusiastic, but the meeting as a whole is not.
- Are there seasoned Friends in the monthly meeting who have the time and interest to visit, nurture, and guide the worship group?

Friends in the worship group may want to open a dialog with the meeting's committee on Ministry and Counsel about the possibility of coming under their care.

Making a decision about which monthly meeting to establish a relationship with gives the worship group the opportunity to practice Quaker decision making and to bring the decision under divine guidance. The first formal step toward establishing a relationship with a monthly meeting may be a letter to the clerk either requesting that the meeting begin a dialog with the worship group about the possibility of a relationship or simply asking to be taken under the meeting's care.

Establishing a New Worship Group Under a Meeting's Care

Sometimes a monthly meeting is asked to establish a new worship group, either by the regional or yearly meeting or by Friends who wish to be part of it. A 40-page pamphlet, "When You're the Only Friend in Town: Starting a New Friends Meeting," offers helpful advice. Here is a possible process for establishing a worship group under a meeting's care, based on the suggestions in the pamphlet:

- If the meeting is approached about helping to start a new worship group, either by its own members or by visitors from outside, the first step is to appoint a "clearness committee" to meet with the Friends making the request. The clearness committee would explore just what is being proposed, and why a worship group separate from the meeting is being suggested, remembering that this may be an important opportunity for the meeting. (See "Releasing a Friend" on page 146134 for more information on clearness processes in general.)

- The next step is to explore whether there are other people who are willing to help establish the new group. These might either be people who intend to be part of the group once it is established, or meeting members who are willing to expend energy in getting it started, but do not intend to leave the parent meeting. Once this group of two or three Friends is identified, the clearness committee meets again with the group to help them clarify their vision.
- If the leading seems to be clear, and the group seems to be ready to proceed, the clearness committee recommends to the meeting that it take the new worship group under its care. It is helpful to be clear what kinds of support the meeting is expected to undertake.
- If Friends approve, the meeting writes a minute that it is taking the group under its care and what that includes in this particular case.

Taking an Existing Worship Group Under a Meeting's Care

> Quakerism tends to be a grass roots religion. Worship groups have been known to spring up spontaneously, and grow into vital meetings on their own. But the process of germination and growth is helped enormously by the active involvement of an established meeting which takes the new worship group "under its care."
>
> (Deborah Haines, "When You're the Only Friend in Town: Starting a New Friends Meeting," p. 31)

When a worship group approaches a monthly meeting about being taken under its care, either informally or formally through a letter to the clerk of the meeting, the matter should be turned over to the meeting's Ministry and Counsel Committee and the contents of the letter or the approach shared at the next business meeting.

The meeting or Ministry and Counsel should appoint an ad hoc[34] committee of three or more seasoned Friends to visit the

[34] An ad hoc committee is created for a particular short-term purpose, and the committee ceases to exist when its work is done.

worship group, join them in worship, and discuss things generally. The visiting Friends can help the people in the worship group understand what it means to be under a meeting's care, and to check that the worship group is clear to move forward. Several visits and additional e-mails and phone calls may be needed.

If the ad hoc committee recommends taking the worship group under the meeting's care, the matter should come before the full meeting at its next business session. If the meeting concurs, it minutes the decision and sends a copy to the worship group. Ministry and Counsel can then plan how to go about nurturing and guiding the group, and arrange for members of the meeting to visit the worship group periodically.

Members of the worship group should try to attend the monthly meeting's business sessions occasionally, but otherwise should expect members of the meeting to come to them. The worship group should report to the monthly meeting at least annually.

Anyone in the worship group ready to apply for membership in the Religious Society of Friends applies to the monthly meeting. Friends in the worship group with membership in distant meetings may want to transfer their membership to the monthly meeting. Couples in the worship group wishing to be married under the care of a meeting apply to the monthly meeting. Usually, clearness committees in such cases are made up of Friends in both the worship group and the monthly meeting.

Having a worship group under a monthly meeting's care is a mutual relationship. The parent meeting should be prepared to provide advice and counsel as needed and to send visitors regularly to worship with the group. Friends from the worship group should plan to attend meeting for business at the parent meeting and report regularly to the parent meeting on their activities and concerns.

Caring for a Worship Group or Preparative Meeting

Here are some ways a parent meeting can support a worship group or preparative meeting:

- Print the time and place of worship and contact information for the group in the meeting's newsletter, along with a notice that they would welcome visitors.

- Encourage the group to send notices of their activities to be printed in the newsletter.
- Help them set up a web page. This could be on the monthly meeting's website.
- Use e-mail to keep in touch. It is certainly not as desirable as face-to-face contact, but much better than no contact at all. Meetings can share business minutes, concerns, and opportunities electronically.
- Make sure that the worship group is on the yearly meeting's mailing list and is in the yearly meeting's records.
- Make the meeting's library available to people in the worship group.
- Get together for social activities to build the relationship between the groups.
- Work together on mutual concerns and projects.
- Invite the worship group to participate in special activities such as retreats and opportunities[35] with a visiting Friend.
- The most important thing is for members of the monthly meeting to join the group's worship on a regular basis.

Moving to Monthly Meeting Status

A worship group or preparative meeting which feels ready for monthly meeting status applies to its monthly meeting. The monthly meeting responds by designating a committee to inquire into the group's state. Ideally, this committee visits the group, joins it for worship and business, and talks with Friends there. It then reports to the monthly meeting on whether the group is ready for full meeting status. If the committee recommends favorably and the meeting concurs, it forwards the application with approval to its regional meeting (or if there is no regional meeting, directly to the yearly meeting). This is then taken up as an item of business at that meeting's next business session.

[35] An occasion when a traveling minister visits a meeting or a group of Friends. These occasions provide an "opportunity" for the Spirit of God to move among the gathered group.

Different yearly meetings have different procedures on whether a regional meeting can establish a new monthly meeting and then simply notify the yearly meeting that it has done so, or whether the request needs to be passed up the regional ladder, with approval required at each level.

There are a number of practical issues that need to be addressed in forming a new monthly meeting:

- Officers and committees. The parent meeting should help the new meeting establish a Nominating Committee and oversee the process to appoint officers and committees as appropriate.
- Finances. The parent meeting should work with the new meeting to see that it sets up appropriate bank accounts and to assist with any other fiscal matters as appropriate. It is especially helpful to figure out how the yearly meeting donation or assessment will be met within the current fiscal year. When deciding on a fiscal year for the new meeting, it is good to check with the yearly meeting to see if a certain end date would work better for purposes of reporting to the yearly meeting.
- Individual's membership: Transfers. When a new monthly meeting is established, Friends should work with their parent meeting to transfer any memberships held by that meeting to the new meeting. If any Friends hold membership in a different monthly meeting, they can ask those meetings to transfer their membership to the new meeting.
- Individual's membership: Applications. Attenders may wish to become members of the new monthly meeting at the time it is formed. It is helpful if clearness committees are set up jointly by the parent and new monthly meeting.
- The relationship and duties of a monthly meeting with its regional and yearly meeting should be made clear to the new monthly meeting. Typically, the yearly meeting offers opportunities and counsel, while asking for financial contribution toward its budget, representatives to yearly meeting sessions, and annual reports on the state of the meeting and statistical information.

- It is a good idea to coordinate the timing of changes in officers and committee members with the yearly meeting.

Issues to Consider in Granting Monthly Meeting Status

Baltimore Yearly Meeting's discipline has a number of useful appendices. One of them gives the following list of queries[36] to consider in granting monthly meeting status:

- Is a sense of community present among members and attenders of the preparative meeting? Is spiritual nurturing experienced within it?
- Are meetings for worship and business held regularly and attended appropriately?
- Is there a core group with the commitment to give permanence to the meeting?
- Is contact maintained with organizations in the wider community of the Religious Society of Friends?
- Is witness for traditional social testimonies of Friends fostered?
- Does the preparative meeting maintain a library of Friends materials? Does it encourage its members and attenders to grow in the knowledge of the Society?
- Has the preparative meeting established relationships with other religious groups in its community?
(Baltimore Yearly Meeting *Faith and Practice*, Appendix H)

Regional Meetings

> The origin of regional gatherings, each embracing several monthly meetings, goes back to 1660 when George Fox was "moved to set up the men's quarterly meetings throughout the nations." These were followed by women's quarterly meetings. . . . They gradually took on considerable responsibilities for discipline, inspiration, pastoral care and records of membership. . . . Overall they functioned as a link in the chain of responsibilities joining local meetings to the yearly meeting.
>
> (Britain Yearly Meeting *Faith and Practice*, 5.01)

---

36 See "Advices and Queries" on page 54 for more information on queries.

Traditionally, two or more monthly meetings in the same geographic area unite in a regional meeting. These go by different names in different countries or areas: general meeting, area meeting, quarterly meeting, or half-yearly meeting (depending on how frequently they meet). Regional meetings, where they exist, serve a variety of functions. Regional meetings may strengthen the life and fellowship of meetings, season concerns, and provide a link in transmitting business and other information between local meetings and the yearly meeting.

In many yearly meetings, however, during the last century the traditional regions have lost many of their traditional functions, since travel to yearly meetings is so much easier. These regional meetings do little or no business but are mainly for fellowship. Some long-standing quarterly meetings now meet only two or three times a year. In some yearly meetings, however, regional meetings have been dropped or the yearly meeting was formed without them. Where no regional meetings exist or they do no business, monthly meetings interact directly with the yearly meeting.

Yearly Meetings

Traditionally, two or more regional meetings in the same geographic area unite in a yearly meeting. The yearly meeting provides a larger group to undertake and discern matters of concern. A yearly meeting consists of the entire membership of its constituent monthly meetings. It can engage in any activity or foster any work that the members consider appropriate, including provision of funds and supervision for common projects. Among its numerous functions, the yearly meeting may issue advices and queries. It reports its proceedings to the monthly meetings. It may accept new meetings into the yearly meeting and release a meeting from membership in the yearly meeting.

"Yearly Meeting" refers to three distinct but interwoven entities: 1) the organization which makes up the yearly meeting; 2) the annual gathering to worship and conduct business; and 3) the body of Friends who make up the yearly meeting (all the members of the constituent monthly meetings). This diversity of meanings functioned for years, as the context always made the meaning apparent. However, in recent times and for the sake of newcomers especially, some efforts have been made to come up with alternate terms. The annual meeting for worship and business is sometimes called the "annual sessions," and this text uses that nomenclature.

Like a monthly meeting, yearly meetings appoint officers and committees through a nominating process. Typical officers and committees are comparable to those for monthly meetings, with the addition of a committee to plan the annual sessions.

Role

A yearly meeting provides a forum for Friends throughout a geographic region to interact, to work together on common projects, to worship together, and to season leadings and concerns. It exercises general oversight and care of regional and monthly meetings and serves as a resource. It maintains contact with other yearly meetings and with other Quaker bodies such as Friends World Committee for Consultation (FWCC), American Friends Service Committee (AFSC), and Friends Committee on National Legislation (FCNL). Yearly meetings also exchange epistles with each other.

Annual Sessions

The yearly meeting holds annual sessions for worship, business, and fellowship. In many yearly meetings, additional activities are scheduled such as talks, performances, opportunities for spiritual growth such as worship-sharing groups and Bible study, interest groups, and programs for children and youth. The purpose of the business sessions is to seek divine guidance for the group as a whole. All members have both the privilege and the responsibility of attending sessions and participating in the deliberations. In order to assure attendance from all parts of the yearly meeting and to carry information and concerns to and from the local meetings, some yearly meetings ask each monthly meeting to appoint representatives. These vary in number from two to five depending on the yearly meeting. These representatives attend business sessions and report to their local meetings on the work and life of the yearly meeting.

The yearly meeting considers reports from Friends organizations and yearly meeting committees, gives attention to epistles from other yearly meetings and prepares an epistle to be sent to them, considers minutes from other yearly meetings, and deals with appropriate business and concerns. There are often Friends visiting from outside the yearly meeting. In most cases annual sessions last most of a week.

Yearly meeting gatherings and work on yearly meeting committees serve as opportunities for getting to know and interact with Friends outside one's local meeting.

Executive Committees, Interim Meetings, and Representative Meetings

Yearly meetings need some way to conduct business between annual sessions. There are several ways they do this:

- An executive committee may be empowered to make decisions that cannot wait for a larger body to gather. It reports its decisions to the next business meeting. Typically, this is made up of the officers and clerks of committees of the yearly meeting or of meeting representatives plus yearly meeting officers.
- A gathering made up of representatives from the constituent monthly meetings may conduct certain types of business. This is called "interim meeting" or "representative meeting," and typically has one or more scheduled meeting times throughout the year. It makes decisions within the scope of its responsibilities and forwards other business for final decision to the annual sessions. Although each monthly meeting is asked to send representatives, any Friend in the yearly meeting may participate.
- Some yearly meetings hire staff to perform tasks throughout the year. These might be clerical tasks (a secretary), providing opportunities for youth to gather (a youth worker), fostering the life of the spirit among Friends in the yearly meeting (a

field secretary), and/or performing administrative tasks (a general secretary or superintendent). Some yearly meetings combine two or more of these.

Representatives

In political systems with representative government, representatives are usually committed to a particular position on behalf of their constituents. This is emphatically not the case with a representative to a Quaker meeting. Meetings appoint "representatives" to ensure that at least a few Friends from the meeting will attend, participate, and report back. A representative to the larger group comes with knowledge about his or her meeting and their concerns, but is not bound by instructions from the local group. Representatives need to be open to the leadings of the Spirit just as they would be in any Quaker business meeting.

Books of Faith and Practice, Books of Discipline

> The term discipline was used by Friends to designate those arrangements which they have instituted for their civil and religious nurture and guidance as a Christian group.
>
> (Western Yearly Meeting *Faith and Practice*, Part I, Origin and Development of the Discipline)

History

> An important step in the development of the discipline was the drafting, by George Fox in 1668, of a body of advices and regulations. . . . This served for a long time as the discipline of the Society. . . . It formed the basis for the discipline of London Yearly Meeting and for all later books of discipline. As the various yearly meetings were established in America, each prepared and adopted its own book of discipline, but there was much similarity, because of the common use of material from older editions.
>
> (Western Yearly Meeting *Faith and Practice*, Part I, Origin and Development of the Discipline)

In the early 1700s, yearly meetings drew up sets of questions on conduct, called queries, that were to be answered by monthly meetings. These, along with minutes of advice and counsel which had been sent out from time to time in earlier years, were compiled into books of discipline. Each yearly meeting compiled such a book. Over the years, as books of discipline were revised, they acquired various titles. Britain Yearly Meeting's 2007 revision is titled *Quaker Faith and Practice: The Book of Christian Discipline of the Yearly Meeting of the Religious Society of Friends (Quakers) in Britain.* Today, almost all yearly meetings issue their own book of "Discipline" or "Faith and Practice" that describes and prescribes the organization, practices, testimonies, and faith normative in that yearly meeting. These books may be referred to as either a "Discipline" or "Faith and Practice"; they are equivalent terms.

Uniform Disciplines

In *The Quakers in America*, Tom Hamm writes, "The early years of the 20th century saw all persuasions of Friends . . . looking for ways to bring their yearly meetings closer together to work on behalf of common causes and interests." In 1897, Gurneyite yearly meetings "embraced a proposal for a national organization composed of the Gurneyite yearly meetings with a *Uniform Discipline* and legislative authority over the yearly meetings."[37] Rufus Jones and James Wood drafted the discipline. "By 1901, all of the Gurneyite yearly meetings except Ohio had endorsed the framework . . . and so the national organization, dubbed the Five Years Meeting [later FUM] held its first sessions in 1902."[38] This *Uniform Discipline* went through several revisions. The last proposed revision, in 1951, never gained general acceptance, and FUM yearly meetings proceeded to revise their disciplines in various ways. The subsequent disciplines bear varying degrees of resemblance to one another. They generally cover the same topics.

[37] Thomas D. Hamm, *The Quakers in America*, p. 55

[38] Ibid.

In 1926, Friends General Conference (FGC), first established in 1900, proposed its own *Uniform Discipline*.[39] All of its constituent yearly meetings except New York adopted it, but with modifications, and New York incorporated much of it.[40] This *Uniform Discipline* was never adopted as a whole by any yearly meeting, and subsequent revisions by yearly meetings introduced additional differences. As with FUM disciplines, however, there are many similarities between FGC disciplines, which tend to cover the same topics, although some yearly meetings have added sections of quotes or appendices.

FGC's *Uniform Discipline* piloted a new understanding of the role of a book of discipline among Quakers. It presented itself as more advisory than authoritative. This is made clear by the appearance of the following quote at the beginning:[41]

> Dearly beloved Friends, these things we do not lay upon you as a rule or form to walk by, but that all, with the measure of Light which is pure and holy, may be guided: and so in the Light walking and abiding, these may be fulfilled in the Spirit, not in the letter, for the letter killeth, but the Spirit giveth life.
>
> (Postscript to a letter from the Meeting of Elders at Balby, 1656)

This new understanding is expressed well in the introduction to Britain Yearly Meeting's *Faith and Practice*:

> Discipline is not now a popular word. It has overtones of enforcement and correction, but its roots lie in ideas of learning and discipleship. Discipline in our yearly meeting consists for the most part of advice and counsel, the encouragement of self-questioning, and of

---

[39] The existence of FUM's *Uniform Discipline* is well known, but until recently FGC Friends had no inkling they shared an original text for their Disciplines. Its existence and history were discovered by Chuck Fager and documented in an article in *Quaker History* in the fall of 2000.

[40] Thomas D. Hamm, *The Quakers in America*, p. 55

[41] This quote had already appeared in other disciplines, but as a historical reference somewhere at the back of the book rather than as a description of the book itself.

hearing each other in humility and love.

(Britain Yearly Meeting *Faith and Practice*, Introduction)

Contents

Most disciplines contain sections on faith and life, organization and business procedures to be followed, and a set of queries. In Pastoral yearly meetings, disciplines also contain doctrinal statements, which usually consist of extracts from George Fox's letter to the Governor of Barbados in 1671 and the Richmond Declaration of Faith of 1887. Some disciplines include a set of advices, a section of quotes, or various introductions or appendices, especially with sample letters and forms. They range from under 100 pages to over 500 pages.

Not all yearly meetings have developed their own book of discipline. In these yearly meetings, Friends are usually referred to another yearly meeting's book of discipline such as those of Philadelphia or Britain Yearly Meeting. A number of yearly meetings have written disciplines for the first time in the last 10 to 20 years, and eventually most other yearly meetings will probably do so as well.

Advices and Queries

Advices and queries serve to engage our minds and hearts in a process which may provide openings to the leadings of the Spirit within us. These leadings may speak to our individual and corporate needs. The advices and queries reflect experiences from many lives as they contribute to the gathered wisdom of the group. They serve to guide us on our spiritual journeys by opening our hearts and minds to the possibility of new directions and insights.

(Iowa Yearly Meeting (Conservative) *Faith and Practice*, p. 44)

Friends have a tradition of reading "queries." These probing questions stimulate individuals, leaders, or people in church business meetings to ask themselves how well they are doing.

(Evangelical Friends Church Southwest *Faith and Practice*, p. 23)

Advices and queries were the first items included in a discipline, and they continue to be used in various ways by Friends today. Advices are principles for the guidance of the meeting and its members. Advices may touch on the life of the meeting as well as on personal discipline, care of children, family life, and the character of our day-to-day living. Each yearly meeting develops and revises its own set of advices and queries to be included in its book of discipline. Some choose 12 different topics to facilitate meetings' considering one each month of the year. Some disciplines now include only queries. Among Evangelical Friends, they may be called "accountability questions."

Advices and queries have unique roles in Quakerism not found in other denominations. While advices, which are phrased as directives, have largely gone out of favor among Liberal Friends, writing and responding to queries remains a distinctive Quaker practice. The first queries were factual, asking such things as how many members in the meeting had been thrown in prison in the last year, but over time their nature and purpose developed more spiritual depth, asking not just for facts and figures but such things as whether members were being faithful to promptings of the Spirit. Queries have become a vehicle for self-examination as much as a means of reporting. Queries have been crafted on all sorts of topics outside those typically found in a book of Faith and Practice as an aid to reflection and to deepen the spiritual life of individuals and the worshiping community. The following observation reinforces the aptness of queries for Quakers:

> The Quaker Way is not so much a system of beliefs as it is a framework for asking the right questions.
>
> (Christopher A. Dorrance, *Reflections from a Friends Education*, pp. 39-41)

Books of Procedure

In addition to books of discipline, many yearly meetings issue a book containing the nitty-gritty details of organization and practice such as the responsibilities of yearly meeting standing committees, how many members each has, how long a term members serve, etc. Because these details change frequently, it is convenient to print them separately from the book of discipline. They are extremely useful to the yearly meeting officers, staff, and committees, but are not of general interest to Friends. They go by various names, including *Policies and Procedures*, *Manual of Procedure*, *Operational Handbook*, and *Procedures and Job Descriptions*.

The Relationship Between Monthly, Regional, and Yearly Meetings

> The relationship between area meetings [monthly meetings], meeting for sufferings [the yearly meeting Executive Committee or Board] . . . and [yearly meeting] committees is delicate and complex.
>
> If there is sometimes tension in the relationships, this is not necessarily unhealthy. It is unhealthy when a matter is shunted from one body to another because a group of Friends lack the spiritual energy and courage to wrestle with a matter that they know may result in uncomfortable plain speaking to a fellow member whose concern, however deeply held, is not shared by the meeting. It is equally unhealthy when any individual or meeting is preoccupied with status, with "getting things through," with efforts to predetermine how another body shall act. We can only be delivered from these dangers by a constant relearning of the nature of true concern.
>
> (Meeting for Sufferings, 1978 in Britain Yearly Meeting *Faith and Practice*, 4.20)

Fostering Healthy Relationships

At each level of organization within a yearly meeting—preparative meetings, monthly meetings, regional meetings, and the yearly meeting—the smaller body submits reports and sends representatives to the larger body, and the larger body provides care and counsel to the smaller body. In this way, a meeting participates in and directs the activities of the larger bodies, while the larger bodies pool the resources of a number of meetings to accomplish common work, to provide care and counsel to its constituents, and to seek God's will.

Unfortunately, some monthly meetings may regard their yearly meeting with indifference or even hostility:

> Many Friends, with no interest in religious affairs beyond their own congregations, see yearly meetings as at best irrelevant, at worst as sources of constant irritation and demands for money.
>
> (Thomas D. Hamm, *The Quakers in America*, p. 136)

There are webs of interconnectedness that need to be in place for a healthy relationship. Clerks of monthly meetings receive information and requests from the regional and yearly meeting, and should handle these expeditiously. Every monthly meeting should have one or more members who are involved in the regional and yearly meeting either through attending their business sessions or serving on their committees. Multiple lines of communication should be in place between the monthly, regional, and yearly meeting. Local committees and their corresponding committees should be in communication and be mutually supportive. Many concerns that arise can best be processed first by monthly meetings and then by regional meetings, before reaching the yearly meeting. Alternately, concerns brought up in the yearly meeting can properly be sent to regional or monthly meetings with the request that they consider them and report back.

Typical monthly meeting responsibilities to the larger bodies include the following:

- Season concerns that arise within the local meeting and forward them to the regional or yearly meeting as appropriate.
- When asked by another meeting to consider a concern or matter, do so faithfully, minute the result, and report where the meeting finds itself on the issue. If the meeting has not reached unity, report what has been done and what the meeting plans to do next and share any preliminary minute.
- Appoint members to attend business sessions and report back to the monthly meeting.
- Support the yearly meeting financially in accordance with the apportionment approved by the yearly meeting.
- At the request of the regional or yearly meeting Nominating

Committee, suggest names of local Friends who would be suitable to serve on committees.

- Annually forward approved monthly meeting reports, for example on peace or religious education, to the regional or yearly meeting for use by the appropriate committees.
- Forward at appropriate times statistical information, names and addresses of officers, committee clerks and members and other information which from time to time may be required by the regional or yearly meeting.
- Annually forward to the regional or yearly meeting an approved report on the spiritual state of the monthly meeting.
- Forward, either directly to the yearly meeting or through the regional meeting, copies of memorial minutes. Some yearly meetings request all memorial minutes; others only those of Friends well-known beyond the monthly meeting.
- Regularly forward the monthly meeting newsletter to the regional and yearly meeting.
- Forward a meeting directory as requested.

Typical business taken up by regional meetings includes:

- Handling applications for full meeting status.
- Considering and forwarding, if appropriate, concerns from constituent monthly meetings.

Typical activities of yearly meetings in addition to considering business include:

- Issuing queries and advices.
- Reporting its proceedings to monthly meetings.
- Sponsoring youth programs.
- Sponsoring service programs and missions.

Seasoning of Concerns

Seasoning means to give a matter attention over a period of time and by disparate Friends; to take the time to seek the Light rather than move into a matter hastily. One seasons a matter by actively working to increase one's understanding and to discern God's will.

Some yearly meetings routinely take up items for business

that have not been considered and seasoned by its monthly meetings. Some yearly meeting committees function without interacting with monthly meetings or appropriate monthly meeting committees. For too many Friends, there is a disconnect between their local meeting and the concerns and activities of the yearly meeting. Local meetings may feel isolated and without support from the yearly meeting. Yearly meeting activities may lack grounding and be insufficiently supported by members of the yearly meeting. This concern is not a new one or limited to certain branches. In September of 1965, Jack Willcuts, an Evangelical Friend, wrote in the *Northwest Friend* magazine:

> The scheme of Friends organization is designed to funnel individual concerns and testimony upward through the monthly, quarterly, and yearly meeting to the world. More frequently these concerns, when manifest at all, are concerns carefully worked out by special committees within a board or department and briefly lifted to the floor of the yearly meeting for approval while most Friends, with one eye on the mimeographed memorandum and the other on the clock, try to determine what is right.
>
> (Jack L. Willcuts, *The Sense of the Meeting*, p. 81)

The regional and yearly meeting can help foster healthy relationships by seeing their roles in large part as serving the monthly meetings. The yearly meeting can help further local concerns by organizing committees and activities that involve monthly meetings throughout the yearly meeting. One of the most important services a regional or yearly meeting can provide is getting Quaker youth together. Someone in each meeting can take responsibility for helping the youth take advantage of such opportunities.

Monthly meetings can help foster healthy relationships by being informed and taking responsibility for the work of the regional and yearly meeting. They should turn to the regional or yearly meeting for advice or help when needed. It is important for meeting youth to have the opportunity to spend time with other Quaker youth. If the yearly meeting sponsors a spiritual formation group, a camp, or conferences, the meeting can encourage members to attend and help them financially if needed. The meeting can encourage and help members to attend larger Quaker gatherings or get involved in one of the national or international Quaker organizations. Monthly meetings can host regional and yearly meeting committee meetings and other yearly meeting gatherings. This is a great way for local members to become acquainted with Friends from other meetings as well as yearly meeting concerns and activities.

Sometimes a monthly meeting will take up a concern, come to agreement on it, and want the other meetings in the yearly meeting to consider it as well. They can send their approved minute to the yearly meeting clerk along with a brief background history of the concern, including who initiated it and what discussions and actions have been taken by individuals and groups. The clerk of the yearly meeting can send the minute and background document to each monthly meeting, noting that this is a request from the particular monthly meeting. Each meeting would be asked to consider the issue and report back to the yearly meeting clerk how they feel—any agreements, actions, or agreements to disagree. It is good if the concern is brought before several or all of the monthly meetings by those bearing the concern. The sense of each meeting is reported back to the yearly meeting. Depending on the response, something could come up at yearly meeting business sessions the next year, or the responses could be forwarded to an appropriate yearly meeting committee to summarize for the sessions the next year.

State of the Meeting Report

Most yearly meetings request an annual report on spiritual vitality from each monthly meeting. This tradition arose out of the use of advices and queries in which monthly meetings would prayerfully consider and write a response to one query each month. Once a year, these responses were compiled and sent to the quarterly meeting. Conservative Friends continue this practice. Some Evangelical Friends still base a State of the Church Report on answers to queries. Drafting and approving a State of the Meeting Report offers the opportunity for self-reflection and honest assessment of how the meeting is doing. Done carefully, this process can help a meeting grow in understanding and fellowship and deepen its spiritual life.

Process and contents

In most yearly meetings, the responsibility of drafting the report is given to Ministry and Counsel. In some meetings, the report gets a first reading and Friends are encouraged to speak later with members of the committee with any suggestions. The committee then revises it and brings it back for a second reading at the next business meeting, where approval is sought.

Baltimore Yearly Meeting's *Faith and Practice* contains a particularly helpful list of things to consider when drafting a report, which is paraphrased below.

The report should cover such matters as:

- The spiritual condition of the meeting and its strengths and failings.
- The nature of meetings for worship during the year, including the quality of the silence and the content and quality of the spoken ministry.
- Meetings for business during the year: the range of concerns considered, attendance of members, and implementation of the meeting's decisions.
- Contributions of Peace and Social Order, Religious Education, Ministry, Overseers, and other committees.
- What is most needed to deepen the spiritual life of the meeting and to strengthen its witness in behalf of Friends testimonies to the world.

There are some common pitfalls meetings fall into in drafting a report, particularly when the yearly meeting provides little or no guidance:

- The report consists of a "laundry list" of activities.
- Problems are glossed over or omitted.
- The report is a collection of individual comments rather than a corporate statement.

Annual Statistical Report

Yearly meetings ask their constituent monthly meetings to supply information each year on such things as the number of recorded members and active attenders, the number of youth, times and places of meetings, and contact information for officers and committee clerks. The yearly meeting provides a form for this information. The number of members and active attenders may be used to calculate an expected or suggested contribution from the monthly meeting to the yearly meeting. It may also be used to calculate the amount owed to a larger body the yearly meeting is affiliated with such as FGC, FUM, or EFCI. Practices on whether and how to count active members, inactive members, active attenders, and youth vary considerably.

Speaking for the Religious Society of Friends or a Quaker Body

There is a wide range of practices and beliefs not only between the different branches of Friends but within most of the branches as well. The only Quaker organization that includes all the branches, Friends World Committee for Consultation (FWCC), makes no decisions on behalf of Friends, but serves instead to help bring Friends in the different branches together for dialog and sharing. Given this situation, there is no organization or person who can speak for the Religious Society as a whole.

Quaker leaders and representatives to other religious bodies tend to describe the Religious Society of Friends in terms of common practices and traditional positions, or to indicate when they are speaking from their personal experience. In making any historical or descriptive claims, Friends need to be careful to accurately represent all members of the Religious Society, not just those in their particular branch, or to be clear about what group of Quakers they are describing. Britain Yearly Meeting's *Faith and Practice* gives the following advice:

> Individuals and groups must be careful not to claim to speak for Friends without explicit authority. Any activity or statement made in public which claims to be undertaken in the name of Friends and

> relating to the corporate life and witness of the Religious Society of Friends must be authorized by the appropriate meeting for church affairs [business meeting]. Any public statement which claims to be given on behalf of Friends in Britain Yearly Meeting as a whole will require the judgment of a more widely representative body than a meeting, area meeting or ad hoc group; it should be considered and agreed by Meeting for Sufferings or by Yearly Meeting before publication. It must be made clear when local initiatives relate solely to local meetings. Similarly, individual Friends or ad-hoc groups should make it clear that they speak only for themselves unless their area meeting has agreed a minute supporting their action.
>
> (Britain Yearly Meeting *Faith and Practice*, 3.27)

Occasionally, someone needs to speak on behalf of a particular Quaker body. This is generally done by the clerk or by an authorized staff person. See "Speaking for the Meeting" on page 18.

Epistles

Friends use the word "epistle" for a letter from one Friends body to other Friends. It may state the condition and experience of the issuing body or express concern for various issues.

> The tradition of writing letters, or "epistles," to use the biblical term, has been part of Quakerism from the beginning. The earliest ministers wrote to each other and to meetings. These letters were informative, but they were also exhortation. This tradition survives among Friends: We write epistles to the Quaker world after our yearly meetings to testify to God's work in our midst. Other important events and gatherings, and times of special concern, call forth epistles.
>
> (Margery Post Abbot, and Peggy Senger Parsons, ed., *Walk Worthy of Your Calling: Quakers and the Traveling Ministry*, p. 284)

Epistle from the Elders at Balby

There is one early Quaker epistle that is well known among Friends, as the postscript has appeared in many books of Faith and Practice, as quoted above under "Uniform Disciplines." In 1656, there was a meeting of Quaker elders at Balby, England, which issued a letter that began,

> The elders and brethren send unto the brethren in the north these necessary things following; to which, if in the Light you wait, to be kept in obedience, you shall do well. Fare you well.

This is followed by 20 advices, including the following:

4. That as any are moved of the Lord to speak the word of the Lord at . . . meetings, that it be done in faithfulness, without adding or diminishing. . . .
6. That care be taken for the families and goods of such as are called forth into the ministry, or who are imprisoned for the truth's sake; that no creatures be lost for want of the creatures [creaturely goods].
9. That husbands and wives dwell together according to knowledge, as being heirs together of the grace of life. That children obey their parents in the Lord; and that parents provoke not their children to wrath. . . .

It is signed:

> From the Spirit of truth to the children of Light, to walk in the Light; that all in order be kept in obedience; that he may be glorified, who is worthy over all, God blessed for ever. Amen

Then follows the note:

> Dearly beloved Friends, these things we do not lay upon you as a rule or form to walk by, but that all, with the measure of light which is pure and holy, may be guided: and so in the light walking and abiding, these may be fulfilled in the Spirit, not in the letter, for the letter killeth, but the Spirit giveth life.

("The Epistle from the Elders at Balby, 1656, as in the copy in the Lancashire Records Office at Preston, from the papers of Marsden Monthly Meeting")

Yearly Meeting Epistles

Typically, yearly meetings issue an epistle "To Friends Everywhere" at their annual sessions, which is then sent out to other yearly meetings and/or posted on FWCC's website. Parts or entire epistles from other yearly meetings are often read during business sessions of the yearly meetings that receive them.

Some yearly meeting epistles contain mostly a description of the annual sessions, both the business and the other activities. Others consist of or include a report more like a State of the Society report, which addresses things such as the spiritual vitality of the yearly meeting, concerns it is wrestling with, and its joys and sorrows. Sometimes they include prophetic messages to other yearly meetings or enjoin them to wrestle with a particular issue.

Typically, a small ad hoc committee of three or more Friends is appointed at the beginning of the annual sessions to draft the epistle. It is good practice to present the draft before the last business meeting so that any Friends who feel they have important input can speak to the committee in private before the final draft is presented for approval.

Some yearly meetings have adopted the practice of having the children at annual sessions write an epistle, usually one epistle from each age group. These sometimes take the form of drawings, skits, or other non-literary forms. There needs to be a common understanding in the yearly meeting whether these are to be considered as reports to the yearly meeting or whether they are to be sent out with the yearly meetings' epistle "To Friends Everywhere."

Other Epistles

Epistles can be generated by any gathering of Friends that feels led to communicate something of substance to the wider body of Friends. If the group is a committee or other ongoing entity, it can represent the epistle as coming from the committee or organization. Sometimes, Friends at a conference or other gathering with no ongoing existence feel led to write an epistle. Typically, they identify the epistle as coming "from Friends gathered at [place and date]," as in the Epistle from the Elders at Balby.

Permanent Records

Every ten years or so, a copy of each monthly, regional, and yearly meeting's permanent records should be deposited in approved archive(s). Facilities for caring for such records are often found at Quaker colleges.

Permanent records for monthly meetings should include:

- A copy of the minutes of each business session, including all the attachments, printed on archival (acid-free) paper and signed by the clerks. The attachments should include the reports of the Nominating Committee and the treasurer.
- Reports of any auditors.
- Any minutes or letters sent under concern of the meeting, such as travel minutes, that may not be part of the business meeting minutes.
- Copies of contracts and significant legal documents.
- A complete file of issues of the newsletter and other publications.

In addition to the above, permanent records for regional and yearly meetings should include:

- Copies of all handbooks, guides, and disciplines pertaining to the regional or yearly meeting.
- A copy of epistles issued by the yearly meeting.
- Copies of minutes of the decision making bodies that meet other than at the annual sessions (Executive Committee, Continuing Committee, Representative Meeting, or whatever bodies make decisions for the yearly meeting).

The meeting should retain copies of all archived materials for its own reference. Friends should continue to produce and preserve paper copies of records. While the overwhelming majority of recording clerks now use computers, rapid advances in technology mean that records preserved in only electronic form may be effectively lost. What would a monthly meeting do now if its records were archived only on five-inch floppy disks?

Section II: Communication Using Technology

Chapter 4: Using Technology

Friends in the developed world have experimented with a variety of remote communication methods which modern technology allows, and will continue to do so as new technologies become available.[42] On-line communication can be uncomfortable for Friends who are unaccustomed to it, though this may wear off with more use. On the other hand, introverts may feel more able to be present to a discussion because they can remain in their element while participating. It is important to provide other means of communication for those who do not have easy access to computers.

E-mail

E-mail is a tool that, if used carefully and thoughtfully, can be used to broadcast information and to support good Quaker process in business and decision making. Many Quaker committees, especially where its members live at a distance from one another, use e-mail extensively. This can be a quick, easy way to disseminate information, minutes, agendas, and do housekeeping such as setting up the time and place for the next committee meeting. Some kinds of committee work seem to lend themselves to e-mail communication, particularly revising documents.

[42] Much of the material in this section is based on a paper developed by the Youth Ministries Committee of FGC, "Best practices for non-face-to-face committee meetings." The full text is available with the Sample Forms, Letter, Minutes, and Reports.

Where deep listening and discernment are called for, however, e-mail communication doesn't appear viable.

When doing e-mail business, everything written in an e-mail should be discerned as carefully as when speaking to someone. Don't write anything you wouldn't say face to face. Employ all the tools that you have for good communication and process with your e-mails. Because e-mail can be sent quickly, there is all the more need to slow down. You need to choose your words carefully as you cannot depend on tone of voice to help carry your meaning. If you need time to respond well, take it. Let the e-mail sit before replying as you consider it. If the response is complicated, let your response sit and review it later before sending it. Write the response in a word-processing program if that helps with the mechanics, and cut and paste it into the body of the e-mail.

If you have agreed to do business by e-mail, you need to make a commitment to check your e-mail and respond in a timely manner for the duration of that business. If there is a period of time when you will not be able to access e-mail or you get too busy, let others know.

Because of the current nature of e-mailing and web communication in general, one problem with e-mails is that every once in a while the e-mail you send doesn't get to a recipient, nor do you receive any notice of this. People change e-mail addresses frequently, which is one reason this may happen. E-mails sent to a group of people are particularly prone to being silently rejected by a computer server that has been programmed to winnow out spam. One way around this is to send each e-mail message individually, which is time consuming unless you have enough software and savvy to automate the process. One way around this is to set up a listserv. Experience has taught that if you don't receive a reply to an e-mail, it may be because it never arrived. A follow-up e-mail may be in order. If that does not elicit a response, it is probably time to pick up the phone or send a letter.

Basic Mechanics

- *The "To" box:* Consider carefully to whom the message should be sent. Don't include those who don't need to see it, but include all who do. Use the "Reply All" button with discretion.

- *The "cc" (copy) box:* Putting someone on the "Cc" line implies that they might want to see this message but no response is expected of them. Sort carefully who goes in the "To" box and who goes in the "cc" box. If it is unclear or could be misunderstood, be explicit in the message about why someone is on the Cc line.
- *The "bcc" (blind copy) box (if available):* Very rarely is the blind copy box appropriate for Quaker business. Generally, either a person should be on the visible list of recipients or they should not be receiving the communication. While there are some exceptions, examine carefully your motives for using the bcc function and if it is in keeping with a full embrace of our truth-telling and integrity testimonies. If it is not, consider whether the message, the process, or your emotional issues need to be examined.
- *The Subject Line:* Make the subject line clear and specific. This helps in filing and accessing business matters. Subjects like "Hi," "Checking in," and "FYI" make it hard to recognize and find the e-mail at a future date. Don't use an old subject line from a previous thread (continuing discussion on a topic) if the content is different. However, having all comments in a single thread be identified by the same "Re: title" can be very useful.

Discussions with multiple people

If a group of people needs to know of something and a central person is taking feedback, e-mail can work well. However, if multiple people are in a discussion on a topic, the process can still work but takes special attentiveness. Generally, someone should act as facilitator. Participants should treat the e-mail conversation as they would a face-to-face conversation. Read all prior messages first, pay attention to where the discussion is going before you respond (don't respond to something said earlier that takes the conversation in a different direction until the current direction is completed), carefully discern if you need to speak now, and leave time between comments.

A facilitator should be constantly discerning if it is necessary to switch to a different communication mode if the conversation is going too quickly, not carefully, splintering in direction, or if some people are not feeling heard. Common face-to-face facilitation techniques that can be translated into e-mail process include:

- Send out an e-mail asking if everyone is feeling heard.
- Ask for feedback from those who have not commented.
- Remind people to leave space between comments if the discussion feels too rapid.
- Feel free to employ Quaker clerking techniques by adding some reflection or direction about the process such as stating, "This is what I have heard," "This is where I hear us going," or "How do people feel about this way forward?"
- Ask for a break (silence) while everyone settles and then send out an e-mail summarizing where the discussion has been going, making a few comments about where the group(s) want to go and reopening the channel for communication.
- Be ready to end the conversation and suggest a phone or face-to-face continuation as soon as needed.

Listservs

A listserv (mailing list server) is a way to automate sending e-mail messages to a given list of recipients. There are many free software options on the Internet; Google provides one that seems to work well. One person with some technical savvy needs to set up the list and maintain it. The larger the list, the more maintainance is needed, but only occasional work should be needed for lists with fewer than 100 people on them. People can sign up to be on a list, or can be invited by the manager.

Listservs can be set up so that anyone on the list can send a message to everyone else simply by typing the group name into the "To" box in an e-mail message. Recipients need to be careful about sending replies, thinking about whether to send their response to the whole list or just to the author of the message so that the people on the list are not subjected to e-mails that don't apply to them. Alternately, the listserv can be set up so that only a few people can broadcast messages.

Many meetings use a listserv as a way to disseminate messages quickly throughout the meeting. In many meetings, e-mail messages have largely replaced telephone trees and printed newsletters. The loss in personal contact is often minimal. Meetings that go this route do need to continue to provide other means of communication for those who do not have easy access to computers or e-mail. Listservs are also used by yearly meetings to communicate to meeting clerks, and may also be used by large committees or other groups of Friends.

Sharing Contact Information

Meetings and organizations that use a directory of Friends often include e-mail addresses as well as phone and cell phone numbers. Unfortunately, people change e-mail addresses frequently, so they may become outdated quickly. This makes listservs, which can be constantly updated, more useful than a directory. Meetings should consider not sharing e-mail or cell phone information for children and youth so they are not exposed to undesirable contacts.

Other Computer Technologies for Communicating

Instant Messaging (IM)

IM software allows two or more people to type to each other in real time, so that a written conversation can be held. The software is free. It can be somewhat impersonal, but is an efficient way to have a conversation and convey information across a distance.

Forums

Forums are often used to hold discussions over the Internet. They function very much like e-mail, but in a setting where everyone can see the conversation and participate. It tends to be more social and feel more personal than e-mail.

Web Cams

Web cams are used to broadcast a live video feed over the Internet. This allows the person on the other end to see the person they are talking to, and if audio is included, it allows for a full conversation between the users. However, there is a sizeable investment involved in purchasing a web cam, and you need a fast Internet connection.

Social Networking Services

Social networking websites are very popular, particularly among young people. Different sites have different focuses (Facebook is geared toward socializing, while LinkedIn is geared toward business networking); however, they all have the same general functionality: users create an account and then receive a home page. Users may visit others' home pages, send other users messages, and upload images. These sites work well to keep up with friends over long distances and for organizing events. There are privacy issues in using services such as this, but usually great lengths are taken to ensure that users' personal information is secure. Networking sites are a good tool for outreach, especially to young people.

Scheduling Meetings on the Web

There are a number of free web utilities that let you pick a range of dates on a calendar and then notify others so they can pick the times and dates that work for them. You then view the responses to find a time and date that, ideally, works for everyone. Doodle is one of the most popular and simple to use. Be sure to set a range of dates far enough in the future so everyone has a chance to respond before the first suggested date has arrived.

Websites

Many meetings use websites for outreach to the larger world. They offer a means of letting others know that the meeting exists, what they're about, and how to join them for worship. There is a helpful pamphlet that addresses aspects of both meeting processes and technical issues, titled "Is Your Quaker Meeting Thinking of Setting Up a Web Site?" You can find a downloadable file for it on FGC's website.

Websites can also be useful for communication within a meeting, but the inherently public nature of the web means that care needs to be taken to protect individual privacy and to post only well-thought-out materials. In particular, meetings don't want to publish draft minutes that have not yet been approved or information about particular Friends, especially contact information, unless they are safely guarded in a password-protected area of the site.

Telephone and Video Conferences

A use of technology that is being used for sensitive work is telephone conferencing, where all members of a committee can join in a phone conversation. This is particularly helpful in moving business forward between face-to-face meetings for committees whose members live a distance apart, such as in yearly meetings and Quaker organizations. With careful use, these can be used for discernment. A similar technology is video conferences, though currently few Friends have access to this.

Suggestions for the facilitator

- Send the agenda and all the materials needed for the call by e-mail in advance.
- Ask people to spend time in worship before the call, then begin the call with group worship.
- Ask people to mute their phone if there is a lot of noise in their background.
- For a large group (over seven people), have each person draw a clock on a piece of paper. Assign each person a position on the clock. Each person should write in the names in the appropriate positions. Then you can very easily go around the clock circle and hear from everyone.
- Have individuals identify themselves before speaking.
- If someone is not heard from for a while, ask them to speak.

- To determine if all are united, ask.
- One hour seems to be about the maximum for effective work. It is better to have more than one call than to let one go on for more than an hour.
- Close with silent worship.

Limits of Communicating using Technology

Although certain kinds of work can be accomplished using different technologies, nothing yet has been found to replace face-to-face meetings. Many Friends suspect that there are certain kinds of communication and group discernment that can only happen when we are in the same room together.

Section III: Life in the Spirit

Chapter 5: The Meeting as Community

The nature of their purpose and quest as Friends binds members of a meeting and of the whole Society into an intimate fellowship whose unity is not threatened by the diversity of leadings and experiences which may come to individual Friends. To share in the experience of the Presence in corporate worship, to strive to let Divine Will guide one's life, to uphold others in prayer, to live in a sense of unfailing Love, is to participate in a spiritual adventure in which Friends come to know one another and to respect one another at a level where differences of age or sex, of wealth or position, of education or vocation, or face or nation are all irrelevant. Within this sort of fellowship, as in a family, griefs and joys, fear and hopes, failures and accomplishments are naturally shared, even as individuality and independence are scrupulously respected.

(New England Yearly Meeting *Faith and Practice*, p. 120)

George Selleck, in his history, *Quakers in Boston, 1656–1964*, observed that:

Friends found that even the proper functioning of the Quaker business meeting depended upon a strong sense of community, or caring in the group. Decisions were reached without a vote, by "gathering the sense of the meeting." But this would happen only when those taking part respected and cared for one another. It was one of the happier discoveries of the early Friends not only that individuals endeavoring to follow the Light of Christ Within would be led to a unity, but that the caring group could be led as well, and might even be given a higher insight than any individual.

(George Selleck: *Quakers in Boston, 1656–1964*. Quoted in New England Yearly Meeting *Faith and Practice*, p. 115)

Where we find Friends doing well at seeking God's will together, we usually find a deep sense of community, a sense of "knowing one another in that which is eternal." This sense of a deep connection is enough for powerful worship and divinely-led decision making, even when many Friends are not well known to one another, as is often the case in large gatherings such as yearly meetings.

Deep worship and divinely-guided decision-making give the participants a sense of community. In turn getting to know and support one another on a more personal level makes deep worship and inspired decision-making easier. Connections between people on the eternal and personal levels reinforce one another.

For many monthly meetings, a vital community is a longed-for goal rather than a reality. We find that we need to work at building community in order to get better at seeking God's will together. We need to learn to communicate and empathize with one another in order to speak and hear the pieces of Truth that each of us has to share.

Entering into community can be scary, however. In *The Meeting Experience: Practicing Quakerism in Community*, Marty Walton writes:

> Being part of a Quaker community is full of risks. If we are to allow the meeting to have any effect on our lives, we must take the risks. We have to work with fire, as in a crucible or tempering steel. We cannot stay in safety, hidden behind our walls of private thoughts with aloof smiles on our faces.
>
> When we move beyond our protective barriers, lift up our shroud of privacy a bit, and begin to ask each other real questions and engage each other in honest searching, we inevitably discover how very different each of us is. We are confronted with experiences both delightful and confounding.
>
> (Marty Walton, *The Meeting Experience: Practicing Quakerism in Community*, p. 17)

Debra Farrington points out that we each look at the world in a different way, and suggests that becoming aware of our own and others' ways of seeing the world can get us past blocks to communication:

> Each of us has a lens through which we look at and evaluate the world around us. It's both unavoidable and healthy to have a lens that helps us make sense of everything we see and experience. We create ways of categorizing information, as well as the things that happen to us that are based in the values of the places we have lived, the institutions we've been affiliated with, our schooling, the values and understandings of friends and family, and our own experiences. All of that is well and good. But when we are unconscious of that lens—when we think that the way we see and understand is Reality—we limit our ability to discern well. We will end up forcing God into our systems of thinking rather than expanding the mind of our heart to accommodate God.
>
> (Debra K. Farrington, *Hearing with the Heart: A Gentle Guide to Discerning God's Will For Your Life*, pp. 96-98)

Building Community

Knowing one another deeply helps us become aware of our own lens and more able to understand where others stand. Within a monthly meeting and in larger gatherings, there are many ways to build community and trust:

- Start from what each of us knows from our own experience.
- Foster deep, satisfying worship.
- Encourage Friends to seek and respond to the Inner Guide.
- Practice careful use of Quaker process in conducting business.
- Encourage regular attendance at both meeting for worship and meeting for business.
- Welcome newcomers and help them integrate with the group.
- Encourage social networks based on friendship, work, hobbies, or shared activities such as music-making.
- Provide a variety of small group activities.
- All contribute financially as able.
- Work together on maintaining the meetinghouse or on service projects.
- Provide opportunities where Friends can share deeply with one another.
- Take individual leadings to the meeting for discernment.

- Support one another.
- Hold one another accountable.
- Actively mentor people into positions of responsibility.
- Provide opportunities for spiritual sharing and growth.
- Provide opportunities to learn more about Quakerism so that there is a common understanding among Friends of what we're about and how we do things.

There is only so much that consciously building community can achieve, however. True Quaker community is grounded in submission to God's will.

> What we believe has profound consequences for how we live, and in particular how we live corporately. A meeting community that firmly believes that, as one skilled clerk put it, "if we shut up and listen God will tell us what to do," will make different choices and, as a result of those choices, will come out looking different from a meeting that believes that "what is most important is our sense of community and how we nurture each other" . . .
>
> (Elizabeth Cazden, *Fellowships, Conferences, and Associations*, p. 19)

Group Formats for Sharing

In the last half of the 20th century, Friends developed a number of group formats for "getting to know one another in that which is eternal." The best known of these is called simply "worship sharing," but there are a number of others. They are used by meetings, at conferences, during yearly meetings, and wherever Friends gather and work on sharing with one another and building community. They all involve responding to questions, sharing one's personal experiences, and leaving worshipful space between each speaker. They provide ways of "creatively listening to each other"[43] and "the achievement of deeper self-understanding and spiritual renewal."[44]

---

[43] Rachel Davis DuBois, *Deepening Quaker Faith and Practice through the Use of the Three-Session Quaker Dialog*, p. 29.

[44] Ibid., p. ix

A common feature is the practice of listening deeply to one another, without commenting on or discussing what another has shared. Another is sharing from one's own experience rather than from speculations or even learned knowledge.

> It may seem irksome, at first, for participants to refrain from making back-and-forth remarks. They should understand, however, that there is positive value in this ground-rule that we do not discuss, or even comment on, what a speaker wishes to share. For this period of time, we are going to hold our too-ready tongues, quiet our too-lively curiosity, forego our too-quick questions and remarks. For the listeners, this voluntary silence can serve as a strengthening and strangely illuminating discipline. For the speaker, the assurance that he will not be cross-questioned may give him a sense of security which will allow him to share areas of feeling he ordinarily keeps closed. For all concerned, this discipline can be a healing ministry. In its receptiveness, the spirit we seek to establish is not unlike that of a meeting for worship. The core of this receptiveness is mutual trust resting upon spiritual faith which, in its fullest sense, is love.
>
> (Claremont Friends, *Fellowship in Depth and Spiritual Renewal through "Creative Listening": Suggestions for Leaders of Group Dialogs Derived from the Experience of Claremont, California, Friends*, p. 8)

Worship Sharing

Worship sharing provides a format for a small group of people to share their responses to a question or set of questions. Each person shares from personal experience without responding to what others have shared. The others listen attentively to what is being said. The questions can have any theme or none at all. Groups of five to twelve people work best.

Preparation

The questions used should be simple and open-ended. They should be framed in a way that invites a sharing of specific experience, rather than opinions, theories, or abstract ideas. Avoid questions that can be answered with yes or no. A question might be about one's spiritual journey: How is God moving in my life today? It might be related to the corporate life of the meeting:

What do I long for most in our community? It might relate to a book the group has been reading together: What touched me most deeply?

Allow at least half an hour for a group of five or six to share their responses to a single question, and at least an hour for a larger group.

The group needs a leader—someone to explain the format and ground rules, to read the questions aloud, to make sure that everyone has had a turn, and to decide when people are ready to hear the next question.

Guidelines[45]

- Reach as deeply as you can into the sacred center of your life.
- Speak out of the silence, and leave a period of silence between speakers.
- Speak from your own experience, about your own experience. Use "I" words. Concentrate on feelings rather than on thoughts or theories.
- Do not respond to what anyone else has said, either to praise or to refute.
- Listen carefully and deeply to what is spoken.
- Expect to speak only once, until everyone has had a chance to speak. You may pass.
- Respect the confidentiality of what is shared.

The worship sharing

- Go around the circle and share names and perhaps one more piece of personal information, such as one's meeting or where one lives.
- The leader briefly explains the format and guidelines, even if most of the people are familiar with worship sharing. It is helpful to have a printed list of the guidelines.
- Decide how the group will speak in turn:
  —In order around the circle?
  —As each person feels ready to contribute?

[45] Adapted from the guidelines developed by FGC's Advancement and Outreach Committee.

—In any order, but passing a speaker's symbol, such as a coin or branch?

- Start with a period of silent centering.
- Read the first question.
- Because the first response will set the tone for the others, it helps if the first person who responds is concrete, honest, and concise.
- The next person should allow a little time before speaking.
- Continue until everyone has either spoken or passed. Before moving on, the leader may invite those who passed to share.
- If there is more than one question, allow a little time, then read the next question.
- End with more silence or a group hug or hand squeeze or whatever seems supportive and appropriate.

Tears

Sometimes someone will cry when sharing with the group. These may be tears of joy or tears from remembering a painful experience. Do not try to cheer up or distract such a person with well-intentioned support. The tears are not the pain. Simply sit quietly, hold a hand or give a gentle hug. Above all, listen with full attention and let the person finish. Be present with loving concern.

Fish Bowl

A new format for sharing has become popular among Quaker teens and young adults. The name, "fish bowl," comes from the format, which is one of an "outside" group listening in on an "inside" group. Friends are divided into two distinct groups. These can be young Friends and adults, women and men, Liberal and Pastoral Friends, or whatever dynamic the group chooses to address. One group shares while the other group listens. This allows for small group work with a large group.

The sharing usually focuses on a particular topic, often by responding to one or more questions. The questions may be written by a facilitator or by the participants. One of the groups sits down in a circle in the center of the space facing one another, while the other group sits on the outside of the circle. The group in the middle often sits on the floor; there may be chairs for the outside circle. The people in the middle are the speakers; the people on the outside are listeners. Leaving space between responses, Friends in the middle respond to the topic or questions. If there are few questions, many Friends will respond to the same question. If there are many questions, only one or two will respond to each.

One way to handle many questions is to write each question on a separate slip of paper and put them in the center of the circle. Each speaker takes and reads a slip, and either passes it on or retains it if it is a question to which he or she feels like responding. This process of silently reading, considering, and passing on or retaining different questions can take quite a while. When the pile of questions has gone all the way around, the speakers begin sharing by reading a question aloud and responding to it out of their personal experience and outlook. Another speaker may add something if led to. When all the questions have been responded to or no one feels led to respond to the rest, the first part of the activity is finished. Sometimes this completes the exercise.

At other times, the inner group stands up and trades places with the outer group, and the roles are reversed. There is a second period of sharing and listening, either with the same or a different set of questions. When both groups have shared and listened, this may end the activity, or the group may regather as a whole and share their reactions.

Quaker Dialog

In the late 1950s, Rachel Davis DuBois developed a three-session format for sharing within a monthly meeting which she called "Quaker Dialog." Quaker Dialog's main aim is "to help local Friends who meet regularly in meetings for worship and business to spontaneously share their experiences in, and their concerns about, the ideal conduct of these meetings."[46]

---

[46] DuBois, Rachel Davis, *Deepening Quaker Faith and Practice through the Use of the Three-Session Quaker Dialog*, p. ix.

Format

The format consists of three two-hour sessions. Group size can be anywhere from eight to twenty; multiple groups can be formed if the group is larger; each needs a leader.

The first session focuses on religious experiences, both outside and within the meeting for worship. The second session focuses on the nature and role of the Quaker method of finding the sense of the meeting. The third session is on one of four aspects of outreach to be chosen by the group: 1) Telling others about Quakerism; 2) Putting into practice Friends testimonies; 3) Wider ministry as outreach (Friends work worldwide), or 4) Sharing with other religious traditions—ecumenicity.

Childhood memories

The first exercise in each session is to go around the circle and share a childhood experience or memory related to the topic. It is amazing how deeply connected a group can feel through this simple exercise.

The use of brief quotations related to the topic

The leader brings a number of pertinent quotations copied onto cards to be read at an appropriate moment. A quotation can be used either for emphasis or for stimulus. These are a way of introducing seasoned reflections, Friends traditions, or other material that will enrich the dialog.

Leadership

> The leader helps participants communicate with each other about things that matter deeply, in an understanding way. When statements become abstract or academic the leader asks for personal experience related to that particular topic, offering his or her own, if helpful. No one gives a lecture; no study program precedes the dialog session; no pressure for agreement or group decision is allowed to inhibit frankness and spontaneity.
>
> (Rachel Davis DuBois, *Deepening Quaker Faith and Practice through the Use of the Three-Session Quaker Dialog*, p. xi)

Quaker Dialog calls for strong leadership. The leader needs to prepare beforehand, plays a major role, and guides the process throughout.

Variations

Quaker Dialog has been adapted for many different settings and for a variety of topics. It has been adapted for use by regional and yearly meetings and for intervisitation between meetings. These use different topics than those prescribed for monthly meetings, and may consist of only one session. Within a monthly meeting, it has been adapted for groups of new members and attenders to meet with a few "seasoned" Friends informally, preferably in a home.

One of its enduring techniques is sharing childhood memories for starting sessions, which works well as an icebreaker, gets a group dynamic going quickly, and models sharing at a personal experiential level that serves well for whatever follows.

Creative Listening—The Claremont Dialog

Creative Listening was developed to answer the need in our mobile society to get to know each other more quickly in depth. It was developed by the Ministry and Counsel Committee of the Claremont, California, Meeting. It was inspired partly by Quaker Dialog and partly by a method developed by West Richmond Friends Meeting in Indiana. Claremont Friends shared it widely, first through an article in *Friends Journal* in 1963, then through a pamphlet (see "Claremont" in "Works Cited").

The format is a series of two-hour meetings, for instance once a week for six weeks. Having eight to twelve people in a group works best. The leadership rotates so there is a different leader for each meeting. The leader selects the questions for the session, often beginning with one that asks for childhood memories. The leader participates fully as one of the group; in addition, the leader monitors the group dynamics.

Each meeting begins with a worshipful silence, after which the leader asks the first question. It works well if the leader or someone else familiar with the method answers first in order to set a model for others. The others then go around the circle taking turns answering. Participants listen in a spirit of understanding and appreciation without questions or judgmental comments.

Anyone who wishes may pass. The topics may range from "deeply satisfying or unsatisfying experiences in childhood" to "turning points in spiritual growth."

Guidelines

- Speak from feeling and experience rather than from theory or opinion.
- Participants have the option not to answer.
- There is no discussion of what participants have shared, and what is said is held in confidence.
- The leader takes part as one of the group.

Common Elements of these Group Sharing Formats

All of the formats described above call for:

- Carefully crafted questions.
- Responding to those questions.
- Sharing personal experiences.
- Listening deeply.
- Beginning, ending, and punctuating the sharing with worshipful silence.
- Except for introductions, allowing people to "pass."

All the formats aim to:

- Create safe spaces for deep sharing.
- Help Friends get to know one another on a deep level.
- Foster communication.
- Build community.
- Build people's listening skills.

They require a substantial degree of self-discipline on the part of all the participants.

Formats for Ongoing Relationships

Spiritual Friendships

Sometimes it is helpful for Friends to pair up for spiritual sharing on an ongoing basis. There are a number of ways such "spiritual friends" can function:

> Spiritual friendships can exist for any length of time, from a weekend at a workshop to a spiritual partnership lasting many years. Ideally,

> spiritual friends can meet face to face on a regular basis, but if circumstances don't allow that closeness, a spiritual friendship can be conducted be means of letters, phone calls, or even email! What is important is that there be an intentionality about the relationship.
>
> (Liz Yeats, "Spiritual Friendships")

A meeting may facilitate setting up pairs of spiritual friends. Ministry and Counsel may ask those who are interested to sign up, and then determine pairings. The pairs are asked to meet regularly for a period of time, usually a year, sharing their individual experiences of spiritual growth with one another. This could be weekly or less frequent. It could include a meal. The common thread is that each person shares his or her spiritual journey and listens to and affirms the other person's journey without judgment or giving advice.

A helpful set of guidelines for spiritual friendships drawn up by Liz Yeats is included in *Fostering Vital Friends Meetings: Volume II.* (Volume II consists of a large selection of resource materials grouped by topic.)

Spiritual Companions Groups

There are many ways groups of spiritual friends can form and function. Nancy L. Bieber has developed a flexible format for a small group that meets regularly to support each one's spiritual journey and to deepen their knowledge of one another. The main idea is to give each member of the group "a time to talk, a time to be the focus person when others simply sit and listen. This is followed by a period of reflective, thoughtful silence out of which arise responses from the other group members." A group may focus on a theme; spend time in silent meditation; or write together on a subject and speak out of their journaling experience. Confidentiality is an important component. Nancy Bieber suggests that the group focus often on the questions, "What is going on in my life; what feelings do I have about it; and how is God involved?"

Nancy Bieber emphasizes that the group's members need to commit to the group: "the kind of sharing that speaks out of one's own experience increases the trust, vulnerability and closeness of group members. Occasional attendance would hurt the group." She suggests that the group spell out the commitment they make to each other by writing out a contract.[47]

Organizing Socializing in a Meeting

Ministry and Counsel or another committee may organize small groups for socializing by asking interested Friends to sign up and then assigning individuals to groups.

Friendly Eights

Friendly Eights are groups of (approximately) eight Friends who get together for a meal and fellowship. These get-togethers are usually held in members' homes once a month for a year (or during the school year). In some meetings, new groups are formed each fall.

Progressive Dinners

Where Friends live relatively close together, meetings can organize progressive dinners in which each course is held in a different home. This means traveling to at least three different houses for an appetizer, main course, and dessert. Different dishes can be provided by the Friends who make up the group. Different groups in a meeting may all meet on the same evening or different ones. This is usually a one-time or annual affair.

A Common Understanding

Tom Gates writes,

> Sooner or later, both the individual seeker and the meeting will come to the realization that acceptance by itself does not provide a sufficient basis to sustain spiritual community. . . . True community

---

[47] Quotes are from Nancy L. Bieber in "The Spiritual Companions Group: A Design for Nurturing Small Groups for Spiritual Growth in Your Meeting," in *Companions Along the Way: Spiritual Formation Within The Quaker Tradition.* The article is on the web at http://archive.pym.org/worship-and-care/s-f-program.htm as of July 2011

> requires something more: a sense of core beliefs, values, and commitments that are understood and shared by all.
>
> (Thomas Gates, *Members One of Another: The Dynamics of Membership in Quaker Meeting*, p. 14)

It is important that this core be based, not on social compatibility, but on a commitment to listen for and act on divine guidance.

> A meeting may find it . . . difficult to extend hospitality to those who do not seem to share our basic values. Although understandable, this attitude risks turning a meeting into an exclusive club of the like-minded, instead of a spiritual community that transcends differences.
>
> (Thomas Gates, *Members One of Another: The Dynamics of Membership in Quaker Meeting*, pp. 15-16)

Howard Brinton suggested the value of diversity:

> The meeting membership should not become so exclusively unified along social and religious lines that outsiders who feel attracted to the principles of the Society of Friends may hesitate to try to gain entrance to it. A meeting is particularly fortunate if it contains representatives of more than one race or economic class. Such variety widens its mental horizons.
>
> (Howard Brinton, *Guide to Quaker Practice*, pp. 59-60)

Lloyd Lee Wilson puts it this way:

> The Quaker testimony of community is that each Friend has been drawn into communion with God and led into a meeting community based on that prior relationship with God. We are in community with those in our meeting not because they are like-minded, but because we each belong to God.
>
> (Lloyd Lee Wilson, *Essays on the Quaker Vision of Gospel Order*)

Just as it is helpful for a nation's people to share a common understanding of who they are and how they operate, it is helpful for Friends to share a common understanding of Quaker faith and practice. Some will delve much more deeply into certain areas, such as history or spiritual practices or business processes, but a basic shared knowledge base is helpful in communicating with one another.

Howard Brinton, in his popular *Guide to Quaker Practice*, pointed out the importance for Friends of two different ways of learning: through experience and through study. He wrote:

> Since the religion of the Society of Friends is based on an inward experience deeper than intellectual concepts, it cannot be taught in the same way that subjects are taught in a school curriculum. Religion of this type is communicated only through practice. A child observing sincere religious acts performed by parents or elders becomes thereby religiously educated. There is only one Teacher of religion, the Divine Spirit working in the heart, either directly or through others. The meeting for worship and the meeting for business are therefore the chief religious educational agencies in the Society of Friends.
>
> (Howard Brinton, *Guide to Quaker Practice*, pp. 54-55)

Howard Brinton recommended that meetings engage in a "ministry of teaching," including the following:

- Teaching the Bible.
- Emphasizing the need for peace and understanding among races, nations, and classes.
- Teaching the history and doctrines of the Religious Society of Friends.
- Holding discussion groups on important books.
- Encouraging members to attend Quaker conferences.
- Supporting members who feel led to participate in Quaker study centers or courses of instruction.

Study and experience can go a long way toward providing common reference points so that communication can flow among us.

We also need mutual comprehension of each others' inward experiences.

> My sense is that to experience a genuine faith community it certainly helps if the individuals have undergone a transformative encounter with the Divine—and for a Quaker faith community the implica-

tion is that this encounter will be understood within the Quaker tradition. That is, traditional Quaker categories and understandings will help to define and provide meaning to the experience.

(Marty Grundy, personal correspondence, 2008)

Whatever each of us can truly say and share from our own experience and whatever we can truly hear of others' experiences will help tremendously in understanding the pieces of Truth we can each contribute to the common pool when we are engaging in communal discernment, worship, and decision-making.

Speaking of God, Christ, and the Divine

Words must not become barriers between us, for no one of us can ever adequately understand or express the truth about God. Yet words are our tools and we must not be afraid to express the truth we know in the best words we can.

(Britain Yearly Meeting *Faith and Practice*, Introduction)

Robert Griswold points out:

I don't wish to minimize the importance of Christ in Fox's ministry, but to note that for much of that ministry he uses a plethora of words for the Divine Within that speaks to us. "Truth," "Word," "Seed," "Power of God," "Witness of God," "Spirit," "Light," "Wisdom of God," "Light Within" and "Light of Christ," "that which is Pure," "Measure"—these are just some of the terms Fox uses to point to that inner experience. Other early Friends had even more. This great volume of pointer words is evidence that, for early Friends and for us today as well, the experience is primary and the name is secondary. Divine reality can be pointed to but it cannot be named.

(Robert Griswold, *Creeds and Quakers: What's Belief Got To Do With It?*, pp. 10-11)

There is a wide range of language used by Friends today to refer to that ultimate truth which is the ground of our worship and our decision making. Different vocabulary can keep Friends from understanding or even listening to one another. In order to talk together about ultimate Truth, Friends must listen deeply both to one another and to the Spirit, getting beyond the inadequacies of the words. There is no neutral language, though, when it comes to ultimate Truth. Friends communicate best when each person uses language that describes how he or she experiences that ultimate Truth.

> We simply need to listen for God's truth in what others are saying, even when it appears hidden among some unhelpful words. Some have used the phrase "listening in tongues" for this process. . . . Careful listening means hearing what people intend to say and discerning the thoughts behind the words, not hearing only the words actually spoken.
>
> (Lon Fendall, Jan Wood, and Bruce Bishop, *Practicing Discernment Together*, p. 44)

When we learn to listen to what lies behind the particular words of a Friend who speaks from personal experience, we find ourselves able to unite with him or her even when we cannot unite on the language. And we, in our turn, must speak out of our personal experience.

Regardless of what we call it or how we think about it, without a source of love, power, and unity greater than each of us individually, Quakerism makes no sense.

What Do We Mean by "God's Will"?

Quakers often say that what we are doing in our worship, our business, and our lives is discerning God's will for us. A problem for some people is that "God's will" implies that God is like a person.

> When we try to describe our relationship with God, one of the most difficult aspects is that we have no way to describe God's actions if God is not a being like us. We say, for instance, that we hear God's voice, but that is a pale reflection of how we experience God "speaking" to us. We talk about feeling guided by God's will, but we don't usually mean that God handed us a piece of paper or sent us an e-mail telling us exactly what to do. We end up speaking about God as if we were talking about a person or being like us, but we do so with the understanding that we are speaking in metaphors, which is the best we can do. . . .
>
> (Debra K. Farrington, *Hearing with the Heart*, pp. 6-7)

It is helpful to keep in mind that God is much bigger than any of our concepts of Him. One of the strengths of Quakerism is that it constantly moves us beyond words by referring us to experience.

Mutual Accountability

Tom Gates writes:

> We need a vision of community that allows not just for loving acceptance, but also for loving challenge, growth, and transformation.
>
> (Thomas Gates, *Members One of Another: The Dynamics of Membership in Quaker Meeting*, pp. 25-27)

Quaker community is characterized by mutual accountability—each of us is accountable to one another. I am accountable to you, and you are accountable to me, not in the sense that we judge one another but so that we can help one another listen and respond to God's leadings.

> Neither the scriptures, my local meeting, nor my closest spiritual friends have authority over me because of their position or inherited tradition; they have authority only insofar as they are faithful in witnessing to the Spirit of Christ and in demonstrating loving care for me. However, loving care may sometimes involve saying things that I do not want to hear.
>
> (Micah Bales, "Individual Leadings and the Body of Christ—Witness and Accountability," a blog posted November 9, 2008, on The Lamb's War blog at http://www.lambswar.blogspot.com)

Conflict

> Intense conflict is an invitation to turn to God, who wants to lead us forward into restored relationships and into new organizational processes.
>
> (Lon Fendall, Jan Wood, and Bruce Bishop, *Practicing Discernment Together: Finding God's Way Forward in Decision Making*, p. 20)

Conflict in a Meeting

History

Strong disagreements arose as the Quaker movement took shape. Those with spiritual implications were dealt with by gathering to discern God's will, just as Friends do today in their business meetings. Conflicts between individuals were handled according to the instructions given by Jesus in the book of Matthew:

> If your brother does wrong, go and take the matter up with him, strictly between yourselves. If he listens to you, you have won your brother over. But if he will not listen, take one or two others with you, so that every case may be settled on the evidence of two or three witnesses. If he refuses to listen to them, report the matter to the congregation; and if he will not listen even to the congregation, then treat him as you would a pagan or a tax-collector.
>
> (Matthew 18:15-17, Revised English)

Friends continued to use this model through the era of Quietism, codifying it in books of discipline. With the Hicksite-Orthodox split in the early 1820s, however, Hicksite meetings dropped it from their disciplines, along with other rules for conduct. Until recently, many Quaker meetings have suffered from a reluctance to face internal conflict openly.

Marty Walton is a seasoned Friend who served as General Secretary of Friends General Conference from 1985 until 1992. In 1996, she gave a series of presentations on Quaker community for Canadian Yearly Meeting. These have been published as *The Meeting Experience: Practicing Quakerism in Community*. In her introduction, Marty Walton explains that "they reflect the observations and experiences I have gathered over the past two decades of involvement in many aspects of Quaker meeting life and repeated visits to meetings and annual sessions in more than a dozen yearly meetings in North America. They also reflect my very personal understanding of Quaker faith and practice."[48]

[48] Marty Walton, Introduction, *The Meeting Experience: Practicing Quakerism in Community*

Marty Walton describes what often happens when a conflict arises in a meeting:

> Friends do not always handle strong disagreement well. I have seen us stop dead in our tracks. We are not sure what to do. We leave things unclear. We go home and think about it. We talk to our friends. We feel uneasy. We wait and see. We go on as we have. We may ask questions, being careful not to commit ourselves. We feel some tension. We talk more with our friends. We open up the question again in a planned session. The disagreement becomes more clear. We still do not know what to do, but we are clearer who stands with us and who does not. We begin to separate into camps. We reaffirm the rightness of our position. We see the flaws in the other position; in fact, we see the flaws in the people who hold that other position. We talk about them, wonder about them to our friends.
>
> And then, we see what has been happening to our Meeting. We see our preoccupation with the conflict. We know inside we have not been feeling or acting loving. Our commitment to the Meeting finally proves itself—we bring ourselves to worship together and ask for help to know the way forward.
>
> (Marty Walton, *The Meeting Experience: Practicing Quakerism in Community*, pp. 19-20)

Marty Walton advises:

> Gospel order[49] is *not* talking about the problem in the parking lot with people who are "on your side," saying things you did not say in the meeting for business. Gospel order is first of all about discerning your own truth and experience and, if a problem exists with someone else, honoring your own truth and that of the other person by going directly to that person with the aim of finding a solution together. How respectful that is of yourself; how respectful of the other person!
>
> Our Quaker meeting communities are where we face our fears and lack of trust. . . . Expressing our solidarity or our opposition is to express our Truth. That is right-ordered action. Truth is good; truth builds community because it is recognizable among us. . . .
>
> But conformism and non-involvement represent our unwillingness to face our own truth or someone else's. Our non-involvement, or worse, our withdrawal—are extremely destructive to community.

[49] See the Glossary for information on "gospel order."

That is one of the biggest fears—that people will withdraw or leave. If conflict arises, some people feel they do not have the energy to deal with it. . . . They want to come to meeting to get away from stress—they need peace and calm.

Is that wrong, to seek an island of calm at the end of a busy week? Well, if that is what meeting means to us, we are not quite seeing the big picture. If we use meeting as a sanctuary from the world, a place of refuge from the onslaughts of our daily life, or a place to get our batteries recharged, then we are seeing meeting as a resource for dealing with the world, a kind of community therapy. And, in fact, meetings do offer this. But to what purpose? . . . Are we only using meeting as a place to heal from the world, or is the world where we help bring about God's love which we know and experience from our life in our meeting? . . .

If all meeting means to us is a soothing place to dip into once in a while, we are missing the substance, the opportunity, the very message that early Friends experienced—that our reality can be changed, transformed through living together with God.

(Marty Walton, *The Meeting Experience: Practicing Quakerism in Community*, pp. 20-21)

Common Sources of Conflict

Trouble comes to meeting
when we come with a purpose
and would have Friends be
an instrument for that.
But we are bid to meet
the Author of our purposes
and make of ourselves
an instrument for That.

(Bruce Nevin, July 2008 *Friends Journal*)

In an excellent article on conflict in meetings by Arlene Kelly in the July 2008 *Friends Journal*, she identifies four common sources of conflict:

- Issues on which people have differing, deeply held views, such as the response to 9/11 or same gender relationships or marriage.

- Decisions about the use of resources, human or financial, within the meeting, such as whether to undertake a building project.
- How to relate to persons in the meeting who have very formed opinions.
- The entry or possible entry of a person into the community who is seen to be a threat to the safety of others.

Conflicts also arise in churches around people in crisis such as a couple who is divorcing, around a person who behaves in a way that some find unacceptable, and around individuals who push their own agendas. The tendency is for people in the meeting to take sides rather than to hold everyone in the Light of Truth. This can tear the community apart.

Arlene Kelly lists the costs of not dealing effectively with conflict:

- A lack of intimacy in many of our meetings when the fear of encountering difference precludes deep sharing.
- People being hurt, angered, or discouraged when initiatives are blocked by differences or a lack of trust.
- The silent exiting of people because of disillusionment.

Arlene Kelly addresses Quaker process when dealing with conflicts in a business meeting. She notes, "In meetings for which conflict avoidance is a part of their pattern we may notice things such as vague minutes that obscure non-decisions."

Addressing Conflict Quickly and Openly

Recently, a number of Friends have looked at how meetings handle internal conflict, and have found that the Scriptural procedure is still sound. Marty Walton describes the traditional Quaker process for dealing with conflict between two Friends:

> Jesus, as Matthew records, would have us respond to conflict immediately. . . . If someone offends you, go directly to that person and try to settle it between the two of you. If that does not work, take a friend or two and go to that person and try again to resolve the conflict. And, after at least two times of that direct an encounter, if the problem still continues, then take it to the church body.
>
> (Marty Walton, *The Meeting Experience: Practicing Quakerism in Community*, p. 20)

Sandra Cronk comments:

> There are a number of helpful aspects of the process of one-to-one admonition described in Matthew 18. It cuts off backbiting, tale-bearing, and general behind-the-scenes, disgruntled murmuring which is destructive to any group. It encourages the persons directly involved in the problem to address their difficulty, asking help from others if they need it. The procedure prevents problems from festering. It does not allow people to shy away from sharing their real thoughts when the behavior of another has caused offense.
>
> (Sandra L. Cronk, *Gospel Order: A Quaker Understanding of Faithful Church Community*, p. 23)

Southeastern Yearly Meeting's *Faith and Practice* points out that "Friends experience is that disagreement is inevitable in any community where people are honestly engaged in dealing with important issues." It advises Friends to "face our difficulties with courage and faith that the Light will guide us." It notes that "the peaceful resolution of disagreements and conflicts that arise in our meetings is vital if we are to carry our testimonies of Peace, Community and Integrity to the wider world."

> The foundation for peacemaking needs to be laid long before conflict arises. Peacemaking is grounded in how we relate to God and each other in Meeting for Worship, Meetings for Worship with a Concern for Business, fellowship, and service. Understanding our faith and practice, knowledge gained from Friends writings, and the regular practice of our spiritual disciplines are important if Friends are to be equipped with the spiritual maturity and guidance to be peacemakers. The development of skills in resolving differences peacefully is acquired over time as we walk in the Light, learning how to handle differences and disagreements with love and forbearance in everyday conversation, committee meetings, and Meetings for Business. Friends need to feel that their meeting is a place where it is safe to disagree; and that when they express themselves they will be listened to because they are valued.
>
> (Southeastern Yearly Meeting *Faith and Practice*, "Blessed Community," pp. 12-13)

The advice to deal with conflicts promptly and lovingly appears in a number of books of discipline across the Quaker spectrum.

Handling Conflict

As in any group of people, conflicts will arise in Friends meetings. It is what we do with them that matters. They need to be acknowledged, named, and worked on. We may need to call on outside help, either from the larger Quaker world or from professionals in our community. Creatively working through a conflict with love and forbearance on all sides tends to deepen and mature a meeting. Ignoring conflicts may lead to a superficial unity, leaving the meeting with no healthy place from which to deal with future conflicts; it may drive a few individuals away, leaving a weakened and less dynamic meeting; or it may lead to an eventual explosion in which large numbers of people walk away wounded.

Southeastern Yearly Meeting's *Faith and Practice* has a long section on "Blessed Community" which goes into detail in describing how to handle conflict.

> The peaceful resolution of conflict requires a covering of prayer and true humility. True humility is not about "being a doormat" or stifling one's light, but means accepting ourselves for who we are, acknowledging our limits and our need for others and for God. It depends upon our understanding that self-respect and respect for others go hand-in-hand. . . .
>
> (Southeastern Yearly Meeting *Faith and Practice*, "Blessed Community," pp. 9-10)

Possible procedures that are suggested include involving Ministry and Counsel, bringing a matter to business meeting, asking for help from another meeting or the yearly meeting, or setting up "some form of structured and facilitated listening for the group" such as threshing sessions[50] or worship sharing.[51]

The following advices are offered:

- Friends may need to be reminded lovingly of their commitment to peaceful reconciliation, and to acknowledge together that their difficulties are shared. In community, it is a fact

[50] See "The Recording Clerk and Minutes" on page 174.

[51] See "Worship Sharing" on page 79.

that we are all in this together, and blaming one another for a problem only works to prevent us from solving it.

- Friends are advised neither to deny their feelings nor to become ruled by them. While it is normal to have strong feelings at times, Friends are advised to learn to recognize them and to avoid any sense of acting out of crisis or anger. . . .
- Friends are asked to set aside agendas, the desire to control outcomes, and any attempts to convert others to their point of view. We are asked and expected not to engage in gossip, make or take sides on an issue, or use other attempts to manipulate others. These behaviors not only show profound disrespect for others, but are also a departure from the Quaker path of seeking God's guidance and unity in the Light.
- Friends are encouraged to strive to dispel confusion and misconception by practicing reality testing and information sharing. Recognize how different issues are interwoven and seek clearness in identifying them.
- Friends are urged to practice compassionate listening, compassionate speaking, and nonjudgmental language.
- Friends are asked to consider what true forgiveness is, and what it is not, and to attend to closure and healing.

(Southeastern Yearly Meeting *Faith and Practice*, "Blessed Community," pp. 9-10)

Arlene Kelly concludes her article by writing that "The good news is that many meetings are increasingly aware of their need to engage the conflict that is inherent to the life of any healthy meeting."

She suggests the following ways to build a meeting that deals creatively with conflict:

- Build community—A strong and resilient meeting has a clear sense of itself as a *community* and not just a place to which a wide variety of persons come for their individual fulfillment.
- Provide opportunities to build personal relationships—meeting work days, intergenerational service projects, book discussion groups, potluck meals, etc.
- Early intervention—Recognize a potentially divisive issue

when it first appears on the horizon and then plan accordingly by setting up a process for working through it.
- Remember the common ground—Start by naming areas of agreement and shared identity.
- Participation from the beginning in a challenging discussion—At the beginning of a process undertaken to deal with a challenging issue, all who are active in the life of the meeting should be reminded of the responsibility to take part in the process from the beginning in a spirit of openness, allowing ourselves to be changed. If we forego that aspect of the decision making, in the absence of a good reason for having done so, then we forgo the privilege of having a strong voice in the decision to be made.
- Address lingering hurts—Acknowledge unhealed hurts from earlier situations. We need to listen deeply to the hurt and anger that is the residue of the past, and to understand the experience from the perspective of each of the parties. But we need to avoid the trap of debating perceptions from the past. Recognizing that the emotion is real, but the act causing it cannot be undone, the question then becomes: what can we do now to enable the parties to lay down the emotions being carried and to begin to rebuild trust? Another key question is: What can we learn from what has happened that will help us avoid getting into a similar situation in the future?
- Tend the roots—The essential challenge is to remain grounded in our faith and what it teaches us.

In planning how to address an issue, a meeting might include threshing sessions, worship sharing, and a mix of large group and small group processing.

Healing

After a conflict, a meeting may need healing. Marty Walton suggests:

> In order to heal after a damaging situation, it is essential that together we name the things that have happened. We need to let the Light shine in that darkness so that our energy can be free to move

on to building something.

(Marty Walton, *The Meeting Experience: Practicing Quakerism in Community*, p. 28)

She suggests some queries to ask ourselves:

- If our meetings have had some tough situations to face, can references to these situations be found in our minutes or in our State of Society reports?
- Have we asked for prayers from other Friends in other meetings?

Conflict Between a Meeting and an Individual

Here is a traditional Friends process a meeting might use with a straying member:

- Ministry and Counsel assigns two Friends to visit the straying Friend.
- The visit takes place on the straying Friend's home turf.
- The visitors should feel loving care for the Friend. They should express this and bring the Friend's troubling actions to his or her attention.
- If there is agreement on the facts, and the visitors judge that the Friend will be open to it, they can suggest changes the straying Friend might make to remain in unity with Friends.
- The visitors should report their visit and what transpired to Ministry and Counsel, which will decide what further action to take, if any.

Conflict Between Groups of Friends

Quakers love everyone, except each other.

(Jack L. Willcuts, "One in the Spirit")

Tom Hamm writes about "Contemporary Quaker Debates":

Friends of all persuasions speak of incredulity, even disorientation, when they encounter Quakers whose ways are different from those they have known, whether they be unprogrammed Friends experiencing Evangelical Friends worship or pastoral Friends being introduced to an unprogrammed meeting. Some Friends will deny

> the bona fides[52] of any Quaker who disagrees with them on matters that they perceive as fundamental. Many find this deplorable. They assert that Friends should model peacemaking among themselves....
>
> Some Friends argue that the differences are exaggerated and the commonalities are greater. Too often, they assert, differences are based on stereotypes and caricatures. Certainly many Friends speak of a conviction that, among all types of Quakers, there is a common spirit.... Still, the differences are real. . . . Many observers still believe this: Friends simply do not speak the same language.
>
> (Thomas D. Hamm, *The Quakers in America*, pp. 146-147)

Tom Hamm enumerates ways in which Friends from across the spectrum are currently engaging with one another:

> Some see hope in respecting differences but finding ways that Quakers of different views can work together in common projects. The oldest organization with this goal is the Friends World Committee for Consultation, which was formed in 1937. Its name describes its function: to encourage consultation among the different bodies of Friends. It supports a range of projects, largely relief or community building, around the world. The Earlham School of Religion is another such organization. It was founded with the goal of bringing together Friends of all persuasions. . . . There are other such enterprises. For almost three decades, there have been periodic gatherings of Friends from North Pacific Yearly Meeting, widely regarded as one of the most liberal in North America, and its EFI neighbor, Northwest Yearly Meeting. . . . Personal contact tends to lessen differences, but not always.
>
> (Thomas D. Hamm, *The Quakers in America*, pp. 150)

Learning to work with and respect Friends of differing flavors can transform our ideas of what being a Friend means.

Caring for the Life of a Meeting and the Role of Elders

The purpose of all ministry and all eldering is to direct attention

[52] Bona fides is Latin for "in good faith." The implication is that others are not really Quakers.

towards the Inward Teacher, who ultimately inspires, corrects, and empowers.

(Jan Hoffman and Kenneth Sutton in *Walk Worthy of Your Calling*, p. 159)

History of Elders

Among the first generation of Friends in the mid–1600s, "elders" were those of whatever age who had been part of the Quaker movement for the longest time and had experience and spiritual insight. They were looked to for help in guiding others. In time, the term was applied to any Friend who showed unusual spiritual maturity and who could mentor other Friends.

In the early 1700s during Quietism, Friends came to identify the role of elders as overseeing ministers—those Friends who were recognized by a meeting as having a special gift of "vocal ministry." Elders were appointed by each monthly meeting. They looked for emerging gifts of ministry, and counseled, encouraged, and rebuked Friends who spoke in meeting, according to their sense of whether the Friend was following a leading of the Spirit or not. An extension of this function became accompanying ministers as they traveled with a call to ministry. "Select meetings" of ministers and elders were set up to jointly oversee the spiritual life of the meeting, and to see that individual Friends did not stray from the fold.

As Friends became increasingly concerned about some Friends assimilation into the wider culture, those with authority became increasingly rule-bound, and disownment for behavior "not according to the Discipline" became common. Elders were considered controversial among Hicksites after the Hicksite-Orthodox split in 1827–1828, and some Hicksites did abolish them. But the main Hicksite yearly meetings did preserve them until the 20th century. Although the function of elder eventually disappeared among Liberal Friends, the idea of eldering as an unwarranted and harsh rebuke remained like a bad odor. This was the only association Liberal Friends had with the concept of eldering until quite recently. Friends in the other branches of Quakerism continued appointing elders for much longer. Some FUM meetings still appoint elders, as do most Conservative Friends.

Sandra Cronk gives a helpful description of the traditional role of elders when done well:

> The admonitory aspect of mutual accountability involved all kinds of situations, including helping people to recognize and exercise their gifts, to see where the broken and unfaithful places were in their lives, to overcome paralyzing fears, to discern leadings, and to know when they had outrun or lagged behind their Guide. Thus, admonition was not simply telling others when they were wrong, at least in the way we usually interpret that idea. It was admonishing a person to be courageous in adversity or to undertake a much needed ministry or service. It was encouraging one another to take a risk in trusting God's leading or letting go of a behavior that was blocking deeper commitment to God. In short, it was helping each other move toward greater faithfulness in all areas of living.
>
> (Sandra L. Cronk, *Gospel Order: A Quaker Understanding of Faithful Church Community*, pp. 24-25)

Elders Among Friends Today

Ken and Katharine Jacobsen, Conservative Friends in Ohio Yearly Meeting, which maintains the practice of appointing elders, reported in 2007 that "in their travels among Friends they have found disappointingly little interest in and much misunderstanding about the spiritual gift and function of elders." The Jacobsens observed that many Friends have gifts of eldership without knowing it. They concluded that "these gifts are underused, and Friends organizations everywhere suffer from the lack of members who prayerfully work to keep the channels of God's love open." They concluded, "Always, the 'how' of eldering, the way of nurturing and guiding, must be Love."[53]

Frances Taber, also a member of Ohio Yearly Meeting (Conservative), has identified ten areas where meetings need care:

---

53 Katharine Jacobsen, "Eldering as a Spiritual Gift," *The Conservative Friend*, Eighth Month 2007

- Nurture of the meeting for worship.
- Nurture of the spiritual life of individuals.
- Discernment and testing of leadings.
- Nurture of community.
- Nurture and oversight of the vocal ministry.
- Identification, eliciting, and nurture of other gifts.
- Teaching.
- Embodying and exemplifying the tradition of the community.
- Fostering accountability.
- Advocating for those who are unheard or invisible.

(Frances Taber, "Applying and Adapting the Tradition of Eldering for Today")

During the 1700–1800s, and still among Conservative Friends today, caring for these areas was the responsibility of elders appointed by the local meeting.

Sandra Cronk notes "the frustration and sense of incompleteness which many feel in trying to deepen their prayer and worship lives or to make a more serious commitment to the work of social justice."[54] A need is felt among many Friends for a deeper grounding of both their individual and corporate spiritual lives. Most Ministry and Counsel Committees don't seem to be meeting that need. Since about 1990, some meetings have created new procedures and committees to specifically address the meeting's role in members' leadings and other areas needing discernment. For instance, in 1995, Central Philadelphia Meeting approved guidelines to be used in "responding to calls to ministry." They explain:

> These were developed out of our desire to be intentional in our discernment and oversight as we found members seeking the support of the meeting for their ministry. The guidelines have served us well in a dual way: First, they have, indeed, been useful in helping us to provide clearness and oversight in a more thoughtful and centered way, and second, by their very existence, they have

[54] Sandra Cronk, *Gospel Order: A Quaker Understanding of Faithful Church Community*, p. 16.

> heightened members' consciousness regarding ministry and have led additional persons to recognize openings to ministry and to seek the support of the meeting.
>
> ("Community Nurture of Members' Faithfulness to the Leadings of the Spirit," presented to Central Philadelphia Meeting for Business September, 2003)

The meeting has experimented with a variety of processes for supporting discernment, and has reviewed and adjusted them over time.

Beacon Hill Meeting changed their Nominating Committee into a "Gifts and Leadings Committee" and added responsibilities for tending to members' leadings. Several yearly and monthly meetings have designated a Sabbath or Jubilee Year during which they concentrated on discernment of Divine leading rather than business as usual.

The following queries from Central Philadelphia Meeting could be used by a meeting wishing to explore its role in members' leadings and other areas needing discernment.[55]

- What does it mean to be a minister?
- How can the meeting support the growth of *all* members in ministry?
- How do we foster gifts of centering and discernment so that service on clearness and oversight committees can be rich in the Spirit and faithful to its leadings?
- How do we develop a process that enriches the meeting community and does not exhaust our energy and attention?

What might elders' role be in current Quakerism outside of Conservative Friends? Tom Gates suggests:

> Elders [are] those who nurture others on the spiritual journey, teaching by example and gentle encouragement. They may not be the most noticeable members of the community, nor the most frequent to speak in meetings for worship or business, but often they

---

[55] "Community Nurture of Members' Faithfulness to the Leadings of the Spirit," presented to Central Philadelphia Meeting for Business September, 2003

> have a "presence" that is evident to others. The recent willingness on the part of some of our yearly meetings to re-explore the positive aspects of the eldering role is perhaps a hopeful sign that this type of service can once again be recognized and valued among us.
>
> (Thomas Gates, *Members One of Another: The Dynamics of Membership in Quaker Meeting*, p. 33)

Some functions that have been named among Liberal Friends for elders include:

- Encouraging and guiding other Friends to grow in the Spirit.
- Giving spiritual counsel.
- Intentionally mentoring other Friends to help them grow in their use of Quaker process and take on positions of responsibility.
- Serving as a companion for a Friend led to travel in the ministry. This often means traveling with and providing spiritual support for the leader of a retreat or conference.
- Grounding worship.

So far, this new recognition of the roles of elders and the recognition of gifts of eldering has been mostly informal, with the exception of the few meetings that have explicitly given traditional eldering tasks to a committee, and the work on the role of elders of FGC's Traveling Ministries Program. There is some talk of actually naming elders for a meeting. In moving cautiously forward with explorations of traditional eldering functions and how they might meet current Friends' needs, there is much that can be learned from those Friends who have maintained the role over the centuries.

Here is how North Carolina Yearly Meeting's discipline describes the role of named elders:

> Elders should jointly feel the responsibility for the spiritual condition of the members and cooperate with, encourage, and strengthen those who share in public ministry and pastoral work. They should have an understanding of the Scriptures, the teaching of Christianity, and a knowledge of the work and purpose of Friends. Because of the delicate and sensitive nature of much of their work, elders must observe the highest levels of confidentiality. Elders share in

> responsibility for appropriate vocal ministry in meetings for worship and should encourage others who give acceptable vocal ministry in meeting for worship evidencing true spiritual leading. They should seek to guide into helpful lines of service those who do not give such evidence. They should be alert to find and suggest avenues of service, especially to new or young members. Elders should tenderly discuss with members of the meeting as to their spiritual condition and, in friendly helpfulness, endeavor to aid all in the attainment of a high standard of Christian life and unselfish service. Elders should exercise watchful care and affectionate oversight for the maintenance of a consistent moral life by the members of the meeting. If the occasion arises, elders should gently counsel any member whose behavior, values, or attitudes are contrary to the Christian faith or out of unity with Friends principles. Elders should endeavor to guide members toward an orderly life and useful service in full fellowship with the meeting.
>
> (North Carolina [FUM] *Faith and Practice,* p. 74)

An important difference to note in the traditional role of elders and much of the current discussion is that traditionally, elders are appointed for life by a monthly meeting. They meet and confer with one another regularly to support one another, hold one another accountable, and to consider together their work in the meeting. The appointment is specifically for work within the monthly meeting. If a named elder moves to another meeting, their role as elder does not transfer; elders must be known and trusted by the meeting they work within.

In contrast, much of the current exploration of elders among Liberal Friends concentrates on individual Friends who might have gifts of eldering, and on their use among the wider world of Friends, rather than being servants of a particular meeting.

Elders probably do need to meet regularly and work with other elders. This would serve several functions: as a check that an individual is acting under the leading of the Spirit and not from their ego; as support and nurture; and for mutual accountability in their work. One of the failings of many Quaker meetings today is the lack of support for Friends in positions of leadership. Providing elders with a peer group would be a step in supporting leaders.

It may well be that there are two kinds of roles for elders today: as a group of named Friends serving a meeting; and as individual Friends who travel and serve the wider world of Friends. How such individuals might be named, nurtured, and held accountable are open questions, along with questions about existing Ministry and Counsel Committees.

Characteristics of People Who Might Grow into the Role of Elders

> Persons drawn to and gifted in the work of eldering tend to be those who are drawn towards listening, observing, responding. They are those who have their antennae out, in terms of a special concern for the spiritual life of the meeting, both corporate and individual.
>
> (Frances Taber, "Applying and Adapting the Tradition of Eldering for Today")

Here are some characteristics of elders from Debra Farrington and Katharine Jacobsen:[56]

- They know how to listen.
- They ask questions rather than give advice.
- They don't judge, but they're not afraid to ask hard questions either.
- They are good observers.
- They use their intuition.
- They strive to nurture.
- They trust God's leading.
- They are willing to pray.
- They are patient.
- They have a concern and feeling for the quality of worship.
- They value spiritual hospitality for and with others.

The Life of the Spirit in Individual Lives

> In Quaker faith and practice, the individual and the meeting are in a dynamic, mutually supportive, and reciprocal relation. Viewed from

---

56 Debra K. Farrington, *Hearing with the Heart*, pp. 121-123 and Katharine Jacobsen, "Eldering as a Spiritual Gift"

> the perspective of the wider culture, our most "counter cultural" claim is that, far from being mutually exclusive, true community and true individuality reinforce one another.
>
> (Thomas Gates, *Members One of Another: The Dynamics of Membership in Quaker Meeting*, p. 8)

Quakers and the Spiritual Life

Much emphasis is placed in this book on the importance of meetings as spiritual communities. In our extremely individualistic society, we need constant reminders of this. However, it is possible to go to the opposite extreme and assume that the meeting will do all that is necessary, and that we need only show up at meeting to have rich, full spiritual lives. This is, of course, not true. Friends need to cultivate their private spiritual lives in order to grow spiritually.

> The relationship of personal discernment and corporate discernment is deep and cannot be broken. If we are to have strength in our individual discernment, we must have corporate clearness supporting us. And if we are to have power in our corporate discernment, we must be gathered as individuals who have already learned the way of obedience and practiced discernment.
>
> (Jan Hoffman, "Comments on Corporate Discernment")

In *Members One of Another*, Tom Gates suggests three opportunities Quakerism offers for individual transformation:

- Deeply exploring one or more of the testimonies—allowing a testimony to search our own life.
- Individual spiritual discipline and practice. Currently, several yearly meetings sponsor "Spiritual Formation Programs" which encourage individuals to commit to some daily spiritual practice and organize participants into small local groups whose members meet regularly to support one another in their spiritual journeys.
- Having a leading and experiencing inward yielding to the divine initiative as we learn to trust God instead of our own

controlling impulses.

(Thomas Gates, *Members One of Another: The Dynamics of Membership in Quaker Meeting*, pp. 20-22)

Tom Gates writes:

> Over the last three years, more than 20 members and attenders from my own meeting have participated in our yearly meeting's spiritual formation program, and this has been an impetus for deepening and growth not only for the individuals involved, but also for the entire meeting.

(Thomas Gates, *Members One of Another: The Dynamics of Membership in Quaker Meeting*, pp. 21-22)

Resistance or even jealousy can arise in a meeting when one Friend is viewed as having grown or having had more direct experience of God than others. It is helpful to understand that growth, mystical experiences, and spiritual gifts are not simply the possession of an individual, but are given to individuals for the building up of the life of the whole community. They are community assets.

Supporting and sustaining individual Friends who come up against trouble because of their faithfulness in following their leadings is an important role of the meeting community. For instance, Friends generally get into trouble when they resist their government's demand for military service and taxes to support war.

In *Hearing with the Heart: A Gentle Guide to Discerning God's Will for Your Life*, Debra Farrington points out places where we might have to struggle with our assimilation into modern culture:

> Maybe we won't be asked to embrace powerlessness, humility, and poverty as a result of discerning and living God's desires, though we never know. But we may discover that we are called to stop seeing ourselves as indispensable at work, as a person who can't take a sick day, who can't manage the workload without working 60 hours a week, or who is defined by what she buys and owns. Perhaps we will find that we really are a slave to something that separates us from God—work, alcohol, drugs, sex, shopping, "being right," or whatever—and we have to admit that we are powerless

> and ask God's help. . . . Each of us has a temptation or two that hooks us easily. The risk of practicing discernment is that we will come face-to-face with them and have to stretch every fiber of our being to banish them.
>
> (Debra K. Farrington, *Hearing with the Heart: A Gentle Guide to Discerning God's Will For Your Life*, p. 43)

Friends in Central Philadelphia Meeting offer the following on what it means for Quakers to work on our spiritual lives:

> The defining element of our faith journey is that it arises from orienting one's life around God, around Truth. Good works, though they may be personally fulfilling, are not synonymous with faithful living. Each of us is called to the continuing work of discerning what is rightly ordered, for me, at this time.
>
> One's *particular* commitment to faithful living is discerned as we reflect on our gifts, our overall life circumstances and what it is to which we feel God is calling us. Faithfulness for some may be outward work in the community; for others it may be quietly holding the community in prayer.
>
> ("Community Nurture of Members' Faithfulness to the Leadings of the Spirit," presented to Central Philadelphia Meeting for Business September, 2003)

Debra Farrington describes the life lived with God at the center like this:

> The process of committing ourselves to God, however, cannot and does not happen all at once. Nor does God ask this of us; the invitation to follow will be issued over and over again throughout the course of our lives. . . . We begin the journey, however, with some expression of willingness to learn to listen to God's desires more deeply, and we do that knowing that obstacles stand in our way. . . . Even so, we continue to try to listen for God. We pray and wait—patiently or otherwise—for the new ears and eyes that give us the ability to really see and hear. And we resist, to the best of our ability, all the personal and cultural obstacles between us and what God desires for us. . . .
>
> This is not the road to glory, fame, and riches, at least not as the world defines them. This is, however, the way to God and the riches of a life lived in God. The journey is not always an easy one, but,

speaking from my own experience, it is worth the effort.

(Debra K. Farrington, *Hearing with the Heart*, pp. 46-47)

Quakers, more than most other religious groups, hold up the model of a religious life as one that is open to change and growth. We expect that, as we learn to hear and follow leadings, our inner and outward lives will go in new directions and take on new aspects. The only constant is the openness to further revelation and change.

Holding Someone in the Light

In announcements during or after worship or at business meeting, Friends are frequently asked to hold someone in the Light. The person may be sick, dealing with difficult life circumstances, struggling with spiritual discernment, or be serving others for a concentrated period of time.

Debra Farrington, in *Hearing with the Heart*, offers some guidance in holding someone in the Light. She writes, "One way of practicing openness to God's will in prayer is to simply hold mental images of those you are concerned about in God's light without asking for anything." She suggests the following steps:

- Find a place where you can pray without being disturbed for five to thirty minutes. Make sure the room's temperature is reasonable, and sit in a comfortable position that supports your back and allows for free circulation of your bloodstream.
- Take a few deep breaths and focus on relaxing your body, letting go of whatever to-do lists or other concerns you have on your mind.
- Find an image of God's love that works for you. That might be picturing God's love as a bright light, or as God's hand open and waiting to receive your concerns, or as anything else that suggests God's receptivity to you.
- Without asking for anything, name the people or the situations that you wish to hold before God, and imagine them being held in God's loving presence. You might see them wrapped in bright light, for instance, or being cradled in God's hand.

Hold them there for as long as you wish, and then move on to the next person or situation you wish to place before God.
- Include all sorts of people and events in this exercise: individuals who are in need of help, your own needs, countries where people are at war or starving, political situations, those suffering after a natural disaster, and even those who are experiencing great joys.
- Conclude with a brief prayer of gratitude for God's loving presence in all these situations.

(Debra K. Farrington, *Hearing with the Heart*, pp. 63-64)

Death

Preparation

Friends should consider their own death and make appropriate provisions in advance to spare their loved ones trouble, expense, and the pain of unanticipated decisions.

(Baltimore Yearly Meeting *Faith and Practice*, p. 66)

Friends are encouraged to plan for their deaths by drawing up a will. Funeral or Ministry and Counsel Committees can ask individuals to fill out questionnaires indicating their wishes and the practical information people will need to know. These should be filed with the committee. (See Sample Forms.)

We feel it is useful from time to time to restate and reinforce the traditional Friends testimony of simplicity. In the matter of funeral practices, the pressures of society seem especially strong. When a family is faced with the stress of bereavement, they find it hard not to do that which they are led to believe their neighbors expect of them. We feel, therefore, that Friends should set down in time of health their wishes as to the disposition of their bodies after death, and the sort of ceremony by which they would like to be remembered. We feel it would be especially useful for families to make these plans together, so that all may be sure of the wishes of the others.

Since this is a tender area, and a matter which people find easy to put off doing, we recommend that a committee meet with members and offer such help as may be needed. For those members who are willing, the committee should keep a file of funeral plans, in order to be ready to serve.

(Ohio Yearly Meeting [Conservative] *Faith and Practice*, p. 73)

A meeting committee can also help by providing information on legal requirements and simple burials and cremations.

In *Meeting the Spirit: An Introduction to Quaker Beliefs and Practices*, Hans Weening suggests that meetings for clearness can be of help and comfort to Friends who are dying.[57]

Quaker Memorial Meetings

A Quaker memorial meeting is a meeting for worship with a special emphasis on remembering the life of the person who has died. Many memorial meetings are celebrations of lives well lived. The monthly meeting holding the service confers with the family, if they will be present, to plan when and where the service will be held, what will be included, and who will do it. Planned elements may include reading a memorial minute, music, or planned messages. A member of the family may plan to speak, or meeting Friends may be asked to speak.

Like Quaker weddings, memorial meetings often have a number of people present who are new to Quakerism, so many meetings begin with a brief welcome and explanation of Quaker worship; it is particularly helpful to let people know how to tell when the service is over. Those present are invited to give personal reminiscences or share something about the deceased person. The group then settles into silent worship. At the agreed-upon time or when the Friend closing meeting deems it right, the meeting is broken by shaking of hands. A reception with food may follow. Photographs or other memoribilia may be displayed.

Memorial Minutes

When a valued member of a meeting dies, a member of Ministry and Counsel, the clerk, or a close friend of the person writes

---

[57] Hans Weening, *Meeting the Spirit: An Introduction to Quaker Beliefs and Practices*, p. 15

a memorial minute. When approved by the monthly meeting, it becomes part of the permanent records of the meeting. Typically, it contains a brief biography of the Friend with special emphasis on his or her activities among Quakers. It may be a few paragraphs to two pages long. If the deceased member was active or well known in the yearly meeting or in the wider circle of Friends, the monthly meeting forwards the memorial minute to the regional or yearly meeting. In some yearly meetings, all memorial minutes are forwarded.

Planning a Memorial Meeting

> Memorial meetings are arranged as convenient for the family. They are conducted as meetings for worship, with Friendly simplicity. If attendance of non-Friends is anticipated, it is appropriate to appoint a Friend to explain Friends' worship near the beginning of the meeting. A memorial minute may be read early in the meeting.
>
> (Baltimore Yearly Meeting *Faith and Practice*, p. 66)

Baltimore Yearly Meeting's discipline lists a number of issues to address when planning a memorial meeting.[58] These include:

- An introductory welcome and explanation is helpful to those who have not been to a Quaker meeting previously. What is to be said? Who will say (or read) it?
- Approximately how long should the service be, and who is going to close the meeting?
- Is there a memorial minute? Who will read it? And when?
- Is there to be music? Who will arrange or perform it? Is special equipment needed? Should it be at a pre-arranged time or as the Spirit moves? Adequate lighting should be assured for anyone who needs to read music.
- Are there any particular people to be asked to speak? Who will make the request?

Practical considerations:

- How many people might attend? Are facilities adequate? If

[58] Baltimore Yearly Meeting *Faith and Practice*, Appendix J

not, what can be done or what other location may be used?

- Parking for a large gathering may be a problem. It is helpful to designate someone (or two or three) to direct people where to park. Reserve a few spaces near the entrance for those who need this convenience.
- Is child care needed? Who can provide it and where will it be?
- Does the family wish to sit in a particular place? How are the places to be reserved?
- Are there to be flowers? Who will supply them? Remove? Transport? Obituaries and death notices may appropriately request donations to a chosen organization in lieu of flowers.
- Does the family want the closed casket or ashes present? If so, where should they be placed? How and when will they be placed and removed?
- Will there be a guest book? Who will obtain it? Where will it be placed? See that a pen is provided.
- Are there to be refreshments afterwards? Who will provide, where will they be served, and who will clean up?
- Can members of meeting offer hospitality to friends and relatives from out of town?
- Should someone remain at the home while the family is at the memorial service? Is there some meeting member not close to the family who might do this?

See also "Healthcare and Final Affairs" in the Sample Forms and Letters.

Chapter 6: Concerns and Leadings

Some older writings use the terms "concern" and "leading" interchangeably, but it can be helpful to distinguish between them.

A Concern

Quakers use "concern" to mean something above and beyond the everyday meaning of the word. In the Quaker sense, a concern is an ongoing urge to do something about an ethical issue, such as the plight of immigrants, care of the Earth, or injustice.

> A Quaker social concern seems usually to arise in a sensitive individual or very small group. . . . The concern arises as a revelation to an individual that there is a painful discrepancy between existing social conditions and what God wills for society.
>
> (Dorothy H. Hutchinson, "Friends and Service")

A concern often is first noticed as a discomfort, a feeling that things are not as God would wish, such as:

- My Quaker meeting does not include many people of color.
- Military recruiting in local high schools seems to target minorities and the poor.
- Perfumes and other scented consumer goods trigger allergic reactions in some people, some to the point of being life-threatening.

Here is a helpful account of the difference between a strong desire and a concern in the Quaker sense:

> "Concern" is a word which has tended to become debased by excessively common usage among Friends, so that too often it is used to cover merely a strong desire. The true "concern" [emerges as] a gift from God, a leading of [God's] Spirit which may not be denied. Its sanction is not that on investigation it proves to be the intelligent thing to do—though it usually is; it is that the individual . . . knows, as a matter of inward experience, that there is something that the Lord would have done, however obscure the way, however uncertain the means to human observation. Often proposals for action are made which have every appearance of good sense, but as

the meeting waits before God it becomes clear that the proposition falls short of "concern."

(Roger Wilson, 1949, quoted in Britain Yearly Meeting *Faith and Practice*, 13.07)

A Leading

Throughout the history of the Religious Society of Friends we have recognised that to anyone may come, at any time, a special inward calling to carry out a particular service. It is characterised by a feeling of having been directly called by God and by an imperative to act.

(Britain Yearly Meeting *Faith and Practice*, 13.02)

A leading is a specific action one feels called to, such as planting native plants in one's flower beds, or talking to an elected official about changing a law. A leading is a glimpse of God's will that arises within an individual, and other Friends may support that Friend in carrying out the task. A leading is God telling you to take a particular action now: *Visit Amanda.* A leading is felt as a discomfort with continuing as usual.

Everyday Leadings

For most of us most of the time, the obedience to which we are called is not great deeds in the world, but small deeds within our intimate circle of community.

(Thomas Gates, *Members One of Another*, p. 33)

Most leadings occur in our daily lives, and may be felt as a tiny nudge or go unnoticed. The Friend who experiences speaking in meeting as an irresistable urge is probably experiencing a leading. Any time a person turns to God for input or clarity is an opportunity for a leading:

Often the discussion of discernment seems to imply that discernment has to do with life's big decisions. . . . Yet, although seeking God's guidance for major decisions is certainly appropriate and wise, we need not save discernment for those big moments. It would probably be silly, not to mention time consuming, to try to

> discern whether parking your car in this place or that helps further heaven on Earth, but it is important to discern what to do with the gifts—financial and otherwise—that we possess. How and when to pray; how to treat others; how to nurture friendships, our spiritual lives, our employees and colleagues; how to vote; how to help those in our communities who have few resources; how to spend the money we have—all these activities and decisions benefit from prayer and conversation with God. In this way, each of us is called to be a partner, or co-creator, with God in building up our world.
>
> Each of us, as God's co-creator, must take responsibility for listening for God's guidance. No one can do that for us. And we must take responsibility for acting on that guidance as well.
>
> (Debra K. Farrington, *Hearing with the Heart*, pp. 20-21)

Friends find that the more they tune in to small promptings and follow through on them, the more easily they notice future promptings and the more clear they may become—like a snowball, gathering more spiritual sensitivity as one exercises the sensitivity one has.

Characteristics of a Leading

The leading comes out of the person's direct experience.

> Leadings start from where we are, from something which touches our lives and hearts in some way, not from an abstract notion.
>
> (Based on information from Margery Post Abbott, 1995. Quoted in Catherine Whitmire, *Plain Living: A Quaker Path to Simplicity*, p. 130)

Knowledge about something generally does not give rise to a true leading or concern. It is when a Friend is intimately acquainted with a situation that the Spirit's call to action arises.

It is a call for one to act, not a desire that someone else do something.

Friends have found that true leadings call for action by the individual with the leading. For instance:

- I will help to teach nonliterate adults to read.
- I will eat locally-grown foods as much as possible.

- I will work on healing broken relations in my family.

Calls to action reached intellectually or through guilt tend to assert that "we" should do something:

- People in the U.S. should use less gasoline.
- Quakers should write letters to their political representatives on issues of concern to Friends.
- Quakers should be vegetarian.

Or that a particular outside group should do something:

- Israel should stop bulldozing Palestinians' homes.
- Large corporations should bring CEOs' wages and perks into line with the company's lowest-paid workers.

> Achieving clarity about a concern is a particular exercise in discernment. It is a process that begins with considerable private reflection and the asking of some tough questions. Is this a desire that someone else do something or is it really a call to act oneself?
>
> (Britain Yearly Meeting *Faith and Practice*, 13.05)

With a true leading, the individual feels compelled into action.

Testing a Leading

It is often difficult to figure out whether we are truly being led by God or whether something else is going on. Here are some queries an individual can use to test a leading:

- Am I motivated by love?
- Do I have direct experience with the area of concern?
- Do I have a right understanding of God's will?
- Am I content with being faithful in fulfilling God's will, or am I focused on results?
- Have I gotten to the root of the situation?
- Is this something I feel led to do regardless of whether others join in?
- Is this in any way self-serving?
- Am I in this for the long haul? Can I be patient?
- Is this consistent with other Friends or am I out in left field?

- Is this consistent with Friends' understanding of the Bible?
- Am I willing to hold fast in spite of possible criticism or censure?
- Is now the time?
- How is this to be done in practical terms? Will it require others' material and spiritual support?

A leading may also need testing by the community. See the section on "Testing a Leading or Concern in Community" on page 140.

Following Through on a Leading

Once you have tested your leading and it rings true, you act upon it. Often, it is only when you begin acting that you get a clear sense of following God's will. There are some leadings that you only recognize as such when looking back. Often, one cannot see further than a first step. Only when you have begun do you get a sense of how to follow through.

> One aspect of a leading is that it rarely comes with a scorecard or set of instructions. So often only a single frame of the movie comes, or at most a preview of coming attractions. Patience—combined with a willingness to do what is clear and take the initial steps required—is what seems to open the way and unwind the movie reel bit by bit.
>
> (Margery Post Abbott in *Walk Worthy of Your Calling*, p. 11)

Following leadings—traveling God's path—builds one's spiritual life.

> Having once had the experience of being faithful to a genuine leading, however small, we become gradually more sensitive to the further movement of the Spirit in our lives. Leadings faithfully followed have a way of begetting more leadings, and eventually, even transformation.
>
> (Thomas Gates, *Members One of Another: The Dynamics of Membership in Quaker Meeting*, p. 23)

Conversely, Friends who have not followed through have reported with sorrow that over time the nudges faded away.

It has been found that leadings tend to follow a recognizable pattern:

The individual's sense of peace is disturbed by a vague sense of disquiet; the person eventually perceives that he or she is being led to undertake some specific task; after a variable period of discernment and resistance, the leading is followed; and upon completion of the task, the sense of inward peace is restored. In Quaker understanding, inward peace comes not by withdrawing from the world, but rather by being faithful or obedient to one's leadings.

(Thomas Gates, *Members One of Another: The Dynamics of Membership in Quaker Meeting*, p. 32)

Discernment

Friends use discernment in appraising a leading or concern. What does this mean? Discernment is a sorting out of what is Truth from what springs from other sources, such as ego. It involves informed thinking, gut feeling, and spiritual sensitivity. Discernment is moving from feelings to clarity about a decision or action for the individual or group.

We believe that God speaks with us all the time, whispering in our ears, nudging our emotions, stirring our senses, and drawing us to the preferred path. Even now, as you read these words, God may be stirring within you, calling, opening, and speaking to you. God desires to be your partner, to journey through life with you.

Both God and humans seek the reality of this dialog and companionship. Spiritual discernment is the process of learning the language and the process of this relationship. For some, it is a spiritual gift that comes easily and that has always been a part of their awareness. But it is also an art and a skill that can be developed. The art of discernment is learning to first be attentive, and then to sift through the many spirits vying for our attention to hear the One True Spirit.

(Lon Fendall, Jan Wood, and Bruce Bishop, *Practicing Discernment Together*, p. 23)

It is not unlike being a good judge of people. Some folks are naturally good at figuring out what people are really like underneath, and whether that matches what they say. For others, it takes practice and help. Those who work in areas where such a skill is useful, such as police or social work, will often get much better at it over time.

> Learning to listen to the Spirit is one of the fundamental disciplines. . . . , and it precedes the ability to discern. We are called to journey through our lives with Christ, as did his disciples, receiving constant teaching, fellowship, and companionship.
>
> (Lon Fendall, Jan Wood, and Bruce Bishop, *Practicing Discernment Together*, p. 27)

Debra Farrington lists some practices that help in discerning God's will for one's life: praying, being silent, paying attention to one's gifts, and feelings.[59] She describes what this might look like:

> When we are trying to discern God's will for our lives or for the world around us, we're not asked to just sit around, be miserable, and smile happily all the while. We're not called to accept the world as it is and just assume that whatever happens is God's will. . . . We're allowed to express our frustration with God. We get to be angry, annoyed, frustrated, and even impatient. Patience, in this context, means that we stay engaged with God, that we keep listening and arguing if need be, that we not leave God out of the process and try to take charge ourselves.
>
> (Debra K. Farrington, *Hearing with the Heart*, p. 179)

> We begin the journey tentatively in darkness—partial or complete. We take classes to learn what we need to know or talk to others about our choices and learn more about what we'll need for the journey. We do something rather than nothing. . . . And if the action is a right one, light begins to dawn. Things and people around us begin to look different. When we persevere and continue to follow the call we've heard with our heart, the light grows, and somewhere along the way, we find ourselves exactly where we are supposed to be, doing just what God called us to do.
>
> (Debra K. Farrington, *Hearing with the Heart*, p. 189)

Debra Farrington writes of finding a leading in one's heart's desire:

---

[59] Debra K. Farrington, *Hearing with the Heart: A Gentle Guide to Discerning God's Will For Your Life*, p. 136

> In order to know the hope of God, we must learn to listen to what our own heart desires instead of what the world tells us we *should* desire, for God often speaks to us through the yearning in our heart. There is a deep distrust of this in some circles today, with good reason. Rampant individualism that focuses only on what you or I want can easily become egotism and run counter to God's will for us. . . .
>
> But assuming that our focus is on God in the first place and that we are part of a community that can offer corrections to our vision when needed . . . our hearts often speak to us of what God desires most. Instead of dismissing what speaks most deeply to us, we need to ask if these desires might be speaking to us of God's will.
>
> (Debra K. Farrington, *Hearing with the Heart*, p. 17-19)

As in all Quaker processes, the best way to learn discernment is by doing it in the company of others with experience:

> Theory, of course, is all well and good, but the only way to really understand discernment is by doing it.
>
> (Debra K. Farrington, *Hearing with the Heart*, p. 136)

Contemporary Examples of Leadings

Writing a book. The text of an interview by Angelina Conti, "Finding a Balance Between Spirituality and Social Action: An Interview with Catherine Whitmire" goes into depth on Catherine Whitmire's process and leadings in writing her two books, *Practicing Peace* and *Plain Living*. The April 9, 2007 article is posted on QuakerBooks' website under interviews (as of Jan. 2011), and may remain available through QuakerBooks.

Walking and talking. Ruah Swennerfelt and Louis Cox of Charlotte, Vermont, have both been heavily involved in Quaker Earthcare Witness, Ruah as General Secretary and Louis as Publications Coordinator. They spent six months from November of 2007 to April of 2008 walking from Vancouver, British Columbia, to San Diego, California, meeting and talking along the way with Friends about the connections among peace, justice, care for the Earth, and personal responsibility.

Providing sanctuary. Breaking the law by hosting and aiding people who lack legal status did not end with the Underground Railroad. Friends all over the country, and particularly those living in border states with Mexico, have engaged in activities to protect immigrant workers and families from deportation. A number of monthly meetings offered sanctuary for people seeking political asylum in the 1980s and '90s.

Service in the community. Kalamazoo Monthly Meeting in Michigan supports one Friend's work with neighborhood youth, which includes hosting a weekly Jumpin' Jammin' and Homework Open House during the school year and organizing summer youth activities.

Serving as a medical missionary. In the 1990s, physician Tom Gates and his wife, Liz, spent three years working at Friends Lugulu Hospital in Kenya in eastern Africa. The story of their struggles to discern whether they were really led to leave a medical practice in rural New England, how way opened as they explored the possibility, and their lives in Kenya is told in *Stories from Kenya*, Pendle Hill Pamphlet #319 (1995).

The Ministry of Sharing a Concern

Sometimes, a Friend receives a leading to make a concern known to others; an individual is led to travel or speak with others or write them to bring the concern to their attention. John Woolman, who traveled extensively in the 1700s with a concern for Quakers releasing their slaves, is a prime example, as are Ruah Swennerfelt and Louis Cox, mentioned above among contemporary examples of leadings.

Such a concern might be:

- Quakers, like other people in the U.S., are gobbling up natural resources at an unsustainable rate.
- Friends may have money invested in companies that are operating sweatshops.
- Chocolate candy may be made from cocoa grown with slave labor in west Africa.

It is important to distinguish between a leading of this sort and simply wanting everyone to get on a band wagon. A true leading is expressed by bringing the concern to the attention of Friends and others and inviting or challenging them to seriously consider whether they feel comfortable continuing as they have been, or whether they feel led to change what they do. One proclaims the Truth as one knows it and leaves the rest to God and the faithfulness of the hearers. God does not lead one to demand that other people do things or guilt-trip them. The prophetic call is for those who have heard to be faithful to God's leading within their own hearts once the Truth has been brought to their attention.

Corporate Concerns

A concern usually arises originally within an individual, but may come to be shared by a larger group. As the concern is made known within the worshiping community, others may feel drawn to it. Such a concern may spread. At some point, it may become necessary to discern whether this is a concern just of individuals or something the whole group is led to take on.

The question here is, "Given that we find this individual Friend's concern to be grounded in the Spirit, are we led simply to support that Friend, or are we also called to take up the concern as a body?" A meeting, if it unites with a concern, may send the concern to other meetings in the yearly meeting for their consideration, and in due course the matter may be brought to the yearly meeting for its consideration. Action by the yearly meeting might be in the form of a minute uniting with the concern, work toward changing the yearly meeting's corporate practices around the concern, setting up an ad hoc group to do further work in the area, and/or sending a minute or advices to its constituent meetings for their consideration. When a task becomes ongoing, a standing committee may be formed. This is how committees of concern are born.

When a concern becomes widespread among Friends in a yearly meeting or a larger Friends decision-making body, further corporate discernment may be needed. The question here is, "Can we, as a gathered community, find clarity to affirm the concern as a matter of enduring guidance for our individual and communal actions?" This is how testimonies are born.

Testimonies

History

Early Friends testified to the workings of the Spirit within them by spreading the good news that Christ had come to teach his people himself, by changed lives, and in all the details of daily living. They testified to the equality of all people before God by treating all as their equals, refusing to abide by such social distinctions as removing their hats in the presence of social "superiors" and addressing their parents and other social superiors as "you" instead of the singular "thou" and "thee." These testimonies served as public witnesses—symbolic acts—to show that they really believed that all are equal before God and therefore should be treated equally in society. They were intended as public challenges to the norms of their society, much as refusing to register for the draft or to pay the portion of one's income tax that goes to paying for war are public witnesses taken up by some Friends today.

> The testimonies of plain speech, non-payment of tithes, and rejection of the oath were all forms of prophetic challenge to the fallen social order. The testimonies were corporate prophetic symbols. . . . [Early Friends] understood [their] testimonies as obedient response to the continued leadings of the living Christ.
>
> (Sandra L. Cronk, *Gospel Order: A Quaker Understanding of Faithful Church Community*, p. 18)

Following the extremes of action and persecution of early Friends, by about 1700, Quakers were settling into Quietism, looking inward at nurturing the existing body rather than focusing on evangelizing. Testimonies became a matter of guidance for personal conduct more than an outward witness to the larger society. The testimonies themselves changed over time. In a changed society with less distinction on social class, there was no need to make a point of keeping one's hat on. It no longer made a statement. During the 1700s, other testimonies arose, such as those against keeping slaves and against the drinking of alcohol. These were first and foremost guidelines for how Quakers should live—100 years before the Civil War, Quakers had divested themselves of their slaves.

Engaging in social and political activities in the larger society, however, was largely frowned on, as working even on causes such as abolition, which Quakers supported, meant working outside the Quaker community with its careful hedges against the influence of the larger world. Tension between Quakers who felt they should engage with such issues in the larger arena and those who felt the need to retain their Quaker distinctives and separate lives helped fuel the schisms of the 1800s. All Quakers at the time were clear, however, that testimonies were rooted in the Divine, and that living according to them was living in right relationship with God and other people.

Current Testimonies

There is no official list of Friends testimonies, but one widely-accepted list includes Simplicity, Peace, Integrity, Community, and Equality (SPICE). These offer guidance for Friends' lives and actions. The testimonies themselves continue to evolve. One that arose in the late 1900s is a call to live more lightly on the Earth, often called Earthcare or Stewardship (giving rise to a new acronym, SPICES).

> It is interesting to note that many of these positions have evolved over time, and while they now seem like fairly straightforward extensions of basic Quaker belief, they involved much discussion and soul-searching in the past. Some issues are still evolving, and you will find that current issues like same-gender relationships, abortion, etc. are topics on which it is very difficult to achieve unity.
>
> (Marc Mengel, www.faqs.org/faqs/Quaker-faq, September 2008)

Chapter 7: The Role of the Community in Leadings, Concerns, Gifts, and Ministry

> Though all journeys through discernment will be different in the particulars, there is one instruction they share: it is difficult and dangerous to journey alone.
>
> (Debra K. Farrington, *Hearing with the Heart*, p. xvi)

Supporting Individuals

The worshiping community has a central role to play in individuals' leadings, concerns, gifts, and ministry. There are many different ways that a meeting can provide support to a Friend who may have a leading or a spiritual gift. Here are some possible ways:

- Prayer.
- Love.
- Nurture.
- A clearness committee or other discernment process.
- An oversight committee or other process for accountability.
- Financial or other practical support.
- Setting up a meeting fund for donations to support the ministry.
- A travel minute or minute of religious service.

Some of these forms of support—prayer, love, nurture—are informal and require no special structure. Others are more formal and require a committee as well as action on the part of the business meeting.

It is important to note that a person who brings his or her leading to the meeting's care is submitting to the meeting's guidance and receiving help in discernment and faithfulness. It does not imply that such work is somehow greater than the work of those who labor quietly in the background, but that the nature of the work calls for additional discernment, support, and accountability.[60]

The final discernment needed is recognizing when a leading or concern is ready to be laid down.

Ministry: What It Is

For Quakers, "ministry" is almost synonymous with "service," but with the added sense that ministry is service that is done under God's guidance.

> We recognize a variety of ministries. In our worship these include those who speak under the guidance of the Spirit, and those who receive and uphold the work of the Spirit in silence and prayer. We also recognize as ministry service on our many committees, hospitality and childcare, the care of finance and premises, and many other tasks. We value those whose ministry is not in an appointed task but is in teaching, counseling, listening, prayer, enabling the service of others, or other service in the meeting or the world. The purpose of all our ministry is to lead us and other people into closer communion with God and to enable us to carry out those tasks which the Spirit lays upon us.
>
> (London Yearly Meeting, 1986, quoted in Britain Yearly Meeting *Faith and Practice*, 10.05)

> Each person has an obligation to serve God by ministering to individuals, to their local meeting, to the yearly meeting, and to the wider community. . . . No sharp line of distinction can be drawn between the importance and value of the different types of ministry.
>
> (Western Yearly Meeting *Faith and Practice*, p. 14)

Spiritual Gifts

The Apostle Paul, in his letters to the Christian communities in Rome and Corinth, included lists of gifts members of the community might be given. These include: administration, teaching, counseling, wise speech, faith, healing, and prophecy

---

60 "Community Nurture of Members' Faithfulness to the Leadings of the Spirit," Central Philadelphia Meeting

(Romans 12:6-8 and 1 Corinthians 12:8-10). The point that Paul emphasizes about these gifts is that they are given to individuals for the good of the group, and he pleads with those in the communities not to be jealous or boastful. He uses the imagery of the human body and its various parts—legs, heart, eyes, ears, etc.—to emphasize that a variety of gifts are needed and that none is to be valued over any other. All are needed to create a functioning whole. This is an apt description of a healthy Friends meeting.

Friends have experienced over the years that individuals in meetings that seek and follow God's will are given the gifts that the community needs. Such gifts might include discernment, teaching, healing, truth-telling, hospitality, and many others.

Naming a Gift or Ministry

An important ministry is the naming of spiritual gifts that have been given to individuals that they may be unaware of. In naming a spiritual gift—in informing a Friend that he or she has a particular gift—that Friend is challenged to acknowledge and develop the gift and the ministry that results from using it.

Naming a gift takes two forms: recognizing a ministry or gift that is already being used but may not have been recognized as such; and calling forth a gift or ministry that is just emerging.

> We tend to think of ordinary actions as inconsequential, beneath God's radar. But God needs all kind of co-creators in this world, including the ones who will give everything they have to the poor and those who can teach a nursery school class with grace and love.
>
> (Debra K. Farrington, *Hearing with the Heart*, p. 189)

Recognizing the things Friends do for the meeting and in their daily lives that make the world a better place—be it mowing the meetinghouse lawn, teaching First-day school, working as a therapist, or being honest and hard working in one's job and treating everyone in the work place with respect—can help everyone in the meeting notice and appreciate the multitude of everyday ministries all around us, and can help us value other Friends' contributions to the life of the meeting and the wider world. Any task undertaken in a spirit of love is ministry, and meetings need all the everyday work its members contribute to hold in place the deeper spiritual work of individuals and the group.

In a report on recognizing and supporting ministries, Chestnut Hill Friends distinguished between these sorts of everyday ministry, and gifts of the spirit that require the discernment and public recognition of the meeting:

> Any Friend may be called to a ministry, but very few . . . require minutes of religious service. For example, for some a ministry may consist of raising children in a Quaker fashion, or living life as simply as possible. For others it may involve engaging in a series of acts of civil disobedience, or running a business according to Quaker principles. All these may be ministries of great importance . . . for they all may contribute in vital ways to the life of the meeting and the transformation of our lives.
>
> ("Report of the Ad Hoc Committee on Recognizing and Supporting Ministries," approved November, 2004, Chestnut Hill Friends Meeting, p. 2)

The report then lists situations in which a "minute of religious service" to recognize a particular ministry might be appropriate. These include a need for oversight, financial support, and carrying a concern to bodies beyond the meeting.

Some examples of gifts that have been named in recent years include:

- Pastoral care.
- Religious education for teens.
- Neighborhood ministry.
- Visiting meetings.
- Facilitating retreats.
- Offering spiritual nurture.
- A ministry of music.

Clearness Processes

History

The original use of "clearness" among Friends was as part of the process of applying for marriage under the care of a meeting. Men's and women's committees were appointed to check that the couple was "clear" of commitments to others. When formal membership was instituted in the early 1700s, similar "clearness committees" were formed for the process of applying for membership in a meeting.

Over the centuries, the Quaker idea of clearness has evolved. Rather than looking for obstructions, we look for clarity. "Clearness" indicates a sense of rightness about a certain decision or action or confidence that an action is consistent with divine will. Clearness is something that we strive for. Clearness committees are used as an aid in reaching clarity in making decisions about membership and marriage. In the 1960s, their use was expanded to help individuals reach clarity about decisions.

> In the 1960s this old Quaker practice took on new urgency as young men facing the draft asked their peers to serve on clearness committees to help them discern what they were led to do. This was not group discernment, as in normal Quaker business practice, but group support for individual discernment. Only the individual could know for sure what kind of witness he was called to, but the clearness committee could provide prayer and caring to move his discernment process forward. The result was a powerful sense of community and mutual accountability around a shared commitment to faithfulness.
>
> Soon clearness committees were being organized around a wide range of issues. . . . They have been used to help members through difficult life decisions, to test and affirm individual witness, and as a powerful way of supporting and holding accountable those engaged in traveling ministry.
>
> (Deborah Haines, *When You're the Only Friend in Town: Starting a New Friends Meeting*, p. 29)

The "evolving purpose" of clearness for individual's decisions "has been to help individuals discern or recognize the inward calling of God in their lives and to offer support during that process."[61]

Currently, clearness processes are used in three situations:

- Individuals apply for membership or ask to be married under the care of the meeting. Clearness committees meet with the applicants to ascertain both whether the applicants are clear and whether the committee is clear to accept them into membership or marriage under the meeting's care.
- An individual feels called to a particular ministry and requests a minute of travel or is being considered for release[62] by the meeting.
- An individual asks for help in making a decision. In this case, the committee's role is to ask probing questions to help the individual look more deeply into the issue and reach clarity. The only decision is the individual's.

Clearness for Individual Decisions

A clearness committee can be set up for a Friend with a leading, concern, or call to ministry. Clearness committees can also be set up for Friends who want help with discernment on a decision in their personal lives, such as changing jobs, giving up a car, or any other matter.

> Committees for Clearness aid Friends in being obedient to the leadings of the Spirit and enable a Meeting to support and nurture its members in building and deepening the spiritual community.
>
> ("A Quaker Path: A Spiritual Journey from Visitor to Attender to Member")

> Clearness committees are not for ordinary, everyday concerns and discernment. For one thing, they require too much work and energy from too many people. But in the midst of a discernment that feels major in your life, or one that you've considered for some time without

---

[61] Debra K. Farrington, *Hearing with the Heart: A Gentle Guide to Discerning God's Will for Your Life*, p. 163

[62] "Release" means that the meeting provides spiritual, financial, or other support. See "Releasing a Friend" on page 146.

finding clarity, this particular method can be enormously helpful.

(Debra K. Farrington, *Hearing with the Heart*, p. 162)

A clearness process where the only decision is the individual's is a bit different from the process when both the individual and the meeting need to make a decision. Jan Hoffman describes this kind of clearness process succinctly:

> A clearness committee meets with a person who is unclear on how to proceed in a keenly felt concern or dilemma, hoping that it can help this person reach clarity. It assumes that each of us has an Inner Teacher who can guide us and therefore that the answers sought are within the person seeking clearness. It also assumes that a group of caring friends can serve as channels of divine guidance in drawing out that Inner Teacher. The purpose of committee members is not to give advice or to "fix" the situation; they are there to listen without prejudice or judgment, to help clarify alternatives, to help communication if necessary, and to provide emotional support as an individual seeks to find "truth and right course of action."
>
> (Jan Hoffman, "Clearness Committees and Their Use in Personal Discernment")

In "Guidelines for Clearness Committees," Deborah Haines describes the process and offers guidelines.

> The basic process is simple. Normally the person seeking clearness asks for a committee to be formed. . . . Five is a good size for such a committee, although it may be smaller or larger. A meeting time and place are chosen to allow for privacy and uninterrupted, open-ended worship. The committee settles into silence. Out of the silence, the focus person describes what clearness he or she is seeking. The role of the other committee members is to hold that situation in the Light, and ask questions, out of silent worship, that may help the focus person find clarity.
>
> The person clerking the committee should explain the guidelines for asking questions:
>
> - Resist the impulse to provide advice or counsel. The purpose of the meeting is not to solve a problem, but to open space for the Light to break through.
> - Do not spend too much time trying to clarify the history of the situation brought before the committee. Focus on opening up the

way forward.

- Keep your attention on the focus person. Sharing your own experiences and insights, even in question form, will be a distraction.
- Maintain an attitude of prayerful listening. Keep your questions simple and non-directive.
- Do not be afraid to ask questions that seem far-fetched or even irrelevant. If they rise up in you with a certain insistence, like a message in worship, they probably need to be asked.
- Pay attention to where God seems to be breaking through, as manifested in love, joy, compassion. Affirm the presence of God.
- Do not enter into the process feeling that you know the answer. . . .
- Expect to be transformed.

(Deborah Haines, *When You're the Only Friend in Town*, pp. 29-30)

Often, the focus person will request that everything shared during the clearness session be held in confidentiality. In addition to a clerk to monitor the process, sometimes it is useful for one of the committee members to record the questions asked for the focus person to have afterward.

Debra Farrington writes of the challenges of being a committee member:

> The majority of the meeting time is spent in asking questions of the focus person and listening to his or her answers. This is the hard part! Committee members may ask any question that seems appropriate to them, though the focus person is entirely free to choose not to answer a given question if it makes him or her uncomfortable. But the questions must be honest questions rather than statements or leading questions. Comments such as "Don't you think it would work if you. . . .?" or "Want to know what I did when I faced the same situation. . . ?" are not permitted. . . .
>
> It sounds very simple, but based on my own experience and that of others, I can tell you that this is the hardest part of the process. We love nothing more than to offer each other advice and counsel. I had no idea how much I loved doing that until I had my first experience as a committee member. Because it is so easy for us to jump in with answers or advice, the clerk (or anyone else who notices that this is happening) is asked to gently steer the conversation back to honest questions whenever necessary.

(Debra K. Farrington, *Hearing with the Heart*, pp. 165-166)

Toward the end, the clerk may ask the focus person if he or she wants to hear the committee members' reflections. Debra Farrington writes:

> Even now, giving advice or interpreting or attaching values such as happiness or sadness is forbidden. The reflections of the group assembled—what Parker Palmer and others call mirroring—should take the form of pointing out things that the focus person might not have noticed in his or her own responses and bodily reactions. Committee members might point out how weary the focus person sounded when discussing a particular path versus the energy in her voice and body when she explored another. They act as a "mirror" for the focus person, reflecting back their observations about what was said and what they saw.
>
> (Debra K. Farrington, *Hearing with the Heart*, p. 167)

Clearness Calling for Decisions by Both Individuals and the Meeting

Membership and Marriage

Meetings use a clearness process to make decisions about membership and marriage under the care of the meeting. See the section on Membership and Marriage for details.

Seasoning an Individual Leading or Ministry

When an individual feels called to a ministry that may involve action by the meeting, such as writing a minute of travel or some other kind of support, the clearness process has two purposes: helping the Friend reach clarity; and determining the right relationship between the Friend and the meeting. This process often includes the following steps:

- An individual initiates the process by asking for a clearness committee. The individual may have been encouraged by Friends to take this step.
- A clearness committee is appointed, usually by Ministry and Counsel. The clearness committee may be composed of at least one member of Ministry and Counsel, one or more Friends the individual has identified, and a Friend or two

Ministry and Counsel judges would provide some balance or contribution. The committee makes the contacts and assists the individual and members of the clearness committee to prepare for the clearness meeting.

- It is helpful for all if the individual writes a description of his or her question or concern, including any relevant background information, and makes sure everyone on the committee has a copy of it well in advance of the meeting so they can read it and pray over it. This provides both valuable information for the committee, and helps the individual process the issue.
- The clearness committee meets with the individual. Reading aloud the description of the issue, followed by worship, is often a good way to begin. Committee members ask questions designed to help the individual reach and express clarity and to explore areas he or she may not have considered. Committee members also ask questions to give themselves enough information and interaction with the individual to guide their discernment of the right response of the meeting (see suggested questions below).
- Sometimes the clearness committee recommends further seasoning, through further work by the individual or by a second clearness meeting.
- The clearness committee reports back to Ministry and Counsel. If the committee is recommending action or support on the part of the meeting, it details those as well as it can. If Ministry and Counsel supports the recommendation for meeting action, and financial support is being asked, Ministry and Counsel consults with the Finance Committee.
- Ministry and Counsel brings the report of the clearness committee to business meeting. If no action for the meeting is recommended, the committee simply reports that the clearness committee met with the individual. If action is recommended, Ministry and Counsel brings a minute or recommendation expressing the nature of the leading, concern, or religious service and the support being requested. The meeting is asked for its discernment on the matter using usual Quaker business process.

- The meeting's decision is minuted.
- If the meeting approves taking action, a committee of some sort may be set up to oversee what comes next. For a short-term committee, the oversight committee reports to the business meeting when its work is finished. For ongoing work, the Oversight or Ministry and Counsel committee may do an annual review and report to the meeting.

Chestnut Hill Monthly Meeting has done some careful work in recognizing and supporting ministries its members have felt led to undertake. A "Report of the Ad Hoc Committee on Recognizing and Supporting Ministries" approved in November of 2004, describes the process they have worked out and their ongoing seasoning of this work. The report includes the following suggested questions for the use of the clearness committee:

- What is the nature of the concern, leading, or proposed ministry?
- What has been the person's experience of the leading?
- How has the person tested the leading?
- What are the challenges the person will face?
- Is the person ready to take on the challenges?
- Is this the right time?
- What kind of support is the person requesting?

Pitfalls to Avoid

- Questions that come from one's own curiosity instead of addressing the focus person's concern.
- Giving advice.
- Trying to push the focus person in a particular direction.

Insistence on a particular direction or idea may come from the best of intentions. While it is okay for committee members to offer information, they need to guard against giving advice.

Testing a Leading or Concern in Community

Because we are fallible, Quakers learned early on to test whether leadings and concerns were truly from God before acting on them.

> [Early] Friends understood that individuals could misinterpret leadings, fall into pride or self-will, run off into notions. The discernment of the broader community was a surer guide to Truth. Fox even put his own leadings under the discipline of the corporate body.
>
> (Elizabeth Cazden, Fellowships, *Conferences, and Associations*, p. 5)

Leadings and concerns often require testing and discernment by a meeting either as a whole or through a clearness committee. *Is this urge from God or are there other motives?* Testing is best done by a diverse group of Friends. This is one of the reasons why taking a leading or concern to one's local worshiping community for discernment is a good idea: different Friends bring different experiences and can look at it from different viewpoints.

Debra Farrington writes:

> Listening to the community is a critical safeguard against fooling ourselves about God's desires for us.
>
> (Debra K. Farrington, *Hearing with the Heart*, p. 162)

Involving the community also helps build up the whole community's faithfulness.

> The private leading must be tested against the experience and collective leading of the worshipping community, not only to check the excesses of the willful or the mistaken, but also to give the support and strength of the religious community to what might otherwise be a lonely, ineffective witness. At its best, such testing strengthens the testimony of both the individual and the group.
>
> (Paul A. Lacey, "Leading and Being Led," p. 15)

Cautions

Here are some red flags that may indicate that something other than God's will is motivating someone.

- Too great certainty.

> One of the surest signs of discerning poorly is being absolutely, positively certain that we know God's will.
>
> (Debra K. Farrington, *Hearing with the Heart*, p. 24)

- The desire to escape an existing situation rather than move toward a new one.
- A sense that others cannot help.

> If you think you have a situation that no one else has ever seen before, and there is no one with knowledge or insight to illuminate your path, you are probably misguided. . . .
>
> In fact, one of the danger signs for us comes when we feel that we can't share what we are discerning with anyone else—that no one will understand our decision. When we feel that we must keep what we are doing a secret from everyone else, we are usually following a voice other than God's. That doesn't mean that you shouldn't be judicious about sharing your heart's desires and your sense of God's guidance with other people, but when a demand for total secrecy exists, either within yourself or given to you by someone else, something is usually wrong.
>
> (Debra K. Farrington, *Hearing with the Heart,* pp. 116-117)

Criteria for Testing

> Throughout the discernment process there should be one overriding principle before the hearts and minds of all: is this individual or group right to believe that this action or service has been 'laid upon' them by God?
>
> (Britain Yearly Meeting *Faith and Practice,* 13.06)

A number of tests and guidelines have been developed over the centuries, and these are good starting points. The most important test, however, is the discernment of a mature worshiping community. Jan Hoffman writes of the futility of relying only on guidelines (such as those that appear below).

> Those persons and meetings which are "in the Life" may find guidelines for discernment (like Scripture, inner impression, the fruits of the Spirit, etc.) affirming and confirming, but also unnecessary. And likewise, when we are "out of the Life," guidelines, no matter how many, may seem tragically mechanical and unhelpful.
>
> (Jan Hoffman, "Comments on Corporate Discernment")

The following tests and guidelines can be very useful, however, especially in helping individuals and communities learning to discern whether a leading or concern is from God.

In *Quakers in Puritan England*, Hugh Barbour identifies five tests used by early Friends:

- Moral purity: The proposed action is not self-serving.
- Patience: The individual can be patient. He or she can wait for better clarity and others' guidance and for way to open.
- Inward unity: The action increases Friends' unity; it is not divisive.
- Consistency with other Quakers: The leading is consistent with other Friends' leadings.
- Consistency with the Bible: The leading is consistent with or at least does not contradict Scripture.

> Books on discernment routinely tell us that when we believe we have discerned God's wishes for us, we should test that discernment against what is written in the Bible. Although I think that's generally true, it is also one of the most difficult ways of testing our call. . . . Perhaps the most helpful suggestion I can make to you is that the more grounded you are in Scripture, the more time you've spent reading and studying it, the more you will develop an overall sense of God's desires for you and the world around you.
>
> (Debra K. Farrington, *Hearing with the Heart*, pp. 204-205)

The test of time

Often, one can only feel confident about one's discernment after one has taken action.

> Perhaps the best test of whether or not you have truly heard God's call with your heart is the test of time. Living in a way that is consistent with God's desires for you and the world around you results in what we commonly call the fruits of the Spirit—a phrase that comes from Galatians: "[T]he fruit of the Spirit is love, joy, peace, patience, kindness, generosity, faithfulness, gentleness, and self-control" (Galatians 5:22-23). When the long-term result of the action you take as a result of discerning with your heart are these fruits, then you have probably discerned clearly.
>
> (Debra K. Farrington, *Hearing with the Heart*, p. 209)

> We try to test the genuineness of leadings by their fruits: Do they draw together the community of faith and give it more power? Do they bring greater harmony and justice into the life of the community or institution? Do they put the needs of the weakest in the fellowship first? Do they address issues clearly, accurately and sensitively? These are not absolute tests of a leading, but they point in the right directions.
>
> (Paul A. Lacey, "Quakers and the Use of Power," p. 30)

Tests for a Social Concern

In her pamphlet on "Friends and Service," Dorothy Hutchinson identifies seven characteristics of a social concern.[63] These can be used as tests for whether a particular concern is under divine leading.

- The individual is prepared for this service by previous experiences and service, though this was not apparent at the time.
- The concerned individual makes direct contact with the evil that needs attention. For instance, "those who visit prisoners or who go to prison as prisoners for conscience' sake may have something to say now which the theoretical penologist, psychiatrist, or sociologist cannot quite match."
- An ability to establish empathy with the objects of the concern, such as prisoners.
- Willingness to work for any minor, unspectacular, partial solution of a big problem. Rather than being a cop-out because they are not directly addressing the big picture, Quakers hold up the ideal at the same time as initiating small, imperfect steps.
- It does not rest until it has penetrated through the superficial evil to its root causes. For instance, if poverty and ignorance are causes of crime, one can work on alleviating poverty and ignorance.
- The person who is sensitive to one social concern becomes inevitably more sensitive to all social evils.

[63] Dorothy H. Hutchinson, "Friends and Service," 1996

- The person with a concern is willing to accept censure and ridicule.

  Dorothy Hutchinson writes:

  > In the last analysis, obedience to the Light is the only satisfying course. Approval is not the criterion. Results are not the criteria. . . . I am convinced that if one is obedient, failure is impossible. If I don't see any results of my work, there are two possible reasons. Either my Light was deficient and I was mistaken about God's will or methods of action. If so, I should be glad there were no results. Or else I was right in my insight and my efforts, but the time is not ripe for results. Then it is for others to build on what I have tried to do until the results become visible. The results, when they appear, will rest upon the foundation laid by many anonymous builders. To be one of these is not to fail.

Anchoring and Oversight Committees

A new name has arisen recently among Friends for an old practice. Many Friends are uncomfortable with the traditional term "oversight." Variously called an "anchoring committee," "a committee for support and guidance," a "care committee," or some other descriptive name, this is similar to a clearness committee but, instead of being a short-term process to aid an individual in making a single decision, it is a longer-term commitment to support, test, and guide an individual's ongoing work or ministry. It provides a framework for mutual accountability between the Friend with a leading or ministry and the meeting.

The term "anchoring committee" arose from the FGC Traveling Ministries Committee, because it anchors the ministry in the body (the monthly meeting/church) that has named and helps to sustain the ministry. It is usually appointed after a clearness committee has reached unity with a Friend about a leading or call to ministry. Three to five members is generally a good number. A clerk is chosen to schedule meetings, prepare the agenda in consultation with the focus person, clerk the meetings, and communicate with the monthly meeting as needed. The committee usually serves as long as the leading continues, but the frequency of meetings might change as the Friend becomes more seasoned in the ministry. Some meetings ask oversight committee members to serve one-year renewable terms.

Meetings can be scheduled at time intervals—at least several times a year—and/or as requested by the focus person. The primary question before the group is, "Is the focus person acting faithfully?" That is, is he or she seeking additional Divine input and then acting on that guidance as the work progresses? Chestnut Hill Friends recommend that oversight committees be listed in the meeting directory in order to recognize the particular leading and the meeting's supportive involvement.

The committee is responsible for helping hold the Friend accountable to God and the meeting. At least annually, the anchoring committee should report to the body that set it up how frequently they have met, how fruitful those meetings appear to have been, and whether the Friend's leading has changed or been fulfilled. If the leading has been accomplished, the anchoring committee should be laid down.

A detailed paper on "Clearness and Anchoring Committees," including how to form an anchoring committee, is available on the Traveling Ministries Program web page at fgcquaker.org (as of January of 2011). Like a clearness committee, an anchoring committee's role is to ask questions that help the Friend hear and follow God's guidance as the task proceeds. Anchoring committees are being used for Friends called to travel in the ministry, for Spirit-led writing projects, and for other work. Ideally, such committees are formed by the individual's local worshiping community. Not all meetings are prepared to set up such a committee, however. In this case, the Friend seeking support and guidance may turn to Friends outside the local group.

Releasing a Friend

It has already been noted that meetings that support a Friend's concern will sometimes assume the financial responsibility for the concern. Whether or not this is so, they may also consider offering other forms of help such as the use of a car, offers of childcare, or the setting up of a support group of people close to the Friend or concern.

(Britain Yearly Meeting *Faith and Practice*, 13.13)

Releasing a Friend covers a range of ways of providing financial and other practical assistance to make it possible for an individual to carry out service that the meeting has tested and confirmed as a true leading. Meetings can also support individuals by releasing them from the usual obligations of members such as donating financially and serving on committees. Someone who spends a significant amount of time acting on a leading or pursuing a concern with support and some form of release is referred to as a "released" or "liberated" Friend.

A very helpful discussion of the financial aspects of supporting an individual's leading is included in Chestnut Hill Meeting's 2004 minute on recognizing and supporting ministries, which is posted on their website as "Chestnut Hill Meeting Minute on Ministries".

"Releasing a Friend" is used in FUM in referring to appointing a pastor.

Ministers

Friends have a different understanding of ministry and ministers than other denominations. Ministry is a spiritual gift. Along with George Fox, we know "that being bred at Oxford or Cambridge did not qualify or fit a man to be a minister of Christ. . . ."[64] This does not mean that no preparation is needed, however. Western Yearly Meeting (FUM)'s *Faith and Practice* notes that "education is not a guarantee of effective ministry, but certainly can be helpful."

The original role for Quaker ministers was evangelism—going out in public and preaching the good news that "Christ is

[64] George Fox, *Journal*, rev. John L. Nickalls, p. 8. Oxford and Cambridge are England's two great universities.

come to teach his people himself."[65] In addition to George Fox, there were almost 100 early Friends who traveled and preached, sometimes in existing churches, sometimes by renting a hall and posting notices inviting the public, sometimes by gathering people in fields. They systematically set up new missions in England and also in the New World, Europe, and a few exotic locales—there was, for example, the Friends minister who felt called to deliver the good news to the Sultan of Turkey.

The second and third generations of Quakers settled in to shore up and maintain the Quaker movement. Friends actively looked for gifts of vocal ministry, and elders nurtured those Friends' growth in the spirit. Naming and recording ministers was a way of both nurturing such a gift and giving public recognition to those who could be trusted to give Spirit-led ministry.

> The Spirit calls forth ministers and the community of faith, the church, confirms them in their call.
>
> (Thomas, Charles F., ed., *The Church in Quaker Thought and Practice*, p. 39)

Such Friends would be recorded—that is, officially recognized in the meeting's minutes—as ministers.

> The original purpose was a kind of credentialing, to decide who had the right to be admitted to the business meetings of acknowledged ministers. By the mid-18th century, being recorded had become a kind of status in the social structure of the meeting, although it did not automatically confer leadership or power of the kind that

[65] George Fox's autobiography contains dozens of renditions of this theme, such as the following passages: "God was come to teach his people by his spirit," p. 48, "Christ was come to teach his people himself by his light Grace power and spirit," p. 113, "There [at the Sedbergh Fair] I declared the everlasting truth of the Lord and the word of life for several hours and that the Lord and Christ Jesus was come to teach his people himself and to bring them off all the world's ways and teachers." p. 42 (*Journal*, ed. Norman Penney; spelling modernized by author)

> ministers or priests in other denominations claimed. But, as has been seen, Quaker ministers, both men and women, often achieved great influence and were at the forefront of all the major developments in American Quakerism in the 18th and 19th centuries.
>
> (Thomas D. Hamm, *The Quakers in America*, pp. 86-87)

Ministers were invited to sit on the facing benches, so that when they spoke they might be more easily heard. Ministers and elders came together in "select meetings" to assess individuals' and meetings' practices and faithfulness, and to nurture Friends' spiritual life and hold individuals accountable. Recorded ministers traveled widely among Friends, serving to nurture and challenge isolated communities of Friends and to weave threads of connection all through the fiber of Quaker society. At the same time, some traveling Quaker ministers continued to advertise and hold meetings open to the public during the 18th and well into the 19th centuries.

During the latter part of this period, ministers and elders became increasingly rule-bound and authoritarian, largely losing the Spirit through upholding the letter. "Following the lead of London Yearly Meeting, which ended the recording of ministers in 1924, the Hicksite yearly meetings stopped the practice. They perceived it as elitist, distinguishing some Friends above others. . . . In contrast, the Conservative yearly meetings continued to record ministers and to look to them as leaders."[66] Most Liberal Friends today no longer record ministers or elders, though New York, New England, and Baltimore Yearly Meetings still occasionally record a minister.

Some unprogrammed meetings are taking a new look at some of these old traditions to see if they might yet serve them. Possible roles of elders are of particular interest, both in anchoring Friends who give workshops and lead retreats and as spiritual anchors and nurturers within meetings.

The question of whether to record someone as a minister sometimes comes up when a Friend takes on paid work as a

[66] Thomas D. Hamm, *The Quakers in America*, p. 87

counselor or minister at a prison or other institution, and asks their meeting to record them as a minister in order to provide them with the expected credentials for the job. This can be a touchy issue. The word "minister" may bring up associations with ministers in denominations Friends left before becoming Quakers. For many unprogrammed Friends, not having a minister is a point of pride.

The situation is different among Pastoral Friends. There is still a tradition of identifying, nurturing, and naming Friends whose ministry is found to be helpful and in line with divine leading, whether or not they intend to go into the paid ministry. Of course, being a recorded minister is desirable for someone serving as the pastor of a meeting.

Western Yearly Meeting (FUM) has the following in its *Faith and Practice*:

> While Friends believe in the ministry of all believers, each with a ministry to render, they also affirm that some gifts may be recognized by being recorded. Friends record those with a public ministry. Within the public ministry, there is a pastoral gift which consists especially in the ability to minister to entire congregations and to do personal work with individuals and families. This gift fits the possessor of it to comfort those who mourn, to lead the members into a closer religious life, to arouse in the young an interest in the things of the Spirit, and to impress others with a sense of the scope and reality of the spiritual life. It is the gift of shepherding and feeding the flock.
>
> The Church cannot make or appoint ministers; it can only recognize gifts where they exist and properly provide for their exercise and development in individuals who have experienced God's calling to this work.
>
> (Western Yearly Meeting *Faith and Practice*, Part III, Ministries)

The Process of Recording a Minister

Pastoral yearly meetings have each established a process for naming, nurturing, and recording gifts of vocal ministry. North Carolina Yearly Meeting (FUM), has the following in its book of *Faith and Practice*:

> When a member has spoken in the public ministry to the edification and spiritual help of the meeting, and has rendered said service in such a manner and afforded a basis for the formation of a judgment as to the nature of his gifts and calling, the Meeting on Ministry and Counsel shall carefully consider whether there is evidence of a gift in the ministry that should be officially recognized. . . . Recording should enhance and improve the opportunity for service, not simply bestow an honor. It should be borne in mind that such recognition in ministry is not only a seal of approval of one who is locally helpful, but that it also involves extension of service beyond the local community. . . .
>
> A recorded Friends minister must be a member. . . , above reproach in character, and a person of deep religious experience and dedication. Such a person must have a thorough knowledge of the Scriptures and of Friends' testimonies and ideals, possessing the skills of a competent leader without being "priestly" or losing the spirit and status of the servant. In financial and business affairs the minister must be of scrupulous honesty and integrity, in all respects an example of Christian living. The minister is expected to meet the standards of daily living set forth in the Queries.
>
> (North Carolina Yearly Meeting *Faith and Practice*, p. 75)

North Carolina Yearly Meeting's process for recording a minister begins with the monthly meeting's Meeting on Ministry and Counsel, which makes a recommendation to the monthly meeting. If approved, notification is sent to the quarterly meeting. The quarterly meeting's Meeting on Ministry and Counsel appoints a committee "to appraise the general fitness of the individual under consideration." If the report is favorable, the recommendation is forwarded to the Yearly Meeting on Ministry and Counsel. If the yearly meeting committee approves, "it shall entrust the person to the care of the Committee on Training and Recording of Ministers." When an individual has completed the prescribed course of study, the committee "shall review again the general fitness, character, and aptitude of the individual for the ministry." If the committee's report to the Yearly Meeting on Ministry and Counsel is favorable, "the Yearly Meeting on Ministry and Counsel may, after full and careful consideration, recommend to the yearly meeting that the member under consideration be recorded as a minister." When the yearly meeting has acted favorably, the recording is completed. Copies of the minute are sent to the quarterly and monthly meeting to enter in their minute books and a copy is given to the individual.[67]

The process in Western Yearly Meeting is similar except that there are no quarterly meetings involved and the yearly meeting has a Committee on Training and Recording of Ministers to oversee the process. The yearly meeting publishes a handbook that provides details of the entire process.

In some yearly meetings, ministers are recognized chiefly at the monthly meeting level, while in others they are only recognized at the quarterly or yearly meeting level.

Paid Ministry and Pastors

While George Fox described the "hireling ministry" of his day in extremely unflattering terms, it is helpful to know that in his day priests in the Church of England were largely educated younger sons of the upper class who needed a source of income and "went into the ministry" because it was respectable and provided a living rather than out of any personal faith or wish to serve. These preachers for the state church were often shallow, uncaring, and completely innocent of any spiritual life of their own. These were some of the people George Fox tried to get help from in his early days of spiritual seeking. They failed to understand him, and prescribed such things as going home and getting married, or taking up smoking tobacco, as ways of snapping out of his depression and becoming a useful member of society. They are not comparable to contemporary ministers who feel called to their work, particularly in countries such as the U.S. and Canada that do not support a state church.

Since the late 19th century, Friends have been "released" for ministry—that is, meetings or organizations have paid a few individuals

67 North Carolina (FUM) *Faith and Practice*, pp. 75-66 and 76-77

> enough so they did not have to hold another job but were set free to concentrate their energies more fully on a particular work. Prior to that, Friends called to travel in the ministry either had sufficient financial resources of their own or had their travel expenses covered, but were expected to earn a living in some other way.
>
> (Margery Post Abbot and Peggy Senger Parsons, *Walk Worthy of Your Calling*, p. 190)

The need for something more than volunteer leadership arose in the 1860s and '70s when midwest Friends brought in vast numbers of converts using the Methodist-style evangelism that was sweeping the country. None of these converts had any experience of Quakerism, some were new to Christianity, and many had acquired a taste for inspirational preaching and revivalism. Originally, meetings released members of their meetings for periods of time to minister to the newcomers, but this fairly quickly transmuted into permanent paid positions. By the end of the 19th century, most midwestern and western meetings in the Orthodox branch of Quakerism had pastors.

Today among FUM Pastoral Friends, a typical pastor leads worship, delivers a sermon, and performs other services such as pastoral care and visiting. There is a wide variety of practice within Pastoral Friends, a few meetings maintaining Quaker distinctives and large portions of open worship (traditional worship based on silence). One Quaker pastor was known to state that, although he prepared a sermon every week, he might or might not actually give it, depending on the movement of the Spirit (though in fact he always did). Most Pastoral meetings include lay leadership during worship—leading singing, reading Scripture, making announcements, and occasionally giving the sermon. Business is conducted using the traditional clerk and committee structure.

The pastor may or may not be paid, though unpaid pastors are generally volunteers from within the community when the work is very part-time. Some small Pastoral meetings share a pastor with another meeting; some offer part-time jobs and get retired pastors to fill them. Financing even a part-time pastor is often a major challenge for a small meeting. Large meetings tend to pay better and offer better benefits, but in general Quaker pastors are not well paid compared to ministers in other denominations.

Usually, these Friends identify themselves as pastors rather than ministers and reject the title of "reverend." Their goal, at least in theory, is to work themselves out of a job—that is, to help everyone in the congregation to grow spiritually and use their gifts so that having a paid leader becomes unnecessary.

The relationship of a Quaker pastor to a meeting is complex. On the one hand, the pastor is certainly not simply an employee, but rather a leader and spiritual adviser. On the other hand, the pastor is an employee, and deserves oversight, feedback, and support from the meeting. Some members' expectations may not match the written job description, if any. If this becomes a problem, it is a matter for the meeting to address. Hiring and firing a pastor is often emotionally charged, and personal ties may take precedence over the good of the meeting in making decisions.

It helps for the meeting to be very clear about what roles the pastor is to fill and to see that members do not make demands beyond that scope. It helps for members of the meeting to be active in all aspects of the meeting and to maintain an independence from the pastor. Although the pastor certainly needs to report to and receive guidance from the business meeting, he or she needs to be sensitive not to unduly influence the group's decisions.

It helps to have some members of the meeting, usually Ministry and Counsel, see that the pastor gets the care and support he or she needs. And it helps very much for pastors to have the opportunity to get together with other pastors for mutual support, sharing, and brainstorming. Yearly meetings with pastors can have a person or committee at the yearly meeting level responsible for overseeing the relationships between pastors and meetings so that they can provide counsel and guidance as appropriate. Yearly meetings or larger organizations can also offer opportunities for retreats, conferences, classes, and other means of helping pastors develop and hone their gifts.

Ultimately, both the pastor and the individual members of

the meeting are accountable to God, and ideally regard one another as co-workers.

Traveling Ministry

> Throughout significant portions of Quaker history the traveling ministry has been the lifeblood of the Religious Society of Friends. Since the earliest days women and men have been called by God to travel to various places among the "world's people" as well as among already established groups of Friends.
>
> (Jonathan Vogel-Borne, "Traveling in the Ministry")

In many ways, early Friends' travels were similar to Paul and other apostles' travels during the first century: to proclaim the Gospel and to return to fledgling groups to provide support and correction. In a short paper written in 1987 on the history and practice of traveling in the ministry, Jonathan Vogel-Borne wrote:

> In succeeding generations, as our religious society became settled . . . and as we became more geographically dispersed, the traveling ministry helped to provide needed communication between the various groups of Friends. . . . Traveling ministers were certified and trusted outsiders to the meeting's "politics." In this capacity they could be of enormous service to the community. Their ability to discern the spiritual health of the meeting, their mediating influence to reconcile differences, and their liberty to speak out on potentially difficult issues both spiritual and temporal were often very helpful to Friends.
>
> During the [1900s], the formal practice of travel in the ministry among Friends had virtually ceased. In the unprogrammed tradition . . . it is thought that no one's gifts in the ministry should be recognized over and above the gifts of others. Along with the advent of modern communication . . . formal travel in the ministry had all but fallen to disuse.
>
> Recently, there seems to be a revival of the traveling ministry. . . .
>
> (Jonathan Vogel-Borne, "Traveling in the Ministry")

FGC's Traveling Ministries Program, established in 1998, has had a tremendous impact among unprogrammed Friends. It matches up seasoned Friends' gifts with the needs of local and yearly meetings. The program has engaged in the work of naming, nurturing, and holding traveling Friends accountable. It has explored and re-energized the roles of Friends engaged in ministry to other Friends and the role of traveling companions to hold the ministry in prayer and to accompany the ministering Friend. This role is variously described as a traveling companion, an elder, or a companion in ministry.

In his paper, Jonathan Vogel-Borne suggests,

> In order for Friends in the home meetings to share more fully in the Spiritual enrichment of the traveling ministry, occasions may be arranged for traveling Friends to speak about their sojourns shortly following their return. The home monthly, quarterly, and yearly meetings will formally receive the returning travel minute at a business session following the return of the traveling Friend. This is an occasion where the endorsements on the travel minute might be read and the Friend would have a further opportunity to share about his or her visit.
>
> (Jonathan Vogel-Borne, "Traveling in the Ministry")

Travel Minutes, Minutes of Religious Service, and Letters of Introduction

A distinction needs to be made between letters of introduction, travel minutes, and minutes of religious service.

Travel Minutes

Travel minutes (or "traveling minutes") are issued to Friends who have worked with their monthly meeting to discern a clear leading to travel and visit other Friends. They may have a specific concern, they may have been asked to visit a meeting for a specific purpose, or it may be that God has moved them to worship with those Friends and to be with them. The Friend who is led to travel lays it before his or her monthly meeting along with the whole nature of the proposed visits as far as can be foreseen. If the monthly meeting unites with the concern or affirms the leading, it writes a minute to that effect and gives the Friend a copy. A travel minute should describe any specific concern the bearer is laboring under. When a meeting comes to unity with a member's concern to travel, it should make sure that finances do not stand in the way by being ready to contribute toward the expenses incurred.

When visits are to be made outside the quarterly meeting (if any), the minute is sent to the quarter for its discernment and endorsement as well. When visits are to be made outside the yearly meeting, the minute is also sent to the yearly meeting for its discernment and endorsement.

> Such a traveling minute affirms that the individual is a Friend in good standing and travels with the blessing of his or her local community. This is reassuring to the meetings visited as well as a real support to the minister. The normal expectation is that such a minute is for a specified time, that the clerk of each meeting visited will sign the letter, including a note about the visit, and that on returning home the Public Friend will bring the minute back to the business meeting and report on the travels.
>
> (Margery Post Abbott and Peggy Senger Parsons, *Walk Worthy of Your Calling*, p. 278)

It is customary, where practicable, for traveling Friends to be welcomed into the homes of those whom they visit. This has the double advantage of saving expense to the traveler and of extending more intimately the benefit of the visit.

While visiting, the carrier of a travel minute presents it to the clerk of the body visited, who reads it aloud as a way of introducing the traveling Friend. (Only the travel minute, not endorsements, should be read.) At the end of the visit, the clerk writes and signs a brief note about the visit. This is called an endorsement. (See Sample Forms, Letters, Etc. for some examples.) Endorsements may be written on the back of the page or on additional pages attached to the letter.

When the proposed visits are completed, the traveling Friend should return the minute and all the endorsements to the body that issued it. The body may ask the traveling Friend to report on his or her experiences as well.

A travel minute represents an activity with a specific form: leaving, traveling under a concern, and returning to report on the completed event. For an ongoing ministry, another form of support, such as a minute of religious service, may be more appropriate.

Companions in Ministry

Since the earliest times, Friends traveling with a concern usually had a companion who could provide both practical and spiritual support. This practice is currently being revived, largely through the influence of FGC's Traveling Ministries Program. Friends who lead workshops and retreats or who travel with other leadings have found that having a companion in the ministry is of considerable spiritual and practical support. The companion prays for the minister as well as those ministered to, being attentive to how the Spirit is moving. The companion helps the minister to deepen his or her faithfulness. It is good practice to provide companions with traveling minutes that describe their supporting role.

Minutes of Religious Service

A minute of religious service is more broad than a travel minute and can include any kind of service. It embodies a meeting's recognition of a call to a religious service in someone's life.

> In recent times Friends monthly meetings within the Friends General Conference have generally moved away from the practice of recording ministers, but have continued to value the practice of issuing minutes of religious service for individual Friends who are traveling in support of an important cause or to nurture the religious life of Friends, meetings, or other groups. During at least the past 30 years this practice has been extended by some Friends meetings to include the recognition of ministries which might or might not involve travel, but which are also intended to support important causes or to nurture religious life either within or outside the Society of Friends. For the past ten years Chestnut Hill Friends Meeting has been engaged in this practice, and as we have found it to be a valued practice, this document is intended to set forth guidelines to encourage and regularize the process for the future.
>
> ("Report of the Ad Hoc Committee on Recognizing and Supporting Ministries," approved November, 2004, Chestnut Hill Friends Meeting, p. 2)

Chestnut Hill Friends suggest that a minute of religious service contain the following components:

- Name the work as explicitly as possible.
- Affirm that the meeting experiences the person as led to do the work; perhaps include how the person's life and spiritual path have led to this work at this time.
- Name the meeting's unity with the work, perhaps making reference to Friends testimonies.
- Name the meeting's specific commitments to supporting this person and his or her work, including the appointment of an oversight committee.
- Ask the reader for his or her support.
- Give the approval date and an appropriate expiration date, with the signature of the clerk of the meeting. The expiration date may vary considerably, depending on the nature of the call.

Letters of Introduction

> Where visiting among Friends is merely incidental to travel for some other purpose, a monthly meeting may issue a letter of introduction for a member in good standing. Such a letter requires no further endorsement. Quarterly or yearly meetings may originate similar letters as occasion warrants.
>
> (New York Yearly Meeting *Faith and Practice*, p. 129)

When members of a meeting plan to travel and wish to make contact with other Friends, they may ask the clerk of their home meeting or the yearly meeting for a letter of introduction. The letter may also convey greetings from the meeting. There are no obligations for financial support, hospitality, or reporting back to the home group. The clerk can issue a letter of introduction on his or her own authority; no consultation or approval is necessary.

Section IV: Conducting Business

Chapter 8: Meeting for Business

The meeting for business, if it be Spirit-filled and properly understood, is a hands-on, laboratory-filled experience in which the whole fellowship comes face to face with the Spirit's demands for the sacrifice of time, treasure, convenience, and prejudice. When opinions differ widely and the need for spiritual discernment becomes crucial, the best are driven, as never in a meeting for worship, to seek that Spirit which can sustain harmony while waiting for the right leading. Thus, God's work among us becomes more real and faith is both tested and strengthened in the business meeting.

(Paul A. Lacey and Bill Taber, "The Purpose of Meetings for Worship and for Business")

What It Is

At the core of the Quaker way of making corporate decisions lies the understanding that the process used is more important than the actual decision. In coming to a decision, Quakers use an inclusive, thoughtful, often slow group process that encourages people to keep their minds open, to turn to the Inner Light for guidance, to listen to one another, and to search their hearts. We expect to learn from the Inner Teacher and from one another, to gain understanding from others' experience, and together to find a way of proceeding that is better than any of the ways we had anticipated individually. As we do that, we rely on the process and our use of it to maintain loving relationships with one another.

[Meeting for business is] about looking for Truth as a body, rather than about our individual senses of truth. We need to enter worshipfully

> into our meetings for business. We need to wrestle with the issues, to share our glimpses of the Truth as we see it, and then we need to let go and listen deeply until all those glimpses give us a sense of the Truth as a whole. This takes time, patience, and surrender.
>
> (Michael Wajda, *Expectant Listening: Finding God's Thread of Guidance*, p. 22)

Group decision making on the basis of seeking God's will, which leads to unity among the group, has characterized Quakers from the beginning. A right and satisfactory decision depends upon the full understanding and unity of the Friends present.

George Selleck, in his short pamphlet, *Principles of the Quaker Business Meeting*, points out:

> When Quakers arose in the 17th century, there were objections on the part of some to the holding of business meetings. Some persons felt that such gatherings placed undue limitations on the guidance of the individual, but the new Quaker movement was characterized by a faith that the *group* could be guided, as well as the individual. The Quaker conviction that the Light of Christ is given in some measure to everyone implies both an individual apprehension of the will of God and also an understanding of God's will mediated through the insight of others. Quakerism has always had within it a strong centrifugal force of individualism, but likewise there always has been a centripetal force of corporate life in tension with it. From the fruitful interaction of these two have come the decisions of the Society. The visions and concerns of individuals prevent the Society from being over-traditional and static; the insights of a gathered group prevent it from moving over-hastily in unconsidered enthusiasm.
>
> (George A. Selleck, *Principles of the Quaker Business Meeting*, p. 3)

In "Some Thoughts on Quaker Process," Paul Lacey lists four principles of the Quaker business procedure:

- Integrity of community is more important than quick, or efficient, or right decisions.
- There is no rush to decide things, since the process is in God's hands.
- Coming into a business meeting with one's mind made up, *even if one is right*, is unfaithfulness to the process.

- The primary aim of the business meeting is to deepen the spiritual life of the community, rather than getting things done.

These are provocative.
George Selleck asserted:

> The Quaker way of conducting meetings for business . . . is of central importance to the very existence of the Society of Friends. The method is primarily an expression of the basic Quaker way of living and working, which creates and preserves the sense of fellowship in the Quaker community.
>
> (George A. Selleck, *Principles of the Quaker Business Meeting*, p. 1)

About Quaker Process

"Quaker process," "business process," and "process" are all used to refer to the practices typically used by Quakers to make corporate decisions, such as sense of the meeting and writing minutes, as well as typical ways the meeting community functions, such as the use of committees and clerks. The key is to use processes and forms that invite the participants to seek God's will and to build a loving community.

Friends have found that using appropriate processes is more important than the decision made. In a short paper on Quaker business practice written for the World Council of Churches in 2001, Eden Grace wrote:

> ***Attitude toward the process:*** We value process over product, action or outcome. We respect each other's thoughts, feelings and insights more than expedient action. The process of reaching a decision yields more "results" than the decisions themselves. . . . Through that experience of the unity of the meeting, we are prepared for faithful discipleship in the church and world. A decision which is made without that experience is of little value.
>
> (Eden Grace, "An Introduction to Quaker Business Practice")

Patricia Loring, in *Spiritual Responsibility in the Meeting for Business*, cautions Friends not to let secular practices creep into

Quaker business:

> Friends spiritual process is extremely demanding; and it is difficult to keep it sorted out from the secular models with which we spend so much of our lives. Yet the process is sufficiently precious to make it worth laboring to keep sight of its spiritual basis while we are in the midst of it. Otherwise it may become a set of empty forms used in a secular manner.
>
> (Patricia Loring, *Spiritual Responsibility in the Meeting for Business*)

When Friends conduct business with a sense of a higher power that can bring us into unity, only then do we realize the full power of the Quaker decision-making process.

> Only as Friends are aware that they are functioning in the Divine presence does the Quaker method work. The commitment to search for unity depends upon mutual trust, implies a willingness to labor and to submit to the leadings of the Spirit, and grows as members become better acquainted with one another.
>
> (North Pacific Yearly Meeting *Faith and Practice*, p. 56)

When we remain faithful to the process, amazing things can happen.

> Quakerism works. Through the extremes of persecution, outward expansion, inward retirement, schisms, separation from the world, and accommodation to the world, the Quaker process for making group decisions works. Too often Friends do not trust it; too often our Quaker faith is weak and our Quaker practice is ungrounded. But when it is trusted and used, when we Friends rely on God's Spirit to guide us as a group, the community grows stronger together. God becomes more visible in our little piece of the world.
>
> (Jan Greene and Marty Walton, *Fostering Vital Friends Meetings*, p. vi)

Being Faithful to the Process

Self-Discipline

Being faithful to the process requires a great deal of self-discipline.

> For this method of seeking the will of God to work, considerable

self-discipline and group discipline are necessary. . . . Mutual respect and trust are absolute necessities. And, at times, Friends must be willing to stop, to wait in silence, in the hope that some new wisdom or insight will come among them.

(Thomas D. Hamm, *The Quakers in America*, pp. 97-98)

In "Some Words on Corporate Discernment," Jan Hoffman identifies disciplines which help us to be rightly guided:

- Silence.
- Humility.
- Obedience.
- Patience.
- Discernment.
- Faithfulness.

Speaking and Recognizing Truth

Everyone has access to a part of the Truth.

(Debra K. Farrington, *Hearing with the Heart*, p. xvii)

Friends find that we have a personal Truth at our deepest gut level. This is Truth that has to have been lived:

Truth is not found by professing correct beliefs and correct actions while actually living outside the life and power.

(Sandra L. Cronk, *Gospel Order*, p. 8)

This is what George Fox was asking for when he challenged the parishioners in Ulverston:

You will say Christ saith this, and the Apostles say this, but what canst thou say? Art thou a child of Light, and hast walked in the Light, and what thou speakest is it inwardly from God?

(Hugh Barbour, editor, *Margaret Fell Speaking*, pp. 8-9)

For modern Friends, the question might well be rephrased, "You say that George Fox said this, and the Scriptures say this, but what can you say? Have you been searched by the Light and heard and followed the leadings of the Spirit? Is what you say in accord with the promptings of the Inner Light?"

Each person's Truth is a small part of Divine Truth. When engaging with other Friends in the search for God's will, we need each of these little pieces of Truth. It is each Friend's right and responsibility to share that piece of Truth when it bears on a matter the group is working on or with which it is struggling. Whatever partial pieces of Truth each of us have hold of, when we share them, we make it possible for the community to discern those greater Truths that individually we probably won't reach.

Sharing or even knowing what our Truth is is not easy for most of us. It takes being deeply centered and in tune with the Divine. Often we find it hard to articulate—to put into words. It is often highly emotional and highly personal. Sharing it involves baring our souls, making ourselves vulnerable to one another. It involves knowing ourselves well enough and allowing God's searching Light to show us to ourselves clearly enough to be able to say, "This is who I am. This is where I stand." This is a point at which the level of trust in the community is critical. People are reticent to share if they rightly fear being bruised.

Over the centuries, Friends have found that how one expresses Truth makes it easier or harder for others to hear it. It is easiest to hear when it comes from a place of love for the individual Friends and the group as a whole. This is not a sentimental love, but a deep caring—God's love being channeled through us. The Truth when told, however, may not come across as loving, but be heard as a rebuke. It may be more like "tough love," telling Friends something that may be hard for them to accept and that may be potentially hurtful. Speaking one's Truth is one of the most practical applications of the testimony of integrity. When it comes from a place of anger, or ego, or frustration, it is harder for others to hear.

John Woolman, who is often thought of as single-handedly convincing Quakers to free their slaves, was not the first Friend to question slavery. Benjamin Lay was fiercely opposed to slavery. One time "in the midst of the solemn silence" during annual sessions, Benjamin Lay walked up the aisle, stopped midway, and exclaimed, "You slaveholders! Why don't you throw off your Quaker coats as I do mine, and show yourselves as you are?" He then cast off his overcoat to reveal a military coat, a sword, and a large Bible. "In the sight of God," he cried, "you are as guilty as if you stabbed your slaves to the heart, as I do this book!" Suiting the action to the word, he pierced a small bladder filled with poke-weed juice concealed between the covers, and sprinkled as with fresh blood those who sat near him.[68] Friends largely ignored him, but he did spark the consciences of several Friends, including Woolman.

In *Quakers in Conflict*, Larry Ingle describes Job Scott, a traveling minister in the late 1700s who saw a need for reform among Quakers and who often gave messages criticizing his hearers. On one occasion, he informed a meeting that God would "as much reject us and our plain form, as any other people . . . where we depart from the life and the power."[69] Larry Ingle comments:

> Although Scott's *Journal* and sermons reverberated with such sentiments, he characteristically refused to be part of any effort to exclude anyone. . . . To reach offenders' minds required laboring with them "in the spirit of meekness and love, with an earnest desire for their amendment, welfare, and restoration."
>
> Scott's approach was reminiscent of Woolman's with slave owners—refusing to compromise with the evil, speaking against it, but laboring with the offender until each saw the Truth. True disciples did not impose their version of the Truth legalistically on others; instead they appealed to the sense of justice in others and permitted the Deity to work. Scott believed in the leadership of the Spirit, a kind of anarchy under God's lordship, a government that ruled not by outward laws but by the inward assent of each of the governed.
>
> (H. Larry Ingle, *Quakers in Conflict*, pp. 8-9)

Sharing one's truth usually happens when one is deeply uncomfortable with the current trend in a meeting for business. One feels led to speak. If one is feeling strong emotions, it helps to name them: "I am feeling angry and hurt," "I am feeling such

---

[68] John Greenleaf Whittier's introduction to *The Journal of John Woolman*

[69] H. Larry Ingle, *Quakers in Conflict*, p. 8

joy," "I am feeling dismayed." Not everyone feels or displays deep emotion, however. Some Friends have the gift of speaking Truth matter-of-factly or posed as an inquiry or question.

Friends need to be tender with anyone who has done such deep sharing. They may feel vulnerable or exhausted. One can hold the Friend in the Light, listen deeply, and continue to love and care for the individual whether one agrees with what they say or not. Sorting out if what they said contributes to the discernment the meeting is engaged in is a separate issue from how one relates to the individual.

Friends need to be able to recognize Truth when they hear it. The question is not, "Do I agree with what is being said?" but "Do I recognize what is being said as authentic?" Getting better at discernment is something Quakers can actively work on, and any given meeting will have participants with varying degrees of sensitivity to Truth. "Weighty Friends" are those whose ability to discern the Truth has been demonstrated over time and whose suggestions have been consistently useful. The meeting can benefit from these Friends by taking their analyses and suggestions seriously. Weighty Friends are not infallible, however; the rest of the meeting needs to test for themselves whether a particular contribution carries weight. Similarly, a Friend not generally known for insight may offer a helpful analysis or suggestion.

How does one recognize someone else's Truth, or one's own? When one Friend's message opens others to speak their Truth, or when the meeting is deepened, these are signs of authenticity. Emotion is not a reliable indicator—strong emotions may also come from a place of ego or defense. Someone with an agenda may have and express strong emotions. A warning sign that a message is not authentic is if others present feel inhibited in speaking their Truth.

A common misunderstanding among Friends is that a true leading for one Friend must apply to all Friends. While we share an openness to new revelation and a set of corporate testimonies, individual's lives will vary considerably. Some Friends are led to spend a year studying at Pendle Hill or a seminary; others are not. Some Friends are led to be vegetarian; others are not.

Some Friends are led to be social activists or to serve people in poverty; others are not. Some Friends are led to spend long periods during the week in prayer; others are not. As the Apostle Paul wrote so eloquently, we are all members of one body; each Friend has a unique function which is necessary for the health of the body as a whole.

I once attended a representative meeting, and after two members of the Peace Committee had given their report, which included admonishing Friends to be active, I reluctantly rose and said, "Friends, I feel harangued." Afterward, several Friends came up to me separately and said, "I'm so glad you said that!" They had been feeling the same way, but had not known how to express it.

After a similar interaction later during yearly meeting sessions, one Friend said to me, "I feel like you're doing my work for me." It is important not to rely on others to speak hard truths. It is bad for the individual who finds her or himself rising to speak frequently, and it is bad for the meeting, which needs to know how widespread a feeling is. One or two individuals who speak frequently can too easily be stereotyped and their messages ignored.

For those who have never attempted such a message, here is some advice:

- Get as grounded as you possibly can.
- Stand up.
- Stay tuned in to the Spirit.
- Use the love you feel coming from the Spirit to infuse you, and channel that love to the rest of the group.
- Speak of your own condition. Name your emotions. Describe any pertinent experience you have that explains or informs who you are and where you stand. If you're not sure why you feel this way, say so. Gut feelings are often difficult to analyze or put into words. That's okay. Traditionally, Friends have used such words as "uneasy," "unclear," and "uncomfortable" to describe misgivings about a proposal. "Easy," "clear," and "comfortable" are used to indicate support for a proposal.

- Be brief. Do not "run beyond your Guide"—when you have shared what others need to hear, stop and sit down.
- Have no expectations of how the meeting will act. You are called only to do and say what is given to you. What the meeting makes of it is up to the meeting. Do not speak again to repeat yourself unless invited to do so for clarification.
- Stay humble. You have shared your Truth; but it is only a part of God's Truth. It may become joined with others' pieces of Truth for an outcome different than you hoped for or expected. Even if the meeting rejects or ignores your offering, know that you have done all that God required of you.
- If you are not sure whether your speaking was rightly ordered, seek out a seasoned Friend afterward and ask.

In addition to our individual, personal Truths, we need Friends who can hear and share the still, small voice of God's guidance for us all.

Preparing Business and Preparing Friends

> Even if Friends are careful to attend meetings for business and to assemble promptly, they may nevertheless fritter away God's opportunity, perhaps because the business has been poorly prepared and presented, or because Friends do not apply themselves promptly and earnestly, or because Friends are self-indulgent, or simply because Friends do not wait upon the Lord.
>
> (Thomas S. Brown, *When Friends Attend to Business*)

The Agenda

Common types of items that come before a business meeting include:

- Reports—no decision needs to be made.
- Recommendations for action—a decision is called for.
- A minute stating the meeting's witness—a communal sense of God's leading is called for.
- Information and announcements.

Reports may come from committees, the treasurer, or other Friends. Items for decision may deal with membership, finance, the quality of worship, appointments, action to be taken to further the cause of peace and justice, or other matters. Who do the items that show up on a business meeting's agenda come from? How do they get there?

Business items may come from:

- A committee.
- The clerk.
- Another meeting officer.
- An individual Friend.

The clerk has the responsibility of drawing up the agenda. A typical agenda might include:

- Worship.
- Minutes of the previous meeting.
- Consideration of business carried over from the previous meeting.
- Treasurer's report.
- Reports from standing committees.
- New matters.
- Announcements.
- Closing worship.

Preparing Business

An important responsibility of the clerk is determining how and when business will be presented, when to lay over a decision for later, and finding a good process that suits each situation. Who will present an item of business? Where will it fall in the agenda? Will the meeting be asked to make a decision now or later? A seasoned clerk will help Friends decide the best process for each item. For routine items, meetings develop traditions on procedure.

For any business other than routine matters, it is important to engage in appropriate research, seasoning,[70] and communicating with the body of Friends. In general, it is good process for a com-

[70] "Seasoning" is the practice of giving a matter attention over a period of time and by disparate groups of Friends.

mittee rather than an individual to look into a matter and bring a recommendation to the meeting for a decision. This helps ensure that pertinent facts and previous meeting actions are considered, and that the matter has been well thought through and prayed over.

When a small group or committee is discussing and coming up with a recommendation, it is important that people in the meeting who have deep concerns about the issue are included in some way. Committee members can talk to people individually or can invite anyone with concerns to a committee meeting. In some cases it is appropriate for the meeting to hold a threshing session or use some other format for the whole group to work on the issue.

Preparing Friends

For any item of business that is complicated or controversial, it helps to bring it to Friends' attention before it comes to business meeting. This can be done through:

- Handing out information.
- Holding a question and answer session.
- Holding a discussion or series of discussions.
- Holding a threshing session or series of sessions.
- Any way that helps Friends share deeply and listen deeply—worship sharing, a fish bowl, or any other format.

> Controversial items are presented and discussed among those in the meeting well in advance of the business session so Friends can come to the business meeting prepared with sufficient information and prayerful consideration to engage in group discernment.
>
> (Lake Erie Yeary Meeting website, "About Quakers: How Quakers Conduct Business" leym.org)

In order for Friends to consider a matter, they need to understand the item, and it may take time for them to digest information. Young Friends of North America (1955–84) instituted "pre-business meetings" to go over upcoming business items in an informal manner with questions and answers and open discussion in order to bring the many new attenders at the annual conference each year up to speed. The items were then handled in the usual formal manner during the actual business meetings.

It is the responsibility of the individual or committee bringing an item of business to consult with the clerk far enough in advance to make sure that Friends can be given sufficient information and time to make an informed decision. If Friends come to business meeting already knowledgeable about items to be considered, they can concentrate on listening for divine guidance during the business meeting.

Occasionally, an item of importance to the meeting arises unexpectedly. To make sure that no one is caught off guard, the clerk or committee bringing the item of business should notify all members about the item or recommendation.

Processing an Issue Prior to Business Meeting

In the case of potentially divisive issues, it is good to use a careful process that includes opportunities for sharing, absorbing information, and discussion or worship sharing in small groups outside of business meeting. These might include threshing sessions, informational meetings, and/or small group processing.

It is important when starting a lengthy process to remind Friends of their responsibility to take part in the process from the beginning. In an article on conflict in the life of our meetings, Arlene Kelly wrote:

> This relates to a situation many of us have encountered: persons holding a strong opinion pro or con show up at the 11th hour when a difficult decision is being made and want their view to be given full weight, though it is absent the benefit of all reflections that have gone before. The lesson is simply this: at the front end of a process undertaken to deal with a challenging issue, all who are active in the life of the meeting should be reminded of the responsibility to take part in the process from the beginning in a spirit of openness, allowing ourselves to be changed. If we forego that aspect of the decision making, in the absence of a good reason for having done so, then we forego the privilege of having a strong voice in the decision to be made.

("Conflict in the Life of Our Meeting: Friends Peace Testimony at Work?" in *Friends Journal*, July 2008)

Threshing Sessions

Threshing[71] sessions offer an opportunity for members of a meeting to absorb information or hear one another's truths on a complex or controversial matter. They may be referred to as threshing sessions, threshing meetings, or listening meetings.

> This term currently denotes a meeting at which a variety of different, and sometimes controversial, opinions can be openly, and sometimes forcefully, expressed, often in order to defuse a situation before a later meeting for worship for business.
>
> (Britain Yearly Meeting *Faith and Practice*, 12.26)

North Pacific Yearly Meeting's *Faith and Practice* offers the following advice:

> Friends should not avoid issues which may be difficult or controversial. It is better for the Meeting to allow full opportunity for differences to be aired and faced. In dealing with such issues, or those of a complex nature entailing information with which some Friends may be unfamiliar, it is often helpful to hold one or more preliminary "threshing meetings" in which no decision is made, but through which the chaff can be separated from the grain of truth.[72] Such meetings can clear the way for later action on the issue. Full notice of a threshing session should be given and special efforts made to see that Friends of all shades of opinion can and will be present. To the extent that Friends of a given view are absent, the usefulness of such a meeting will be impaired. If factual material

---

71 Historical note: to thresh is to separate wheat from chaff, or any grain from its seed coverings and stalks. In earlier times this was done by beating harvested stalks of grain with a flail or by stomping them underfoot. In either case, it was a noisy, chaotic activity. "Originally the term was used to describe large and noisy meetings for convincement of 'the world's people' in order to 'thresh' them away from the world." (Britain *Faith and Practice*, 12.26) In other words, among early Friends, threshing meetings were meetings for evangelism.

72 "Chaff" is what is left after threshing—the husks. "To separate the wheat from the chaff" means to sort out what is important from a confusion of information or opinions.

> needs to be presented, persons knowledgeable in the area should be asked to present such material and be available to answer questions.
>
> The clerk or moderator of a threshing session should make it clear at the start that the meeting not only expects, but welcomes expressions of the widest differences. Friends are urged not to hold back whatever troubles them about the issues at hand. Hesitancy to share a strong conviction, because it may offend someone, reflects a lack of trust. The clerk's job, then, is to draw out the reticent, limit the time taken by too-ready talkers, and see that all have an opportunity to speak. It is useful to ask someone to take notes of the meeting for later reference. At times the threshing meeting may forward a recommendation to the meeting for business.
>
> (North Pacific Yearly Meeting *Faith and Practice*, p. 58)

The clerk has the additional responsibility of closing the meeting at the appointed time.

Several different formats are used for threshing sessions.

> Normal practices of a Quaker meeting for business are relaxed so that Friends can speak more than once to an issue, can speak to a point just made, or can ask a question of a previous speaker. The clerk might even ask for a "straw poll" of opinions at "this point in our discussion so far," or go around the circle giving each person an opportunity to speak in turn. The special role of a threshing session is that it allows everyone to say what they think without the burden of needing to make a decision. It enables folks to speak strongly yet be able to change their position and not merely defend their point of view in anticipation of a decision about to be made.
>
> (Arthur Meyer Boyd, "When Quakers Disagree")

The following ground rules have been found helpful:

- No decision will be made in this gathering.
- Come with a sense of humility and openness to new insights and to learn about differing experiences.
- Listen to each person and receive their thoughts.
- Each person has the opportunity to declare what he or she is thinking, feeling, and perceiving.
- Speak from personal experience.

The important thing is that no decision will be made during

the gathering, that Friends are encouraged to share their deeply held convictions, and that all are listened to with respect.

Informational Meetings

When there are a lot of facts to share or Friends need to gain an understanding of a subject, a gathering separate from business meeting can be useful. This may consist of a presentation by Friends or by others with expertise in the subject, followed by questions and answers. This has been found helpful for meetings faced with a pedophile in their midst.

Small Group Processing

Sometimes it is helpful to process a matter in small groups. This could be done using a worship sharing format, a fish bowl, or other small group processes. See "Group Formats for Sharing" on page 78 for a description of some formats.

> From time to time, a meeting may benefit from looking at itself and identifying specific areas needing attention: pastoral care, outreach, or major changes such as rebuilding or developing premises. The discussion of such matters in small groups, properly constituted, can help to involve the whole meeting and prepare it for decisions which must eventually be taken in the regular meeting for church affairs. Valuable suggestions and solutions may come from individuals who would not feel able to voice them in the more formal meeting.
>
> (Britain Yearly Meeting *Faith and Practice*, 3.26)

Seasoning an Item of Business

It might appear to Friends who regularly attend meetings for business but are not involved in the preparation or follow-up that items of business make their first appearance in meeting for business, where they are dealt with. Actually, an item of business may be forwarded for seasoning between an individual, a committee, and business meeting several times before it is completely dealt with.

An item might:

- Be passed by the clerk directly to a committee to be worked on before coming to business meeting.

- Be brought before the meeting for decision there and then.
- Be presented to the meeting as a report. Friends "receive" the report but do not need to approve it.
- Be announced to the meeting and be assigned to a committee or officer who will work on it and bring it back to the meeting when ready. In some meetings, this is standard practice for applications for membership and marriage under the care of the meeting.
- Be brought before the meeting for Friends' consideration with a final decision to be made at a later meeting for business.

When Friends are unable to reach a decision during a meeting for business, they may decide to have a small group do further work and report back to the next business meeting. The group could be a standing committee, one or more meeting officers, or a committee created for the purpose which will cease to exist when its work is done, which is called an ad hoc committee. The current state of the meeting's discernment should be recorded in a minute, traditionally called a Minute of Exercise or in some places a Minute of Process.

> Minutes have several functions. They should represent gathered distilled truth. They should record the extent to which the meeting has been able to come to unity on the subject. Not to have full unity is not a failure. It is better to record the extent of the unity achieved and to leave the rest to God's right timing, allowing for further action at a later date. If there is remaining disunity, the minute should gather the points of disagreement for the record. Again, this should not be considered a failure, but rather a statement of the understanding of the gathered meeting at that time.
>
> (John Smith, in *Friends Understanding of the Word of God*, Ohio Yearly Meeting)

Outline of the Business Meeting

Business meeting begins with worship:

> Don't be lulled into thinking that you are there to get the job done and can dispense with the worship. Hold the work of the meeting in the Light. Listen deeply and speak tenderly. Begin with worship;

end with worship; and call for worship whenever tempers fray or weariness sets in.

(Deborah Haines, *When You're the Only Friend in Town*, p. 21)

During the worship, it is often helpful if the clerk reads something brief that will help the meeting settle into a worshipful but attentive attitude. After the opening worship, the meeting turns to the business at hand. Sometimes the clerk will go over the agenda to give Friends an idea of the scope of the business to be brought forward or to see if there are additional items that need to be added to the agenda.

The clerk introduces the items of business one at a time. The meeting goes through the following steps in considering each item of business:

- Worship—it is helpful to pause between each item long enough for the group to settle.
- Present the business—done by the clerk, a member of a committee, or an individual.
- Make sure that the item is widely understood. This may require some questions and answers or providing written copies of reports, recommendations, or proposed minutes.
- Share or discuss—each contributes toward the whole.
- Discern the sense of the meeting—usually vocalized by the clerk.
- Write, read, and approve a minute. Some clerks will ask if Friends are "easy" with a minute rather than asking if they "approve" it.

It is good practice to:

- Present budgets and nominations at one meeting but defer decision to the next meeting so that any errors or concerns can be raised privately. Written copies of budgets and nominations should be made available. This method of giving items a first and second reading can also be used for other complex business.
- Have the written minute of a decision or of anything controversial read and approved while the meeting is still in session.
- Call for a period of worship when Friends lose their focus.

- Have short periods of worship between items of business or whenever Friends start to stray.

  Business meeting ends with worship.

Responsibilities

The Role of the Clerk in Conducting Business

> The clerk's task is to help those present at a business meeting discern the will of God.
>
> (New England Yearly Meeting *Faith and Practice*, p. 224)

> The clerk facilitates a collaborative process. The giftedness and skills of a clerk are as important to the group as a coach is to an athletic team. Yet the responsibility for the decision does not rest upon the shoulders of the clerk, for it is God who makes known the decisions and next steps. The clerk does not control the content or the outcome of the meeting, yet he or she does maximize the conditions under which people can work helpfully together.
>
> (Lon Fendall, Jan Wood, and Bruce Bishop, *Practicing Discernment Together*, p. 117)

The clerk is easily identified during a meeting for business; he or she, along with any assistant or recording clerk(s), is at the front of the room facing everyone else, standing or seated behind a table to facilitate handling papers and writing minutes.

The clerk decides if an item needs to be held over, seasoned further, or talked over by some Friends before a decision is made.

The clerk is responsible for drawing up an agenda and presiding at business meetings. This often involves consulting with committees or individuals with business to bring before the meeting beforehand and determining whether the business will come directly to the meeting for business or be seasoned by a committee or other process first. If there is a recording clerk, the two clerks are jointly responsible for seeing that accurate minutes are kept. In some Quaker branches, the clerk takes the minutes. The clerk is responsible for seeing that those given a responsibility in a business meeting are notified of it. This may be done by providing them with a written copy of the minute.

The clerk is responsible for conscientiously carrying through any tasks assigned to the clerk.

When working with committees and other officers to prepare and follow up on business, the clerk sometimes needs to address tensions, problems, and personalities. A clerk who can function in a supporting, healing, and mediating role is invaluable. The clerk may work with Ministry and Counsel to see that good work is acknowledged through a note or comment outside of business meeting, that committees are encouraged to grow in their understanding of Quaker process and to come to know one another in that which is eternal, to privately confer with Friends whose actions or understandings are problematic for the meeting as a whole, and to address other issues that affect the community and its decision making.

> For the most part we have to wrestle with . . . humdrum down-to-Earth business.
>
> (Britain Yearly Meeting *Faith and Practice*, 3.07)

One of the tasks of the clerk is to discern what decisions are a matter of Friends' convenience and can be handled expeditiously. Most writings about Quaker business process only deal with big decisions—the ones that take much care, may take a long time, and in which Friends need to come to a sense of unity, often called "the sense of the meeting." In most meetings, however, much of the business is routine, and some of it is trivial. God probably doesn't care if we meet on Tuesday or Wednesday, or if we paint the bathroom blue or green. Nor is it of ultimate significance if the members of a committee are appointed for one year or two. For matters such as these, consensus, that is, general agreement, is fine. It gives the group functional, utilitarian decisions reasonably expeditiously.

> Discernment of God's will should be used only on substantive matters: matters essentially neutral to the spiritual life (like the time of meeting) do not require disciplined discernment.
>
> (Jan Hoffman, "Words on Practical Aspects of Meeting for Business")

The clerk's role during the group's consideration of business is to monitor and adjust the flow of the discussion or sharing. In order to help Friends discern the will of God, the clerk needs to concentrate on the rhythm and pacing of the business and any emerging sense of the meeting.

> A chief art of the clerk is to set the pace of the meeting so that its business may be accomplished without either undue delay or undue hurry. A sense of proportion and a sense of humor are helpful.
>
> (Baltimore Yearly Meeting *Faith and Practice*, p. 74)

The clerk serves the meeting by remaining calm in the face of disagreement or strong feelings.

> When disagreement or strong feelings are present, the greatest hope for change comes when someone is able to remain in a place of centered calm. . . . [This] means being able to hold the tension of others without catching it or needing to release it. When we merely avoid tension, we limit our ability to face conflict and to enable transformation from the tension. In contrast, staying in a place of conflict in a respectful and centered way, knowing that we need inspiration to resolve the conflict, releases the full transformative potential of meeting for business and increases the likelihood that those present will be able to hear and respond to the motion of the Spirit.
>
> (Debbie Humphries, "Four Pillars of Meeting for Business," *Friends Journal* Sept. 2009, p. 25)

It is emphatically not the job of the clerk to direct the discussion or sharing toward a particular conclusion. This would be inappropriate.

> There are errors into which a clerk may fall. One is acting as head or president of the meeting—presenting optional outcomes from which the meeting should choose, arranging a presentation to facilitate a certain decision, stopping deliberation before unity is reached.
>
> (Susan Smith, "Friends Business Meeting, as Conservative Friends Experience It," p. 5)

However, it is the clerk's job to help keep the business on track.

> The clerk is responsible for seeing that only one subject is discussed at a time. The meeting is at liberty to change the subject, but it is the clerk's duty to keep discussion to the subject in hand until the meeting itself has decided to shift it. The clerk must also remind Friends regarding items of unfinished business and must ask a speaker who addresses an individual to address the meeting as a whole. If a speaker's remarks are not easily heard or understood, the clerk may repeat them to the meeting. If certain members take up too much time, the clerk or some other Friends may feel it right to ask that their remarks be concluded.
>
> (Howard Brinton, *Guide to Quaker Practice*, p. 40)

In order to monitor the meeting, the clerk needs to set aside his or her own opinions on the matter before the meeting.

> The clerk of a business meeting is preeminently a leader as servant. The job requires the fullest measure of self-denial. The good clerk uses his or her skills to discern where the group is prepared to go and to reflect back to the group what agreement it is reaching.
>
> (Paul A. Lacey, "Quakers and the Use of Power," p. 28)

In *Practicing Discernment Together: Finding God's Way Forward in Decision Making*, Lon Fendall, Jan Wood, and Bruce Bishop present a lovely analogy:

> The clerk is the symphonic conductor of a group with many gifts. Every group preparing to make a decision has a musical composition in the making. No one really knows the tune until each part gets offered up in its rightful place. There will be no music if the drummer insists on drowning out the oboist. The rests are as important as the note to be played. The holding back is as important as soaring into a solo. The Holy Spirit calls forth the tune; the clerk facilitates that process.
>
> (Lon Fendall, Jan Wood, and Bruce Bishop, *Practicing Discernment Together*, p. 83)

Some aids for clerks

Annual calendar. Certain business gets transacted at certain times every year—the budget, nominations, reports to the yearly meeting, etc. It is helpful to draw up a list of when things need to come to business meeting or be sent to the yearly meeting, and then to look at when work on that business needs to begin, so that the Friends doing the work can be reminded when it is time to start.

Suggested scripts. Some yearly meetings maintain a notebook with a script of business done every year to help the clerk in presenting annual business clearly and in a useful order. This gets handed down from clerk to clerk, and any changes are incorporated along the way. This could cover such things as beginning and ending sessions, welcoming visitors, introducing the reading of memorial minutes, or any other usual business. This could also be done at the regional or even monthly meeting level, and might prove a great aid to an inexperienced clerk.

The Role of the Recording Clerk

See "The Recording Clerk and Minutes" on page 215 for details of the recording clerk's tasks.

Quakers have found that writing things down and reading them aloud helps the group ensure that everyone understands and is in agreement with a decision. Groups that have recording clerks assign to them the tasks of writing minutes and maintaining a book of minutes with all the pertinent attachments. Some groups, particularly Conservative Friends, assign these tasks to the presiding clerk.

In *Before Business Begins: Notes for Friends Meeting Recording Clerks and Recorders*, William Watson emphasizes the importance of collaboration between presiding and recording clerks:

> Where the functions of the clerk have been divided into presiding and recording, the division of labor is often blurred, and I think for understandable reasons. The labors of both clerks are directed to the same end of helping the meeting find its way to meaningful decisions and actions. In order to do this effectively, they must cooperate at every step and in ways that suit their own temperaments and abilities.
>
> (William Braasch Watson, *Before Business Begins*, p. 29)

> Effective collaboration between the clerks . . . is the foundation on which the timing and rhythms of the meeting for business are constructed. When this collaboration works well, as it usually does, the meeting is free to conduct its business unhampered by delays and confusion, and the pacing . . . takes care of itself.
>
> (William Braasch Watson, *Before Business Begins*, p. 37)

William Watson points to the recording clerk's task as primarily listening to the Spirit and putting the sense of the meeting into words:

> Although it is useful to have clear and concise phrases . . . , the heart of the recording clerk's task, like that of the presiding clerk, lies elsewhere. Both clerks must be willing to pursue something that can never be stated precisely, to listen for meanings that are sometimes more implied than spoken, to search for unity in the midst of a discussion in which that unity may never be stated in so many words. . . . Listening for the Spirit that sustains this unity and striving to give it adequate expression is central to the task of the clerks. . . . By listening for the Spirit rather than to the words, the recording clerk can contribute to the collective effort.
>
> (William Braasch Watson, *Before Business Begins*, p. 30)

If a Clerk or Recording Clerk is Unable to Serve

From time to time, clerks and recording clerks can't perform their usual duties. This may be because:

- They are away.
- They are incapacitated.
- They are too personally involved in an item of business.

If they can anticipate the problem, they can often arrange for a substitute beforehand. If not, a substitute needs to be found at the business session itself. Some Friends to look to for such service include:

- Assistant clerks.
- Previous clerks or recording clerks.
- Seasoned Friends that the meeting is comfortable with taking on the task.

Whoever is tapped, the first action of the meeting should be to approve that the Friend serve as acting clerk or acting recording clerk.

When a clerk or recording clerk needs to "step aside" for a particular item of business, that item may be clerked by someone else and then the usual officer may resume service. Clerks are advised that stepping aside voluntarily serves the meeting better than trying to clerk an item of business about which they feel personal concern. Friends need to support a clerk in stepping aside. It is important that the clerking be done; it is not important who does it.

The Role of Participants

> If the Quaker method of arriving at unity does not succeed, the difficulty is generally due to the participation of some members who have not achieved the right attitude of mind and heart. Dogmatic persons who speak with an air of finality or assume the tone of a debater determined to win may be a serious hindrance. Eloquence to appeal only to the emotion is out of place. Those who come to meeting not so much to find the Lord's will as to win acceptance of their own opinions may find their views carry little weight. Opinions should always be expressed humbly and tentatively in the realization that no one person sees the whole Truth and the entire meeting, as the Body of Christ, can see more accurately than one person can see any one part of it.
>
> (Jack L. Willcuts, *Why Friends are Friends: Some Quaker Core Convictions*, p. 82)

The clerk presents business or calls on someone else to present it; the recording clerk writes the minutes. What is everyone else to do?

The first responsibility of meeting members is to attend meeting for business—to be there. But if the meeting never addresses challenging business, or breaks down into wrangling over it, it may be hard for Friends to feel that attending is worthwhile. Some Friends may never have experienced grounded deliberation, or may not have experienced coming to a sense of the meeting.

> The interest that the meeting's members take in the business of the monthly meeting will largely depend upon the variety and validity of the activities engaged in and reported upon.
>
> (Howard Brinton, *Guide to Quaker Practice*, p. 49)

Bill Taber suggests that participants can find meeting for business transformative for both themselves and the meeting:

> We can be severely tested by two ever present and very real hazards in the Friends business method; impatience and a vacuous boredom. The Friend who recognizes that these hazards can be a spiritual call to go deeper into worship brings great power to the work of the church as well as an opening of his or her own spiritual gifts, including discernment. Thus the Friends business meeting cannot be described as just the peculiar Quaker form of getting things done; rather it should be seen as an essential part of the spiritual formation and the spiritual growth of every seasoned Friend, for it is that place through which we learn to walk hand-in-hand with each other and the Spirit out into the world to do the work of committed and obedient disciples.
>
> (William Taber, Jr., "Friends Consultation on Discernment")

All Quaker meetings where business are conducted are basically committees of the whole; that is, each person present shares responsibility for the process, for contributing as appropriate, for keeping the group on task, and for staying open to the leadings of the Spirit. This takes a great deal of self-discipline.

Susan Smith, longtime clerk of Ohio Yearly Meeting (Conservative), suggests the following guidelines for participants:

- Speak only when moved by God, but do speak then.
- Be concise; speak to the question.
- Do not quibble with each other or with the wording of a minute, but
- Be willing to say so if something seems to be wrong or more should be added.
- Expect to speak only once on a topic; avoid an ongoing interchange with one or more other people.
- Listen carefully, to God and to each other.

- Actively pray, probably silently, when contention or confusion arises.

(Susan Smith, "Friends Business Meeting, as Conservative Friends Experience It," p. 3)

Marty Walton writes of temptations associated with meeting for business:

> Sometimes we move too fast, avoid hard questions, sweep things under the rug of our own awareness. We may give unwitting agreement to processes or positions that, if we really prayed about, we would discover we could not support.

(Marty Walton, *The Meeting Experience: Practicing Quakerism in Community*, p. 27)

One role for participants is to hold the meeting for business in the Light. This may be done by particular Friends with a gift for this who choose to not participate in the meeting in other ways, but also by the whole body, particularly during worship and when a clerk is working on creating a minute.

> Friends are reminded that inspired clerkship requires the continued prayerful support of the gathered body.

(Ohio Yearly Meeting *Faith and Practice*, p. 15)

Listening deeply is the responsibility of all present—both to one another and to the Spirit. Concentrating on this listening role helps Friends maintain a worshipful atmosphere and resist temptations to chatter or behave in other disruptive ways.

> Friends are urged to seek divine guidance at all times, be mutually forbearing, and be concerned for the good of the meeting as a whole rather than to press a personal preference. Time should be allowed for deliberate and prayerful consideration of the matter in hand. Everyone must want to reach a decision and be open to new understanding. Friends should come to each meeting for business expecting that their minds will be changed. . . . They should speak briefly and to the point, express their own view, avoid refuting statements made by others, and give each other credit for purity of motive. When someone has already stated a position satisfactorily, Friends need offer only a word or two

> expressing agreement.
>
> (North Pacific Yearly Meeting *Faith and Practice*, p. 57)

> In a rightly-ordered meeting for business, all participants share responsibility for the spiritual discernment that occurs, and hence for the actions that flow from it. Creation and maintenance of a spiritual climate in which corporate discernment can flourish will naturally fall to the clerk(s) and other "weighty Friends" more than to those who are inexperienced, but the discernment itself is made collectively by the gathered meeting. . . . Authority for all decisions rest with the meeting as a whole, and ultimately with God.
>
> (Australia Yearly Meeting, "Quaker Business Method: The Practice of Group Discernment")

In order to listen to and hear one another, it helps for Friends to know one another.

> The Quaker method is likely to be successful in proportion as the members are acquainted with one another; better still, if real affection exists among them.
>
> (George A. Selleck, *Principles of the Quaker Business Meeting*, p. 3)

Friends need to actively work at understanding what each Friend says, getting beyond the inadequacies of the words.

> We simply need to listen for God's truth in what others are saying, even when it appears hidden among some unhelpful words. Some have used the phrase "listening in tongues" for this process. . . . Careful listening means hearing what people intend to say and discerning the thoughts behind the words, not hearing only the words actually spoken.
>
> The effective clerk will insist that the group take some time between the statements to listen to God. Participants must support the clerk in this effort by waiting until the words of others have soaked in. Then and only then should participants switch from listening to speaking. And that speaking should flow directly from their listening to God.
>
> (Lon Fendall, Jan Wood, and Bruce Bishop, *Practicing Discernment Together*, p. 44)

> Leaving the direction of the meeting to Christ may be very hard. Many of us who have had extensive secular education and who have not grown up in this yearly meeting are accustomed to using our knowledge and our intelligence as our own tools in a discussion. Some of us are no doubt quite good at interpreting the interplay of dynamics within a meeting and, by adding comments or information strategically, directing the group's decision toward the goal we think right. There can be a fine line between a person's manipulating a business meeting and someone's witnessing clearly under God's direction—just as it is sometimes difficult during meeting for worship for a person to discern the difference between his or her own concerns and a message that God would have spoken aloud. Waiting for clearness about whether to speak is useful.
>
> (Susan Smith, "Friends Business Meeting, as Conservative Friends Experience It," p. 2)

Here are some guidelines for participants:

- Pay attention.
- Make sure you understand each item of business sufficiently before the group moves into discernment. This will help the meeting move along without wasting a lot of time.
- Be open to the leading of the Spirit and expect to be surprised.
- Listen attentively and lovingly to others' views. Consider what experiences inform them. If you can maintain an attitude of loving concern for all present, that will help you to hear what others say.
- Keep your heart and mind open. If the meeting is floundering, listen for divine guidance in finding a different solution than has yet been suggested.
- Remember that this is not your meeting; it belongs to God.
- When in doubt, return to silent worship.

> We must befriend silence if we are to practice discernment, because silence lets us hear God's part in the conversation.
>
> (Debra K. Farrington, *Hearing with the Heart*, p. 58)

Bill Taber's "practical suggestions" include the following:

- Get to meeting early and settle into worship as soon as possible.

- Absorb as well as hear the words spoken, and bathe speakers and clerks in wordless prayer.
- Wait for the deep inward motion, which is deeper than a surface emotion or idea; and then, before speaking, wait to see if Love is also there.
- Stay in worship, in a special state of consciousness. In a wider, softer mind, a nonreactive mind, a quieter mind, thinking can be even keener; our thinking does not get in the way of feeling, of waiting for leadings.
- Recognize the value of the spaces in the meeting. There needs to be enough space between messages and minutes to reconnect with a deep underlying unity beneath and beyond words, even when we seem to have a strong disagreement on the level of words.
- When there is disagreement, be prepared for the process to pause long enough for God to reveal a new, more creative perspective.
- Do not be afraid to say no. That can be an obligation.
- Be aware of the clerk.

  Jack Willcuts wrote:

> We protect ourselves too carefully from . . . dreaming, from expecting the impossible. . . . Boldness, creativity, confidence, adequacy for Christian living and serving result from His taking over. . . . Our hope is in the raw, real power of the Holy Spirit at work among Friends. . . . Being convinced that Friends have convictions based on Truth and that Quaker values are important may still result in a sterile spiritual emptiness. With all the benefits of an impressive past and an exciting future it is still possible to drift into mere religious routine and tradition unless the power flows. . . . Power is channeling and using the created resources of God. . . . Spiritual power is not a human talent skillfully used, but rather, an availability to the guidance of God.
>
> (Jack L. Willcuts, *The Sense of the Meeting*, pp. 94-95)

Weight

Weighty Friends are those whose ability to discern the Truth has been demonstrated over time and whose suggestions have been consistently useful.

> This matter of weighing the individual utterances in arriving at the sense of the meeting is quite fundamental to the Quaker method. Several Friends may quite sincerely speak in one direction, and then one Friend may express an insight which carries weight and conviction in the meeting in a different sense. This one acceptable communication may outweigh in significance several more superficial ones.
>
> (George A. Selleck: "Principles of the Quaker business meeting," p. 8)

> In the process of reaching a decision, the clerk and the meeting may quite properly take into consideration that some Friends have more wisdom and experience than others. . . . The meeting, however, must be on guard against always accepting words of weighty Friends as final and must also be wary of accepting the traditional pattern only because it is traditional. Fresh, powerful insights are often granted to new and younger members.
>
> (North Pacific Yearly Meeting *Faith and Practice*, p. 57)

A potentially controversial question is whether to give more weight to members of the meeting than to attenders. Traditionally, and still in some yearly meetings, only members participate in business meetings. In other yearly meetings, long-time attenders who are active in the meeting are encouraged to participate in meetings for business.

When a legal question arises, it makes sense for members to be given more weight than attenders, as it is the members of the meeting who will incur any potential liability. In other matters, a meeting has to fall upon its traditional practice and best judgment in determining whether to make a distinction between members and attenders when weighing their input on a decision. It is helpful if Friends discuss this and have a common understanding before it becomes an issue in making a particular decision.

Time

Quaker business process takes time.

One reason that Friends conduct of business is so slow is that is takes time to sift ourselves and the matter at hand for ego, self-will, sincere mistakes, matters of individual conscience, and for reasons which may be excellent intellectually but not necessarily for God's will. In a meeting which is seeking at the deepest level, there must be time and opportunity for all these matters to rise to the surface, to be examined in the Light, and to settle again to a deeper level of quiet. There must be time not only for those whose interest and concern for the matter has impelled them to go deeply into it, but for those whose inward processes and flow of words are moving at a slower pace—and perhaps at a deeper level as well. There must be time for change to take place inwardly—not just in the head but in the heart and gut—as members search the matter and are searched by it.

(Patricia Loring, *Spiritual Responsibility in the Meeting for Business*)

It is the practice of Friends to give unhurried and sympathetic consideration to all proposals and expressions of opinion.

(Wilmington Yearly Meeting *Faith and Practice*, p. 55)

Taking time is difficult for many of us.

Patient spiritual waiting is a hard discipline for us moderns to practice. Our minds are quick. We spend too much time thinking and analyzing. We are easily distracted or enticed by our own thoughts. . . . We also like to be in control, to will all that happens in our lives. It is difficult to learn to let go of our will and to sink deep to where the Holy Presence is waiting to lead us.

(Michael Wajda, *Expectant Listening: Finding God's Thread of Guidance*, p. 15)

Even for routine decisions, it is important not to feel that the clock is ticking.

A sense of urgency is, in itself, uncentering.

(Barry Morley, *Beyond Consensus: Salvaging Sense of the Meeting*, p. 22)

A proper concern for giving all matters due consideration is no excuse for wasting time, however. Deborah Haines puts it well:

> As Quakers we are committed to taking as long as necessary to reach unity, but we are most certainly not required to take longer than necessary.
>
> (Deborah Haines, "A Practical Mystic's Guide to Committee Clerking")

In setting an agenda and in preparing both the business and Friends, it is a good idea to anticipate concluding monthly business within two hours. In "Words on Practical Aspects of Meeting for Business," Bill Taber offers three reasons why business meetings should not go beyond two hours:

- The group loses its mental acuity.
- Some people won't come back.
- People start to leave physically.

To complete business within two hours, participants must practice a high degree of self-discipline.

Presenting Business

Written or Oral Reports?

Whether a report is given from memory or from a written report should be decided jointly by the person giving the report and the clerk of the meeting—different means are appropriate for different kinds of reports. A written report is useful in several ways: it helps the presenter pull their thoughts together and usually leads to a more concise and helpful report; it helps the clerk understand the business; and it is an invaluable aid to the recording clerk. If at all possible, copies of written reports should be given to the clerk and recording clerk before the report is given.

Use of Paper and Alternatives

A question often arises about whether printed copies need to be distributed, and if so, how many copies to make. It is up to those involved to decide whether printed materials are necessary in individual cases. One thing to keep in mind is that faithfulness to God's guidance does not usually lead us to completely reject the use of resources; instead, it leads to a weighing of how best to serve God while using a minimum of resources. When copies are needed, a general guideline is that two people can look on together.

Sometimes technology can be an aid here. Our small yearly meeting has discovered that projecting budgets and other reports from a laptop computer is effective, and only a few paper copies need to be made. For Central Committee meetings, FGC has gone to sending out electronic copies of reports, with paper copies mailed only to those who request them. This allows many Friends to read them online and only print out those they want on paper.

Presenting a Report

Treasurer's reports and reports from committees are standard fare in meetings for business. It is often appreciated if Friends who have attended regional gatherings, yearly meeting business sessions, or other Quaker gatherings give a brief report on their experience. Young people who have attended Quaker conferences can also be asked to report. These reports can summarize what the Friend(s) did, what their experience was, and what issues of interest to the meeting were raised and how they were dealt with. The clerk should advise the Friend(s) who are reporting on the amount of detail to include and approximately how long the presentation might take. Any items arising from the gathering that need the meeting's action should be reported separately from the general narrative.

Approval vs. Acceptance

Friends approve decisions and minutes. Friends receive or accept reports (the group is not deciding anything). To maintain this distinction, the clerk can refrain from asking for approval of a report, and minutes can record that the meeting received or accepted the report. It helps to present reports from a committee separately from items brought by the committee for decision.

Tips on how to Give a Financial Report without Having Friends' Eyes Glaze Over

Some meetings have patterns of giving financial reports which serve them well. Particularly in yearly meetings and in committees that handle large sums of money, however, it is common to observe a number of Friends' eyes begin to glaze over partway through a financial report. Below are some suggestions for helping all Friends present to follow and understand the report.

- Hand out enough copies so everyone can see one or project a readable copy.
- Assume that your hearers are interested and intelligent but that many have no previous acquaintance with financial statements.
- Orient Friends to what is contained in the report: the time period it covers, what is in the different sections. Describe sections in layman's terms with words like, "how the money is to be used" for the budget; "where that money is" for bank balances, and "how we spend our money" for expenses.
- Don't read the line items. People should be able to look at a copy and see those for themselves. Give them time to do so when discussing each section. Instead, summarize and put things into context. Bring people's attention to those things that have changed and explain why.
- When reading totals and balances, round off. "Twenty-four thousand dollars and change" is more readily understood than "twenty-four thousand two hundred twelve dollars and sixteen cents." If someone wants to know the details, they're in the report.
- After hearing three numbers, many people's capacity to listen wanes. Choose carefully which numbers to announce.
- Tell Friends if there are outstanding bills or income that are not included in the report.
- Explain those items that are not routine or that are of particular interest or concern. Do your best to explain in layman's terms

why they matter or what the implications are.
- If something difficult to understand is done purely for bookkeeping reasons, say so.

Presenting an Item for Decision

In bringing a matter to business meeting for its consideration, it is useful to supply a concise summary of background material and a clear statement of the kind of response wanted from the meeting. Make sure that all needed information—history, actions taken, possibilities considered—is provided as part of the presentation of the item. Pertinent minutes from previous meetings should be read. The more clear and concise the presentation of the item, the better Friends can process it.

It is helpful if items for decision come in the form of clear written recommendations for what to do, proposed next steps, and/or decisions that need to be made. For certain matters, copies should be made available during business meeting for all there to see—budgets and financial reports; slates of nominations; other reports involving a lot of detail, all of which is important and may take some time for people to digest. The clerk should be told of the upcoming business and any recommendations as far in advance of the meeting for business as possible. Copies of any written materials should be given to the clerk and recording clerk.

Most items for decision can be presented using the following guidelines:

1) This is the item of business.
2) This is where it comes from: this is what has happened in the past that brought the matter to this point. Give a historical review of one to ten sentences, including how the meeting has handled it in the past. This may involve some digging in old minutes, or conversations with others who remember what happened because they were present and part of past actions.
3) This is who worked on it (the standing committee or an ad hoc committee with the names of the people serving on it and anyone else involved).
4) This is the process by which we arrived at our recommenda-

tions: what we've considered, who we've talked to, what we've done, etc. Anticipate people's questions of whether someone has been consulted or an option considered.

5) Make a recommendation. In a few cases, it may be reasonable to present a few alternatives, but generally it is most helpful to the meeting in its deliberations to bring forward one specific suggestion, whether that is what is ultimately decided or not.

See if there are questions; it is good practice to allow the clerk to ask for questions rather than the person presenting the business. Once any questions have been answered, the presenter should turn the running of the meeting over to the clerk.

Anticipating Concerns when Presenting Business

Sometimes, a committee will carefully deal with an issue and bring a specific recommendation to the larger group, and then people in the group raise questions that the committee has already dealt with and put behind them. This situation should be avoided. When bringing a recommendation, try to be aware of concerns about the issue in the group and address them up front when making your recommendation.

For instance, your report might include, "When looking at what age groups to put together for First-day school classes this year, we took into consideration whether siblings would end up in the same group, and decided it was more important to have fewer groups than to have siblings in separate groups." This will ideally keep someone from objecting, "But the Baker sisters will be in the same group."

Presenting an Item for Approval vs. Presenting an Item for Consideration

> When a committee brings a recommendation for consideration . . . the committee must avoid being so attached to its recommendation that it forgets that new insights can develop as the Meeting considers the matter.
>
> (North Pacific Yearly Meeting *Faith and Practice*, p. 58)

Some Friends speak in terms of asking for the meeting's approval when presenting an item that requires a decision. This implies that the meeting is being asked to rubber stamp the work already done. While meetings often do approve recommendations, occasionally the group will reject or amend the recommendation or send it back to the committee for further work. This can be appropriate. The work of the committee is on behalf of the larger group and needs to be approved by them. A committee's recommendation is just that: it is recommending that the larger group do something. It is then up to the larger group to discern if that works for them and is consistent with their understandings. Someone in the larger group may bring up an issue the committee had not thought of, or come up with an idea better than anything the committee had come up with, or simply be Spirit-led to go in a different direction than the committee had anticipated.

This is the essence of discernment: hearing and obeying God's voice. Quakers do this by taking individual leadings to a group for testing and discernment; the understandings of the larger group are taken to a yet larger group for testing and discernment; etc. In Quakerism, it is not really true that decisions are made by consensus,[73] that is, by everyone agreeing; rather, our decisions are formed by being bathed in the Light and assessed by a variety of Spirit-led people and groups, so that the final course of action can be honed to its core and set on a sure path, leading to clarity and empowerment and widespread support.

It is helpful when presenting an item for decision to ask for the meeting's consideration. Only when the clerk has suggested a sense of the meeting should the meeting be asked, "Do Friends approve?" Here is a simple rule of thumb: only the clerk should use the word "approve."

If it becomes the rule rather than an occasional occurrence for Friends to labor over a committee's recommendations, Friends may need to consider how much trust they are placing in their

---

[73] See Barry Morley's pamphlet, *Beyond Consensus: Salvaging Sense of the Meeting*, for a helpful distinction between consensus and Quaker decision making.

committees. It becomes discouraging for committee members if they faithfully consider a concern on behalf of the meeting and it seems the meeting is continually redoing or questioning their work on the floor of the meeting.

> In the meeting for business, Friends need to consider carefully the recommendations of a committee, and at the same time not re-do the work of the committee. Mutual trust between the meeting and a committee and faith in the power of God over all will help achieve the proper balance.
>
> (North Pacific Yearly Meeting *Faith and Practice*, p. 63)

Asking the Larger Group for Input

Occasionally, it is appropriate for a committee to ask for input from the larger group. This may be presented as, "We would like your input before making a recommendation. If Friends will share briefly on the matter under consideration, that will help us in coming up with our proposal." If the timing of the meeting allows, you can even do brainstorming—coming up with ideas—in the larger group (check with the clerk first!). But do not expect the whole group to decide on a detail. Trying to do this usually leads to a lengthy and unfruitful discussion. A meeting should be reluctant to function as a committee of the whole when it has already appointed a committee to work on the matter; working out the details is the committee's job.

Considering Business

> The right conduct of our meetings for church affairs depends upon all coming to them in an active, seeking spirit, not with minds already made up on a particular course of action, determined to push this through at all costs. But open minds are not empty minds, nor uncritically receptive: the service of the meeting calls for knowledge of facts, often painstakingly acquired, and the ability to estimate their relevance and importance. This demands that we shall be ready to listen to others carefully, without antagonism if they express opinions which are unpleasing to us, but trying always to discern the truth in what they have to offer. It calls, above all,

> for spiritual sensitivity. If our meetings fail, the failure may well be in those who are ill-prepared to use the method rather than in the inadequacy of the method itself.
>
> (Britain Yearly Meeting *Faith and Practice*, 1995)

When an item for decision is presented all Friends need to understand the issue. Thorough preparation beforehand, a written draft of a recommendation or minute, and a clear presentation of the item to the meeting for business help tremendously. Any confusion should get cleared up and people's questions should be answered before the group tackles making a decision. This may mean postponing the decision until any necessary additional information or advice can be obtained. Once the issue is understood, the meeting should be given the opportunity to quickly express if the recommendation is in the right ballpark. Before addressing any details or discussing any wording, the meeting needs to be clear whether this is an item that Friends want to address and that the approach suggested is agreeable, or whether one or more Friends are uncomfortable with the whole thing. Friends can be encouraged to address the issue at this holistic level by a practice of silent waiting while Friends digest the information that has been presented. It is helpful for one or two Friends to drop a few words or phrases into the waiting silence that express general approval or discomfort.

When presented with a recommendation, a meeting has a variety of possible responses. These include:

- Agree to the recommendation.
- Agree to the recommendation with some changes.
- Agree to something completely different.
- Reject the recommendation and take no further action.
- Decide that the item needs additional work/seasoning/information. The meeting should assign who will follow up (clerk, committee, or someone else), make clear whether they are authorized to decide or just to report back, and suggest or assign when they will report.

George Bliss advises clerks, "Try a sense of the meeting early and often, trust that the Spirit might work quickly sometimes.

If you have unity, the meeting can move on, and if you don't have unity, Friends will tell you. Just because there is a potential for controversy, it doesn't need to develop."[74]

It is the duty and privilege of all present to honestly share their personal views and experiences that are pertinent. Discomfort of mind is an indication that one is not in unity with what is being suggested. It is incumbent upon Friends to express that discomfort as best they can. When expressing disagreement, Friends should strive to speak from a place of love and humility, but without any sense of apology for being who they are and thinking what they think. It is in sharing our deepest experiences that we come to know and understand one another. When our deep sharing helps others get a glimpse of the Truth or Divine Love that underlies our experience, we are brought closer to unity. When a Friend speaks with deep emotion or otherwise forcefully, a period of silence helps to absorb any shock waves.

> Friends should allow Friends whose feelings have been aroused to release those feelings. Tears, harsh words, raised or shaking voices, difficulty with articulation—any of these might accompany release. Friends who release their feelings should be listened to lovingly. No effort should be made to intervene—to correct, argue, analyze, criticize, clarify, or explain away. Sometimes we need to get something off our chests. Release should be encouraged and appreciated. It clears the air. . . . By emptying themselves of anguish, anxiety, fear, anger, perhaps even joy, Friends open their minds for an inpouring of Light.
>
> (Barry Morley, *Beyond Consensus*, p. 16)

Friends should expect to listen deeply to others, to seek common experiences and understandings at a deep level, and to change their views.

> Don't panic because the things people are saying seem to conflict with one another! Don't ignore the negative-sounding statements. Don't automatically discount what sounds like an "inappropriate"

---

[74] George Bliss in "Words on Practical Aspects of Meeting for Business"

comment because of someone's age, lack of social skills, inarticulateness, or strong emotions. Simply let all these statements come out and rest on the proverbial table in the middle of the room. They are all part of the unfolding of God's guidance, like the scattered pieces of a jigsaw puzzle before the puzzle gets assembled.

(Lon Fendall, Jan Wood, and Bruce Bishop, *Practicing Discernment Together*, p. 102)

Considering Concerns

North Pacific Yearly Meeting's *Faith and Practice* offers the following advice for an individual with a concern:

> The appropriate place for a concern first to be considered and tested as a true leading of the Spirit is within the monthly meeting, the basic unit of the Society. Before a Friend brings a concern to the meeting for business, the Friend should consider it prayerfully, to be sure that it is rightly motivated and of more than personal or passing importance. The Friend should season the concern through consultation with qualified Friends, a standing committee of the meeting, or a specially requested Committee on Clearness. The concern should come to the meeting for business in mature form with a clear, concise, written statement of its purpose, means, and the support requested from the meeting. Public expression implying meeting support for a concern is to be avoided unless and until such support has been received, especially when possible disobedience to law or conflict with custom may be involved.

(North Pacific Yearly Meeting *Faith and Practice*, p. 59)

Britain Yearly Meeting offers helpful guidelines for a meeting considering a concern.[75] The meeting "needs to be absolutely clear" whether it is:

- Recognizing a concern seen as religiously valid.
- Supporting the concern and accepting responsibility for its furtherance, including financial support where necessary.
- Adopting the concern as one it shares, whereupon the concern becomes a concern of the whole meeting.
- Recognizing the concern and forwarding it with its support

[75] Britain Yearly Meeting *Faith and Practice*, 13.12

to a more widely representative meeting.
- Deciding that the matter before it is not a religiously valid concern.

Sometimes a meeting will not see the validity of a concern brought to it at first, but over time may come to unity with it.

> If a Meeting fails to unite with a member's concern, the member generally reconsiders it very carefully. If the Friend feels called upon to continue, the meeting may be able to encourage the member to go forward with the concern even when the meeting is unable to unite with it. Occasionally, an individual who is strongly convinced that the corporate life of the meeting and of the Society will be enriched if it can grow and unite with a particular concern brings that concern to the meeting repeatedly over an extended period. Many of the Quaker testimonies have evolved because of the patient persistence of a valiant Friend who has perceived the Light more clearly than other members. Such persistence has helped some meetings and the Society come to unite with an insight which they could not at first accept. Sometimes when a concern does not arise from a genuine spiritual leading and the Friend is "running ahead of his Guide," the Meeting continues to be unable to unite with the concern.
>
> (North Pacific Yearly Meeting *Faith and Practice*, p. 60)

Speaking to Business

> We are called to love those present enough to listen to what they have to say and to speak what is worth their hearing.
>
> (Thomas S. Brown, *When Friends Attend to Business*)

It is important that Friends speak on matters they feel deeply about openly, honestly, and tenderly.

> In meetings for business, and in all duties connected with them, seek again the leadings of the Light; let our utterances be brief and without repetition. Let us keep from obstinacy and from harshness of tone or manner and admit the possibility of being in error. In all the affairs of the meeting community, let us proceed in a peaceable spirit, with forbearance and warm affection for each other.
>
> (New England Yearly Meeting *Faith and Practice*, p. 206)

In *When You're the Only Friend in Town: Starting a New Friends Meeting*, Deborah Haines suggests that Friends use a process similar to worship sharing when speaking to business.

> Present each item as if it were a question for worship sharing. Explain the guidelines for worship sharing. Make clear that you expect Friends to approach the business in hand in a way that is radically different from ordinary discussion. Here are the basics:
>
> - Allow silence before and after each person speaks.
> - Listen attentively and respectfully.
> - Do not react to or critique what others have said, but express your own concerns and insights as deeply and honestly as you can.
> - Speak as much as possible from your own experience.
> - Expect to speak only once during consideration of a given item.
>
> Paradoxical as it may seem, this approach is likely to achieve a decision grounded on a sense of the meeting far more quickly than a back-and-forth discussion would. Everyone has a chance to speak, and to be listened to. Everyone is encouraged to dig more deeply and share more honestly than they normally would. When everyone has spoken once, there may well be a clear sense of how the meeting is led to move forward. The clerk may want to reframe the question in light of what has been said and ask for another round of worship sharing. If there is no unity, further discussion is unlikely to help. Ask a few Friends to explore the question further and bring back a recommendation to the next meeting. Then move on to the next item of business.
>
> (Deborah Haines, *When You're the Only Friend in Town*, pp. 22-23)

Here are some guidelines for speaking to business:

- Follow any customs for allowing the clerk to decide when someone will speak. Holding up one's hand or saying, "Clerk, please" are used in some meetings to get the clerk's attention. Wait to speak until you are recognized by the clerk (unless this is not the group's practice). There should be a pause between speakers so that all can digest what the previous person has said. You may find that someone has already expressed what you had planned or that your views have shifted.

- Except in a very small meeting, stand to speak if you can do so.
- Direct all comments to the group (not one's neighbor).
- Help the meeting stay on track. Do not indulge in personal reminiscences or raise side issues. Carefully consider whether your point is relevant and needed by the meeting. There is no need to rephrase a point that has already been made or to confuse the issue with considerations that might be better addressed elsewhere or at another time.
- Speak briefly and from personal experience. Do not indulge in theoretical debates. Speak for yourself and of yourself. Say "I think this is too expensive" rather than "This is too expensive" or "I am concerned about . . ." not "Some Friends are concerned about . . ." If you can maintain an attitude of loving concern for all present, that will help you to communicate without offending.
- If you agree strongly with a speaker and feel that the meeting should know you agree, do not make the same point. Instead, simply say, "That Friend speaks my mind" or "I agree."
- "Be certain of your facts. Avoid stating as facts things which are matters of opinion."[76]

It is important to let the clerk direct the flow of the meeting, even if that means that one is not given the opportunity to speak on a matter.

> It could be that a given speaker says what a person who had a hand raised and was not recognized at that moment would have said. . . . Or it could be that a sense of the meeting is clear . . . long before everyone present has spoken to the question. . . . So from both the clerk and the body of the meeting, after a given contribution, there needs to be a testing to see what that contribution has done to the "ecosystem" of the meeting—to see if more words are necessary at all, or if different words need to be spoken. . . . The clerk needs to give people a chance to change their minds about whether to speak or not, and people need to be ready to change their minds

[76] Britain Yearly Meeting *Faith and Practice*, 13.10

about needing to speak.

(Jan Hoffman, "Words on Practical Aspects of Meeting for Business")

Those who speak easily should hesitate before speaking; those who find it difficult to speak should push themselves when they have something pertinent to contribute.

There is a certain dry humor given to some Friends as a gift to lighten Friends' deliberations:

> Humor may have a rightful place, restoring perspective, lifting spirits, and diminishing tensions.
>
> (Thomas S. Brown, *When Friends Attend to Business*)

Queries for Speaking to Business

- Have I truly listened and heard and understood before I respond?
- Are my comments furthering the business or taking the group off-task?
- Am I laying down the law or speaking in humility?
- Have I already spoken to this issue and need to leave space for others to speak?
- Am I giving little side comments to the person next to me rather than actively listening?
- Are my comments Spirit-led, or am I just maundering on or chatting about something of interest to me?

Sense of the Meeting

In the 20th century, many Friends referred to our corporate decisions as being achieved through "consensus." In the last twenty years or so, a renewed emphasis on the Divine role in Quaker decision making has led to the use of "sense of the meeting" instead. Among some Friends, "unity" is used instead of "sense of the meeting."

Barry Morley, in his influential 1993 pamphlet, *Beyond Consensus: Salvaging Sense of the Meeting*, wrote:

We understand by now that Alcoholics Anonymous works because individuals turn their alcoholism over to their higher power. Sense of the meeting works because we turn our decision making over to a higher power.

(Barry Morley, *Beyond Consensus*, p. 5)

What It Is

We are cautioned that, like a gathered meeting, sense of the meeting must be experienced to be fully understood:

Individuals may talk about the sense of the meeting, but until one experiences it as an inward process, it cannot be understood fully.

(Barry Morley, *Beyond Consensus*, p. 6)

Eden Grace describes sense of the meeting like this:

Friends commit themselves to discovering and implementing the will of God. . . . What we call 'the Sense of the Meeting' is not the collected wisdom of those present, but the collective discernment of God's will. . . . Our bold affirmation is that God does indeed have a will for us, that God is actively trying to communicate that will, and that we are capable, through corporate prayer, to discover that will. A sign that we have achieved our goal of discerning God's will is the experience of Unity which is recognized and affirmed by those gathered.

(Eden Grace, "An Introduction to Quaker Business Practice")

Sometimes a clerk will articulate a sense of the meeting that is somewhat different from any view that has been expressed but incorporates all of them so well that all present unite with it.

Barry Morley describes what happens when we come to unity:

When we seek the sense of the meeting we allow ourselves to be directed to the solution that awaits us. It is a process of surrender to our highest natures, and a recognition that, even though each of us is possessed of light, there is only one Light. At the end of the process we reside in that Light. We have allowed ourselves to be led to a transcendent place of unmistakable harmony, peace, and tender love.

(Barry Morley, *Beyond Consensus*, p. 12)

As we continue to address an issue, as we lay aside any need to win, as we turn increasingly inward in order to transcend differences, long focus brings us to the Source of resolution and clarity. It is in this Light that God's voice is heard. From the Light we sense an influx of enveloping harmony. Peace tinged with triumph settles upon individuals and over the meeting. When we feel the Presence settle among us, and silence overtakes us, we have arrived where we want to be. Silence is an inward and outward sign that the process has been completed.

(Barry Morley, *Beyond Consensus*, p. 19)

Through the process by which Quakers attain the sense of the meeting, transformation occurs. We are changed. We feel, in a literal way, the loving Presence which hovers over us. It manifests in the love we have for one another. We form invisible bonds among ourselves which transcend the petty and make the next sense of the meeting more desirable and more readily attainable. We are participants in each other's well being. . . . We sense that the sense of the meeting came through us and for us, but not from us. We are amazed that it works—exactly as it's supposed to.

(Barry Morley, *Beyond Consensus*, p. 24)

Reaching unity may come easily or may be a lengthy process. Quaker business procedures are designed to allow all Friends to come to unity on a decision before the group acts. When it does act, however, it is usually with whole-hearted support.

Learning Sense of the Meeting

I have heard people say that Quakers don't teach each other sense of the meeting because it can't be taught. Perhaps this is true. However . . . sense of the meeting can be *learned*.

(Barry Morley, *Beyond Consensus*, p. 28)

Barry Morley suggests ways to foster skills that will be used in seeking the sense of the meeting. These include:

- Sharing one's experience with a group.
- Listening attentively.

- Encouraging one another.
- Reflecting on spiritual matters.
- Using silence to begin, punctuate, and wrap up personal sharing.
- Meeting for worship.

Barry Morley's point is that "opportunities for developing the mindset needed to learn sense of the meeting can be provided."[77] He suggests that Friends can schedule sessions that encourage such learning in religious education programs, in workshops at regional and yearly meetings, and at Quaker conferences. He suggests that clerks get together for mutual encouragement, mutual instruction, or mutual Spirit searching, and that yearly meetings could sponsor suitable teachers who could visit meetings. [78]

Moving Business Forward When There Is Conflict

> Decisions do not need to be unanimous, but they do need substantial unity.
>
> (Evangelical Friends Church Southwest *Faith and Practice*, p. 49)

> Guess what? Quakers have disagreements among themselves and in their monthly meetings for business. Nothing unusual about that—we're human, after all. What is unusual is how Friends address disagreements.
>
> (Arthur Boyd, "When Quakers Disagree")

Conflict in a meeting for business is not something to be avoided, but something to be worked through. It is an opportunity to engage in deep, meaningful sharing, and a challenge for the whole community to open to the guidance of a higher power.

> In the process of receiving new light, God's will may very well be

---

[77] Barry Morley, *Beyond Consensus: Salvaging the Sense of the Meeting*, pp. 28-29

[78] Ibid., p. 31

for us to be in disunity, struggling to find a new unity.

(Jan Hoffman, "Words on Practical Aspects of Meeting for Business")

It has been the experience of this yearly meeting in the past to know that Friends have met in division and uncertainty, and that then guidance has come, and light has been given to us, and we have become finders of God's purpose. This gives us ground for confidence. We shall not be held back by the magnitude of the questions which are to come before us, nor by a sense of our own unworthiness.

(London Yearly Meeting, 1936, quoted in Britain Yearly Meeting *Faith and Practice*, 2.91)

There are several things that can be done to help Friends move forward.

- A period of worship is always in order. Anyone can suggest it. If Friends use this time to lay aside their own egos and open themselves to the Light, hearts and minds can be transformed.
- The clerk or anyone else with a gift for gathering and articulating the sense of the meeting can offer a summary of where things stand. This helps to clarify that upon which Friends do and do not currently agree.
- The clerk or recording clerk can offer a trial minute—something for Friends to consider that will help them focus. This assures those who have spoken that they have been heard and do not need to repeat themselves, for they hear their views reflected in the developing minute. It can show that the meeting's efforts thus far have uncovered some grounds for unity even though others remain to be found. Articulating the different views that divide the meeting may help Friends hear and understand one another.
- When Friends have labored faithfully over a period of time but there is still disagreement, it can be useful to clarify where individual Friends stand by polling the meeting. This means having Friends in turn state whether they are in agreement or not with the current proposal. This is not a vote—though

it looks like one—as no decision is based on who or how many support or oppose a proposal. It can be a useful means of clarifying the general tenor of the group.

It helps for Friends to remember that it is the faithful use of the process and maintaining loving relationships within the meeting, not the ultimate decision, that is of first importance.

> In all our meetings for church affairs we need to listen together to the Holy Spirit. We are not seeking a consensus; we are seeking the will of God. The unity of the meeting lies more in the unity of the search than in the decision which is reached. We must not be distressed if our listening involves waiting, perhaps in confusion, until we feel clear what God wants done.
>
> (London Yearly Meeting, 1984, quoted in Britain Yearly Meeting *Faith and Practice*, 2.89)

Objecting, Standing Aside, and Standing in the Way

> There is Quaker lore that any individual can stand in the way of a decision and prevent the decision from being taken. This is not entirely true. "Standing in the way" is a mutual responsibility between the individual and meeting to test our sense of Truth as we are imperfectly able to sense it at the time. But no one, after prayerful consideration by the meeting, can "stand in the way of a decision" without the meeting's permission. The meeting can proceed, in loving tenderness to those who cannot join in the decision.
>
> (Arthur Meyer Boyd, "When Quakers Disagree")

Occasionally one or two Friends object, and feel they cannot withdraw their objection to the meeting's taking action in a matter on which all other Friends in the meeting unite. In such a situation, the opposing Friends may well question whether their objections should be considered binding on the meeting. On the other hand, a meeting may too readily agree to an action on plausible but superficial grounds, so it is well to ponder objections voiced by a few Friends, or even a single Friend, which may reach to the heart of the matter at hand. If the meeting, after prolonged laboring, is convinced that it is following divine guidance, it may set aside the objections and proceed. It may include reference to the objections in the minute recording the action.

(North Pacific Yearly Meeting *Faith and Practice*, p. 57)

When there is a clear sense of the meeting but one or a few individuals are not comfortable with it, several things should happen:

- The individuals should make their discomfort known.
- The individuals should search their hearts and minds and test whether they can unite with the sense of the meeting.
- All other Friends should strive to understand and sympathize with the individual(s) and to search their hearts and minds for any resonance with the reason for the stop.[79]
- All Friends should seek divine guidance.

> In group discourse not focused on discerning God's leading, it is difficult to back away from strongly expressed positions. . . . In challenging cases, the opponent of the proposed action continues to say the same things over and over again. In the worst cases, there is a hint or an open threat that the person will leave the group if that person does not get his or her way. This is a sign of dysfunction in the group and should prompt its members to pray for the healing of the individual's spirit and the spirit of the group.
>
> (Lon Fendall, Jan Wood, and Bruce Bishop, *Practicing Discernment Together*, p. 141)

Friends who cannot agree with a decision may choose to stand aside, which means that in good conscience they cannot agree with the decision, but they will not stop the group from proceeding.

> The person who stands aside needs to understand that the decision is the best achievable by the meeting as a whole so that he or she is prepared to support the decision's implementation.
>
> (Australia Yearly Meeting, "Quaker Business Method: The Practice of Group Discernment")

[79] When one has a gut feeling that something is not right, Friends say that they have a "stop" or a "stop in the mind."

> Although the meeting may then proceed with the action proposed, it must do so in humility.
>
> (Thomas S. Brown, *When Friends Attend to Business*)

However, no one who feels that a decision is against God's will should stand aside until he or she reaches clarity. Clarity should not be achieved through persuasion by others, but through the attention of *all* participants to the Inner Light. Many business meetings have been enriched because individual Friends expressed sentiments that led to an eventually deeper and more satisfying outcome. This system is cumbersome, but it works. Often a lone dissenter turns the group toward a final solution that is richer and more satisfying to all than any of the original proposals.

On rare occasions, a Friend refuses to stand aside. When this happens, it is the responsibility of the meeting to discern whether the Friend is acting from a Spirit-led place. The meeting then decides whether to leave things as they are, to postpone the decision, or to override the dissenting member.

> Occasionally [an] individual may not feel clear about standing aside. . . . In that case, it *is* possible for the clerk to move ahead despite the objection, even though that would be a rare situation. In that case, the resulting minute might indicate that the person was "unable to unite" with the decision. In such a situation, the dissenting individual has been unable to trust the discernment of the meeting. This broken trust causes a rift—a wound that needs to be healed with diligent effort on the part of all parties. The goal is for the dissenting individual to once again become spiritually and emotionally free to participate in group discernment.
>
> (Lon Fendall, Jan Wood, and Bruce Bishop, *Practicing Discernment Together*, pp. 114-15)

Postponing a Decision

> Sometimes it will be right to leave the decision to a later meeting, but the clerk should bear in mind that this can be the "lazy" option. Sensitivity is required in recognizing when the meeting is really too tired to proceed further. It may be realized that more background work would be beneficial or that time is needed for everyone to

> consider the options more carefully. A decision to come back to the subject on a later occasion will then be a positive and important part of the process.
>
> (Britain Yearly Meeting *Faith and Practice*, 3.07)

The current state of the meeting's discernment should be recorded in a minute, traditionally called a Minute of Exercise, or in some places a Minute of Process.

> When the group decides to wait until another time to take definitive action, a minute very helpfully provides the context for resuming the discussion later. The minute of process lets the group feel heard. It documents the flow of the concerns so that these concerns do not have to be repeated at the next meeting.
>
> (Lon Fendall, Jan Wood, and Bruce Bishop, *Practicing Discernment Together*, pp. 116-17)

Special or Called Meetings for Business

Sometimes it is useful to hold an extra meeting for business. This may be in order to act in a timely fashion or to provide a session dedicated to discernment of a difficult topic. It is important that all Friends be made aware of the called meeting sufficiently in advance to be able to attend. It is also important that no additional business be addressed of which Friends were not notified. A concerted effort to both appear to and to actually include all Friends is necessary to establish a context of trust for the called meeting. Providing babysitting or rides or other accommodations to make it more possible for some Friends to participate may help.

Here is how two yearly meetings handle called meetings:

> A special meeting for business may be called by the clerk to consider a specific matter of business. Advance notice of such a "called meeting for business" should be given, and no business should be considered other than that for which the meeting was called.
>
> (North Pacific Yearly Meeting *Faith and Practice*, p 58)

> Special meetings of the monthly meeting may be called by the clerk, or by the clerk upon request of three members. Notice shall

> be given at a regular meeting for worship at least seven days before the date of holding the special meeting; it shall name the business to be considered and the persons calling for the special meeting. No business may be considered at a special meeting other than the business for which it was called.
>
> (New England Yearly Meeting *Faith and Practice*, p. 234)

Following Up

Any time a meeting sends a Friend out as a representative or assigns a task to one or more Friends, the individuals should report back to the next convenient business meeting. When a task is assigned, it may be helpful for the minute to include who is going to perform the task and when they will report back to the meeting. This helps to ensure that each task is actually performed and that the meeting is informed in a timely fashion. In drawing up an agenda, the clerk can go through previous minutes to identify reports that are due.

Lon Fendall, Jan Wood, and Bruce Bishop offer clerks a checklist for following up after a meeting for business:[80]

- Follow through on any action items requiring implementation.
- Letters to be written; documents to be signed.
- Necessary communication with people/committees.
- Further meetings to be scheduled.
- Notes/e-mails of appreciation.
- Follow-up conversations that might be wise.

The Recording Clerk and Minutes

Overview

> The drafting of a minute is a spiritual exercise. Every clerk needs the full support and attention of the meeting, so that together they may achieve high standards of clarity and accuracy.
>
> (Britain Yearly Meeting *Faith and Practice*, 3.14)

[80] Lon Fendall, Jan Wood, and Bruce Bishop, *Practicing Discernment Together*, p. 119

> Composing a minute to express the unity that was achieved in the sense of the meeting is a weighty spiritual practice, not a clerical function.
>
> (Australia Yearly Meeting, "Quaker Business Method: The Practice of Group Discernment")

Quakers have found that writing things down and reading them aloud helps the group ensure that everyone understands and is in agreement with a decision. The writing down, reading back, and approval of minutes is part of the process of Quaker decision-making. The recording clerk takes minutes during business meeting and presents them for approval by the group as directed by the clerk (or, among some Friends, the clerk writes the minutes, and instead of a recording clerk may be aided by an assistant clerk). The clerk should provide the recording clerk in advance with as much pertinent information as possible: agenda, names, dates, places, and the precise recommendations of those proposing some action.

Before a minute can be drafted, the clerk needs to articulate the sense of the meeting and get Friends' agreement. A minute is the written expression of the sense of the meeting and may or may not use the same words and phrases as those used by the clerk.

> In the truest sense it is not the recording clerk, but the meeting and the Spirit that guides it that prepare the minutes.
>
> (William Braasch Watson, *Before Business Begins*, p. 5)

Some clerks fashion a minute instead of formulating the sense of the meeting, successfully combining these tasks, but with other clerks the attempt may lead to confusion and arguments over wording. It may work better to first express the sense of the meeting verbally, and then turn to fashioning a written minute.

Minutes that record decisions traditionally record only the conclusion; no details of how the decision is reached are included. The final decision is the one the group perceives as God's will; who said what along the path to coming to that decision is not pertinent. Sometimes it is appropriate for minutes to record why a particular decision was made. This can be noted very briefly.

For instance, the minutes might include, "The meeting decided to change banks so that we no longer have to pay monthly fees." If Friends later revisit the issue of what bank to use, they will be helped to know why a change was made.

To paraphrase Deborah Haines, while the minutes should be detailed enough to carry the sense of the meeting, they certainly do not need to be longer than that.

Ways to aid in the process of writing good minutes:

- The recording and presiding clerks may study the agenda together in advance of the meeting.
- A routine minute may be drafted in advance for on-site editing as discussion of the matter takes place. (Examples: membership, marriage, matters having clear alternatives.)
- To the extent possible, make minutes complete and interpretable without reliance upon attachments (which may go astray).

Minutes also serve as a written record to refer to later as needed and are an important means of communication between monthly, regional, and yearly meetings and their committees.

For both these reasons—helping Friends in the decision making process and as a record for the future—the accuracy and completeness of minutes are crucial.

> Finding appropriate words to clarify the decision for those who are not present is a key part of the spiritual discernment process, so it is important to resist the temptation to offer a loose approximation.
>
> (Australia Yearly Meeting, "Quaker Business Method: The Practice of Group Discernment")

Accuracy includes both accuracy of detail—dates, numbers, etc.—and also of the sense of the meeting, the spiritual leading. Completeness means including in the written minute any decision along with the pertinent details—who is going to follow up, dates, times, and places. A good question to ask when deciding how much detail to include is, what will be useful for Friends 10 years from now?

Each minute must receive the assent, spoken or tacit, of the meeting. Once approved, minutes are not open to revision except by further action by the meeting. In coming to a decision, however, Friends seek unity, not uniformity.

> Assent to a minute . . . does not necessarily imply uniformity of judgement. Rather it is recognition that the minute records what the group feels is right at the time. There may be Friends who would wish the meeting to move forward more adventurously and others who fear what seems dangerous experiment. Each might have wished the meeting to take a different course from that agreed upon. But each will consider what is right for this meeting with these differences of judgement sincerely held and will give assent to a minute which seems to reflect the sense of the meeting, even if not wholly acceptable to oneself.
>
> (George A. Selleck, *Principles of the Quaker Business Meeting*, p. 13)

Because announcements are often given at the end of a business meeting, they often get included in the minutes. Only announcements of continuing interest need be included—ones that are mini-reports. Announcements of upcoming events or other things that will be moot within a few months need not be minuted. If desired, a simple statement that announcements were given may be included in the minutes.

When business is not finalized during a particular meeting, a minute can be written summarizing the state of the business and what remains to be done. This is called a process minute or minute of exercise.

Conventions

Naming Individuals

In some Quaker traditions, individuals who present business are not named in minutes, instead being referred to as "the clerk" or "the clerk of the So-and-so Committee." No record is kept of who attended a particular business session. This emphasizes the communal aspect of Quaker decision making; it is not the individual contributions that are important, but where the group ended up. Other Friends keep a record of who attended a business meeting. Some Friends report the name of the person presenting business; for instance, "Mary Baldwin presented the So-and-so Committee's report."

No Closing Phrase

It is typical in the secular world for minutes of a meeting to end with a closing such as "respectfully submitted," followed by the name of the secretary. This is not a Quaker practice; it is precisely the sort of hollow gesture that early Friends witnessed against in their testimonies of not giving hat honor and using plain speech. There is no need for a closing phrase.

Numbering Minutes

Many yearly meetings number their minutes, often using the date as part of the numbering system. For instance, YM07-27 would be the 27th minute recorded during the 2007 annual sessions, while RM07-7 would be the 7th minute recorded during the 2007 representative meeting. This makes it easy to refer to a particular minute later, and is especially useful for yearly meeting minutes because there are so many minutes recorded at one time.

Monthly meetings may or may not find a numbering system useful. Typically, there are many fewer minutes recorded at one time and so it may be easier to refer to "the minute on such-and-such a topic at the August 2008 business meeting." If a numbering system is used, it can consist simply of numbers without a date; references to the minute may be made by referring to Minute 5 of the August 2008 business meeting.

The disadvantage of referring to minutes by number is that usually the topic and contents of the minute are not included, so to understand the reference one has to look up the original minute.

Recording Minutes in the Face of the Meeting vs. Writing Them up Afterward

Some monthly meetings approve all the minutes of a meeting at that meeting, and read them at the next meeting for information only. In other meetings, the recording clerk takes notes and prepares minutes later. Those minutes are read for correction and approval at the next monthly meeting. For many years, all minutes were written and approved "in the face of the meeting." At a time when minutes were all handwritten, this made sense. Since the advent of typewriters and word processors, many meetings have instead adopted the practice of approving in the face of the meeting controversial minutes or those that have required considerable consideration by the meeting, but allowing the recording clerk to make sense of his or her notes on the remainder and bring carefully crafted minutes to the next meeting for business for approval.

There is currently a move among some Friends to return to the practice of fully formulating and approving all minutes as decisions are made, which they find works better. This is greatly facilitated when business has been properly prepared, when the clerks have been made aware in advance of the substance of items for business, when matters are presented to the meeting clearly, and when the group has thoroughly digested and come to unity on matters. Where any confusion or inattention to necessary details prevails, it is impossible to write complete and accurate minutes on the spot. There are advantages and disadvantages to each practice.

Advantages to recording minutes in the face of the meeting:

- There is no confusion about what was decided.
- The same body of Friends who made the decision approves the minute.
- The need to pause while a minute is written can build in periods of worship when the meeting can resettle.
- Some recording clerks take minutes directly on a laptop computer, enabling them to rearrange portions and produce a finished minute that is ready to be printed.

Disadvantages:

- It takes time during the meeting for business.
- Details that should be included in a minute may be omitted.

Depending on how you look at it, the following is either an advantage or a disadvantage:

- To enable the recording clerk to write a clear minute on the spot, it helps if Friends give the clerks advance notice of items of business in some detail. Each item of business also needs to be carefully prepared, presented, and processed.

Advantages to writing minutes up afterward:

- The recording clerk can consult privately with others on wording and what to include.
- The recording clerk can take the time to make sure pertinent details are included and to write a carefully crafted minute.
- The business meeting may take less time.

Disadvantages:

- There is sometimes confusion about what was decided.
- Too much information may be included in a minute simply because it is easy to do so.
- When a different body of Friends listens to and is asked to approve a minute from a previous business meeting, the business may get rehashed. If the situation has changed since the minute was written, it can give rise to confusion as to what the minute should say. It is difficult to stick to what was known and approved at the time.

Wording of Minutes

> Remember that any minute you present is only a draft minute until the meeting has accepted it as its own. . . . Be ready to minute a decision of the meeting which is different from all the possibilities you had in mind. Accept with good grace improvements to your draft made by the meeting.
>
> (Britain Yearly Meeting *Faith and Practice*, 3.14)

The better prepared the meeting is to make a decision and the clearer the presentation of the item at business meeting, the easier it is to record the decision. While writing minutes is the particular responsibility of the recording clerk, the entire body is responsible for seeing that the minutes are accurate. Elegant or even concise phrases are less important than capturing the essence of the decision.

When a minute is proposed, Friends may suggest corrections or clarifications. It is best if these are kept to a minimum.

> When considering the wording of documents to be sent out by the meeting or included in the minutes, Friends need to exercise restraint in suggesting improvements. . . . God's work may very well go on even if perfection of expression is not achieved.
>
> (Thomas S. Brown, *When Friends Attend to Business*)

When a meeting is not entirely clear about a decision or its details, it is difficult to write a clear minute. If Friends seem to have gotten bogged down in the minutiae of the wording, they might consider whether the problem is not the minute but lack of clarity. At such times it is best to enter a time of silent worship. At the end of that time, often the clerk or recording clerk can offer a revised minute that is acceptable, or a Friend can express the issue that is unresolved.

When the wording of a minute continues to be problematic, the meeting may:

- Grant to responsible persons the power to make purely editorial changes as needed.
- Ask a few Friends to withdraw and make the needed revisions based on Friends' objections and suggestions and bring it back to the meeting.
- Continue to struggle with it in the full meeting if suggested changes would change the meaning or tone, trying to focus on the meaning rather than the words.

If the recording clerk feels unable to make headway, she or he can ask the meeting for help. This could be in the form of holding the recording clerk in the Light while she or he works on the minute, commenting on a trial minute, suggesting alternate wording or an entirely new minute, or clarifying what the meeting has decided.

Sometimes a lawyer, the treasurer, or someone with specific expertise needs to be consulted before a correct minute can be written. Friends can approve a draft of the minute in principle with the understanding that changes will be brought to the next business meeting for final approval.

Recording clerks should be authorized to correct mistakes in spelling, grammar, and typing. They should not be authorized to make changes that might affect the meaning. If an addition or correction to a minute is deemed necessary after it has been approved, the recording clerk should report the suggested change at the next business meeting and get Friends' approval.

Clerks and recording clerks should not put themselves in the position of defending a proposed minute. Either the body is going to accept it as is or change it; the clerks' jobs are to discern and faithfully record the meeting's decision.

> The minute, if properly drawn, will reflect a collective decision that will be supported, if necessary, by the meeting. If it is not properly drawn and needs to be changed, one would hardly want to defend it.
>
> (William Braasch Watson, *Before Business Begins*, p. 33)

Types of Minutes

While all items that come before a business meeting are minuted, not all are decisions. Many items of business are reports of one kind or another that do not call for a decision or approval. Minutes for different kinds of business have been given descriptive names. Use of these names is more prevalent among older established and more traditional Friends. Here are some types of minutes to record the various sorts of business that commonly come up.

- *Minute of Record.* This sort of minute merely records for archival purposes a significant event that has taken place in the life of the meeting such as a marriage, funeral, or public action.
- *Minute of Decision.* A record of what was decided.
- *Minute of Conscience.* A longstanding tradition among Friends is to record in a paragraph or two a moral or conscientious position on a topic of concern in contemporary society. For instance, a number of minutes have been written and circulated in recent years among Liberal Friends on issues around homosexuality, the rights of homosexuals, and whether a group of Quakers feels clear to perform marriage ceremonies

or ceremonies of commitment for same-sex couples. This kind of minute expresses the meeting's standard for behavior by members individually and as a corporate group. It is intended as a witness for all time on the issue, and proceeds from a palpable sense of the meeting, not just a lukewarm "okay." Often, it is reached after a long struggle and represents a new understanding.

- *Minute of Exercise.* A minute of exercise, also called a "process minute," affirms where the meeting is at a given moment when there is as yet no clarity to act. These minutes simply state the various perceptions in the meeting on a given matter at that moment and can be helpful in building a sense of the meeting. Often if Friends can clearly affirm where they are, it frees them to perceive new Light. Such a minute is used in lengthy processes of discernment.

> A minute is above all true to the real state of the meeting without evasion or embroidery. Therefore, the minute must on occasion record uneasiness, a lack of unity, a wish that a way forward be taken but uncertainty as to what such a way should be.
>
> (Madge Seaver, "On Minutes of Exercise")

> Not every decision has to be the final resolution of the issue, and recognizing this can be very helpful. . . . Sometimes the group does not know the final resolution, but it does know the next step.
>
> (Lon Fendall, Jan Wood, and Bruce Bishop, *Practicing Discernment Together*, pp. 112-13)

Dissemination of Minutes

Approved minutes are circulated or published so that all Friends may read them. This can be in a meeting newsletter, via e-mail, or posted to a website.[81] It is important to remember than not

---

81 Meetings are advised not to post unapproved minutes to a website, which is available to anyone in the world, as this could lead to a misunderstanding if they are taken out of context or the reader does not understand that they have not been approved.

all Friends use computers, so meetings need to provide information in at least one way each person in the meeting can access.

Making it Easy to Look Up Items in the Minutes

The recording clerk should be prepared to research previous minutes that bear on current business. To facilitate this, it is helpful when writing the final version of minutes to indicate each minute's subject in some way that will make it easy to pick out topics later. Future recording clerks will bless you.

Here are some possible ways of helping future Friends find particular minutes:

- Underline key words such as "mortgage" or "membership."
- Add a lead-in to each topic in the margin or in a distinctive font (such as italics or bold) that can be easily skimmed, such as "State of the Meeting Report."
- Create an index by date and minute number (if numbers are used) of matters that are likely to be referred to later. These might include:
  —Legal matters such as owning a building.
  —Minutes stating the meeting's stand on a social issue.
  —Meeting policies and practices.

The index can be updated after each business meeting.

Finished Minutes, Other Records, and Archives

The recording clerk is responsible for keeping one complete and accurate set of official minutes on acid-free paper (most computer and copy paper these days is acid-free). The minutes should be signed by the clerks and include any amendments made at later business meetings. The minute book should also include financial reports and the reports and minutes accepted by the meeting from its committees. It is convenient to keep the minutes in a three-ring binder or similar apparatus.

A meeting's minutes serve as a permanent record and should be complete and accessible. The recording clerk should have access to copies of all minutes approved by the meeting so that he or she can research the meeting's previous dealings on recurring issues. A good practice for recording clerks is to maintain a minute book with the minutes from the last four or five years as well as documents one might want to refer to such as committee lists, a directory of members and attenders, and the budget.

Every ten years or so, a copy of the meeting's permanent records on acid-free paper should be deposited in the approved archive for the meeting's records. Permanent records should include:

- A set of minutes, signed by the presiding and recording clerks. Reports from the treasurer and committees should be attached as noted in the minutes.
- Any financial records not included in the minutes, for example, copies of deeds or contracts.
- If the meeting is incorporated, records of incorporation and minutes of annual meetings.
- A list of marriages under the care of the meeting.
- Membership records of current and past members, including records of births, marriages, divorces, deaths, transfers, and terminations of membership.

  Other records to include might be:
- State of the meeting reports.
- For meetings with pastors, the pastor's annual report.
- Whatever other records the meeting wants permanently kept.

Usually, yearly meetings make arrangements for all records to be archived in the same place. The meeting should retain copies of all archived materials for its own use.

Queries on Meeting for Business

San Francisco Monthly Meeting has developed a helpful set of queries on meeting for business:[82]

[82] Jan Greene and Marty Walton, *Fostering Vital Friends Meetings: Part II*

- Are your meetings for business held in a spirit of love, understanding and forbearance? Do you seek the right course of action with a patient search for unity and a willingness to accept the authority of the Truth?
- Do you come to meeting eager to search for God's will rather than to try to win acceptance for a previously formed opinion of your own? Are you prepared to assist by silent, prayerful consideration, speaking only if you feel you have a helpful contribution to make?
- Do you give each member credit for purity of motive, notwithstanding differences of opinion? Is your love for your neighbor so strong that you are as eager to understand as to be understood?
- When your clerk is searching for the sense of the meeting, do you overcome diffidence and express your view without undue delay? Do you maintain silence while the minute is being composed?
- Do you avoid bringing to the meeting matters that should first be considered by a committee? Do you allow unimportant matters to be disposed of quickly? When a decision is being reached with which you disagree, do you accept your responsibility to speak at that time rather than later?
- Do you refrain from pressing your own views unduly, if the judgement of the meeting obviously inclines to some other view?
- When the meeting has come to a decision, do you accept it as "our" decision, rather than "theirs"?

Chapter 9: The Nominating Process

Each Quaker group, whether it is a monthly meeting, a yearly meeting, or an international organization, discerns what committees, officers, and other personnel will best serve its needs at any given time. It has become the custom among many Friends to limit the duration of service on any given committee or office. The exceptions are treasurers, trustees, recorders, and webmasters, where continuity is greatly to be desired and for whom the necessary qualifications limit the pool. This did not used to be the case. There was a time when clerks, committee clerks, and others would remain in a position for years, as long as they were willing and able to do the job and the group was satisfied with their work. This is still done in some places, especially among Conservative Friends.

There are advantages and disadvantages to both approaches. One of the advantages of moving Friends about from time to time is the opportunity for individuals to grow into new positions. This works best when there are seasoned Friends who mentor the new Friend and help him or her grow into the new position.

> Among Friends everywhere, the Nominating Committee is one of the most important committees in a meeting. The meeting depends upon this small group of spiritually sensitive, wise, tactful, and dedicated Friends to find appropriate persons to fulfill meeting responsibilities, to see that Friends learn Quaker process, and sometimes to draw out spiritual gifts by asking Friends to stretch themselves. Beacon Hill Friends Meeting (NEYM) has renamed their Nominating Committee "Gifts and Leadings Committee," and added responsibilities for tending to members' leadings. The Meeting is concerned not only with appointing the most qualified person to each job but also with developing and using the talents and resources of all members and attenders. In asking people to assume various responsibilities, the meeting recognizes that different individuals have different gifts which are not equally appropriate for all positions in the meeting. Members and attenders should not be asked to take on inappropriate responsibilities out of a sense of

"equality" or "taking turns."

(North Pacific Yearly Meeting *Faith and Practice*, p. 61)

At its best, a Nominating Committee finds a good fit between the gifts that individuals have to offer and the needs of the group. The Nominating Committee can discern which individuals have been called to work in certain areas and to create committees that function well as a team. The Nominating Committee can identify latent gifts or suggest new areas of service. The committee can see if there are new people or young people it would be good to involve. The committee can confirm and nurture Friends' growing spiritual maturity by asking them to serve in positions that call for discernment and experience. All of this takes time and prayerful consideration. The result can be officers and committees that perform useful jobs under the leading of the Spirit as well as a lively spiritual community.

At its worst, a Nominating Committee can fill slots with whoever can be coerced into taking a position or with individuals who are eager to take on responsibilities that call for more wisdom and discretion than they possess. The result can be officers and committees that function erratically if at all, a fragmented and contentious community, and a place where it is difficult to hear or follow the promptings of the Spirit.

The committee must begin its work well in advance of the date when its slate is presented to the meeting. Although most of the committee's work is seasonal, it continues to serve as a standing committee throughout the year to nominate persons to fill vacancies that may occur or new positions that the meeting may establish.

Appointing Friends to a Nominating Committee

The meeting is advised to establish a careful process for the selection of knowledgeable, sensitive, experienced, caring, and forthright Friends to serve on the Nominating Committee.

(Baltimore Yearly Meeting *Faith and Practice*, p. 56)

> It is important to ensure openness and to prevent any suggestion of an inner group.
>
> (Britain Yearly Meeting *Faith and Practice*, 3.24d)

Nominating Committees are appointed in a variety of ways:

- A special committee may be asked to bring forward names of Friends. This could be an ad hoc committee (sometimes called a Naming Committee), an existing committee such as Ministry and Oversight, or several meeting officers.
- Names may be suggested from the body of the meeting. This only works well in a well-disciplined body. It is frowned upon in some places because it tends to encourage insuffiicently seasoned suggestions. Britain Yearly Meeting's book of *Faith and Practice* states that "Receiving nominations from the body of the meeting is not generally a good method of making appointments."[83]
- The existing committee may nominate its successors. Great care needs to be taken, or the character of the committee will become self-perpetuating.
- Names come from representative bodies. For instance, in Iowa Yearly Meeting (Conservative) and Northwest Yearly Meeting (Evangelical), names for new appointments to the yearly meeting Nominating Committee are suggested by representatives from the monthly meetings.

As with other committees, members of a Nominating Committee should serve overlapping terms so there is continuity.

Desirable Qualities for Members of a Nominating Committee

> Members of this committee are chosen with regard to their discernment, seasoned judgement, and general knowledge of the membership.
>
> (New England Yearly Meeting *Faith and Practice*, p. 226)

[83] Britain Yearly Meeting *Faith and Practice*, 3.24a

Ideally, Nominating Committee members should:

- Be familiar with the function and structure of the meeting and with the "good order of Friends."
- Be familiar with the purpose and work of each committee.
- Have the ability to discern.
- Have the ability to keep information confidential.
- Be comfortable asking others to serve.
- Have the ability to say what they think, frankly but without offending, to other members of the committee about a Friend's suitability for a committee or office.
- Be aware of the interests, talents, proven experience, latent gifts, and potential leadership of various meeting participants.
- Be members of the Society, and preferably of the local meeting.

In addition to these qualities, the committee also needs one or more of its members to have the following abilities:

- Be organized and able to keep accurate lists of multi-year terms, the positions that need to be filled, the people asked, whether they have agreed or not, etc.
- Be willing and able to clerk the committee.

It is helpful if members of a Nominating Committee are representative of the meeting so that all ages, races, and areas of concern can be included in its deliberations. It is good to include a mature young adult on the committee for this reason as well as someone who is in touch with new people. Ideally, someone on the committee should be familiar with the work of each committee and position that needs to be filled.

It is important for the committee to remember that it is not appointing anyone—it is bringing names to the business meeting for consideration.

> The Nominations Committee is not the appointing body and must bring the suggested names to the body for which it acts. Members of this body have the responsibility for approving the names or not and must be given the opportunity to express any doubts they might have.
>
> (Britain Yearly Meeting *Faith and Practice*, 3.24g)

Suggested Steps for the Annual Nominating Process

Preparation

- Someone, usually the clerk of the committee, needs to procure an up-to-date list of the slate of positions, the Friends currently serving in them, when those appointments expire, and whether there are any new positions not on last year's slate. This work can begin several months before the committee needs to bring a report to business meeting.
- Someone, usually the clerk, needs to draw up a list of what positions need to be filled and the pertinent details: for how long a term, if they need to be members, etc. This should include all the positions that are expiring, including those of Friends who will probably agree to continue. Also check if there are Friends who have served as long as allowed and therefore cannot continue.

Committee Work

- Hold a committee meeting to go over the list of positions to be filled. Hold the process in the Light and look for divine guidance in proceeding. Begin the meeting with worship—not merely "a brief period of silence" but a deep enough and long enough stillness to become gathered as a group ready to do the Spirit's bidding. Giving this settling process long enough to work makes the subsequent work of the committee flow more smoothly and take less time overall. Close the committee meeting with at least a brief period of silence.
- Usually, Friends already serving who are eligible to serve another term are asked to continue. However, if members of the Nominating Committee don't know whether specific persons are valuable members of a committee, it is good to ask that committee's clerk and then decide whether to ask them to serve another term. If questions have been raised about an officer, those need to be addressed. If the officer has indicated a desire to continue, that may include a face-to-face

discussion about the concerns that have been raised.

- Discern who to ask to fill the positions (see "Discerning Who to Call" for ideas on structuring this).
- Divide up the tasks. Which member of the Nominating Committee will talk with which Friends? To whom will they report the responses? The Nominating Committee often finds it effective to use a cell phone to telephone Friends during the committee meeting. At the end of the meeting, there may be only a few Friends left to contact. Decide when and where the committee will meet next.

Presenting a Slate to Business Meeting

- Before anything is reported to business meeting, two things need to happen:
  —Each Friend on the slate needs to be asked to serve.
  —Each Friend on the slate needs to agree to serve.

If the Nominating Committee designates clerks of committees, these also must be asked and agree to serve as clerk. If it is probable that a Friend will agree to serve, but there has not been an opportunity to ask or respond, the Friend may be appointed "subject to consent." If the Friend does not consent, the Nominating Committee is responsible for finding someone else. If possible, avoid this situation.

- It has been found very helpful to present the entire slate at one business session but postpone making any decision to the next session. In the meantime, the Nominating Committee can make copies of the proposed slate available. If time does not allow for this, the list can be made available before being presented at business meeting. Both of these procedures allow Friends time to digest the information, find and notify the committee of any mistakes, and raise any questions or qualms privately. Having someone challenge a nomination on the floor of the meeting inevitably results in hurt feelings, and can get ugly.
- Revise the slate if appropriate and present it at the next business session, where a decision will be asked for.

Follow-up

- Make sure clerks of committees know who has been newly appointed.

Discerning Who to Call

> Our ability to discern the gifts of others is not perfect and we will recognise an element of God's grace in our deliberations. Be bold; welcome the chance to give opportunities to younger Friends and to those more recently arrived, and encourage those who underestimate their own potential for service.
>
> (Britain Yearly Meeting *Faith and Practice*, 3.25)

There are many processes that a Nominating Committee can use to help discern who to call for what position.

A Suggested Process for a Monthly Meeting

At the monthly meeting level, the Nominating Committee is usually responsible both for identifying who might be suitable and for discerning who to call. Where the pool of possible people is limited and all are known to at least some members of the Nominating Committee, the committee can review who there is without yet thinking in terms of where they might serve. A meeting directory can provide a list of potential Friends. After a period of worship, the committee can hold up each Friend in turn and share where they think each Friend is in his or her spiritual journey. The committee can explore whether a Friend may be ready to take on a new challenge or serve in an unexpected way.

It helps to think of each Friend as either someone who needs mentoring (training up in the life of the Spirit and the life of the meeting) or as a seasoned Friend who can mentor others on a particular committee. Rathern than focusing narrowly on the committee's task or how it is currently operating, be open to new possibilities. Consider those who are new or young but may be ready to take a first step into Quaker service. Consider those who are infirm but may have valuable insights and experience. This builds the groundwork for discerning a match between gifts and service.

If not all members of the Nominating Committee are familiar with the positions to be filled, it is good to review what the committees and officers do and how they operate. What skills and abilities do people need in order to serve in different positions?

One way of approaching how to match up people with positions is to hold up each committee or position in turn and see what names to serve in that position rise from the members of the Nominating Committee. This can generate a list of possible names. Once this is done for all the committees and officers, each possible name can be held up and members of the committee respond as led with brief comments on the suitability of the person for the position. The committee clerk may be able to generate a proposed slate from this exercise by gathering the sense of the meeting, or further discernment may be needed.

It is helpful to anticipate that not all Friends will agree to serve and to have alternate names held in reserve.

A Suggested Process for a Yearly Meeting or Other Large Body

In yearly meetings and other large groups, the members of the Nominating Committee probably do not know all the Friends who might serve. In this case, the whole yearly meeting must take on the responsibility for suggesting who might be suitable, leaving the task of discerning who to call to the Nominating Committee. Members of the Nominating Committee should actively solicit suggestions. They can ask Friends to bring them names of those in their monthly meeting or others they have gotten to know who might serve in a particular capacity. Existing members of committees should consider who they know who might serve and suggest those names to the Nominating Committee. Committee clerks should let the Nominating Committee know if they are in need of someone with particular skills. The nominating process takes longer in these circumstances than in a monthly meeting where more people know one another. The task of the Nominating Committee is more difficult, and its members need to rely on the recommendations and discernment of others.

It may work well to assign certain officer positions, committees, and other appointments to different members of the Nominating Committee. Each Nominating Committee member can then confer with the clerks of "their" committees or the current holders of "their" offices or other appointments to find out how things are working and what the needs are for the coming year.

A yearly meeting Nominating Committee starts the discernment process with a list of all the suggestions it has received for various positions. Where do you have ample possibilities? Where do you have too few? The committee should solicit additional names so that all necessary positions can be filled. Members of the Nominating Committee may need to contact meeting clerks, committee clerks, and others asking for additional suggestions for certain positions.

When the committee begins fitting people to positions, it is best to start with the most critical positions, such as officers. There may be times when a position on a committee goes unfilled if people are scarce.

How do you discern whether people are appropriate for positions if you don't know them? Members of the Nominating Committee may have to rely on the discernment of others. Who suggested the name? Is it an off-the-cuff suggestion or a recommendation? Does anyone on the committee know that person? Are committee members willing to rely on that person's discernment? Are there people who you can ask about the person whose name has been suggested? The clerk of a committee may be consulted about members proposed for that committee. Consider whether you yourself would be willing to serve on a committee with a person under consideration, knowing what you know.

The Strawberry Creek Meeting Process

Strawberry Creek Monthly Meeting in California has developed a Spirit-led nominating process which has been found helpful by other Friends. "This process, also known as the Strawberry Creek Method, has been adopted by a number of meetings as a helpful way to discern the gifts that members and attenders bring to committee work. This process is exceptionally useful when the committee is having some trouble with a particular position, but is not always practical for filling every position."[84] Here is a summary of the process.[85]

Focus on the position or committee to be considered. When all committee members feel they understand what is being sought, the committee goes into silence out of which people name whatever names occur to them, without commenting on the name. When it seems clear that no more names are forthcoming, questions may be asked about names which are unfamiliar to some on the committee. When all are clear that they know enough about each name, the committee enters into silence again. One person slowly reads all the names that have been suggested. Out of the silence, each committee member names the one name which rises to the top for them. Again, no comment is given on any name.

When all committee members have shared who rose to the top for them, there may be only one name, and the clerk can call a sense of the meeting on that name. If one name seems to dominate, the clerk can ask if the committee is clear on that name or wishes to continue in worship. If the clerk feels there is no sense of the meeting, committee members then share why they think a given name rose to the top for them. After this sharing, committee members go back into silence and once again name the one name that rises to the top for them. Usually, the clerk will be able to call a sense of the meeting after this second period of worship. If not, the committee needs to discern its next step.

---

[84] Strawberry Creek Monthly Meeting website at strawberrycreek.quaker.org/about.php, September 2008. More information about the process can be found in "Spiritual Discernment within the Nominating Process" by Perry Treadwell, in the October 2005 edition of *Friends Journal.* The process is also described in *Fostering Vital Friends Meetings: Part II.*

[85] Summary by Marty Walton in *The Meeting Experience: Practicing Quakerism in Community*, p. 32

Strengths of this process:

- The person to be asked is chosen out of worship and a sense of their gifts for a particular task.
- The process does not focus on what gifts people do not have. There are fine names who are just not right for a given position. In worship, these names will drop away without comment on what they cannot do. No negative comments need be given.

Asking and Being Asked to Serve

> Members ought to feel a sense of rightness of their service—a sense of divine calling. Appointments should not be accepted nor declined lightly. Their acceptance should mean willingness to be regular in attendance, to work with others, and to share and to listen. Preparation for effective service is important, involving the ordering of personal affairs so that it is possible to give fully of time, energy, and spiritual resources.
>
> (New England Yearly Meeting *Faith and Practice*, p. 226)

Suggestions when asking a Friend to serve:

- In approaching a person, see that details of the nominating process are understood, including the fact that the meeting, not the committee, is responsible for the ultimate appointment.
- The approach should not be made casually. The duties involved in any position should be fully understood by the Nominating Committee member and by the person approached for nomination. A written job description, if available, should be given to a prospective nominee, and the length of service made clear.

When you are approached by a member of a Nominating Committee, consider the request carefully. You need to discern whether you are suited to carry out the task, as there are things about you and your commitments that the members of the Nominating Committee may not know. In order to make a decision, you need to know what you are being asked to do. Nominating Committee members should tell you how long an appointment is for and in a general way what is involved. Within a monthly meeting, you may already know this, but members of a Nominating Committee should be prepared to provide any information requested—what the committee does; how often, when, and where it meets; and anything else germane. If members of the Nominating Committee do not have complete information, they should be prepared to provide the name and contact information for a person who does, such as the clerk of the committee.

Until the Friend who has been asked has sufficient information, no decision can be expected. Nominating committees should expect Friends to take time to gather information and discern whether this is a task they are willing and able to take on. Do not insist on an immediate response, but do let the person know the committee's time schedule. Time can be built into that schedule so that Friends have sufficient time for individual discernment between being asked and needing to let the committee know.

Agreeing to serve on a committee or as an officer is a commitment. Committee members need to arrange their personal schedules to allow them to attend committee meetings regularly. They should expect to have tasks to carry out between committee meetings.

Presenting a Slate to Business Meeting

When a Nominating Committee presents a proposed slate, everyone should be able to see a copy. It has been found helpful for the meeting to postpone action on the proposed slate until the next business session. In the interval, members may seek clarification, express concerns, or catch mistakes.

It is important that the Friends presenting the slate avoid language that indicates that the slate is already approved. Such phrases as "Our new clerk will be" or "We are happy to announce that so-and-so has accepted the position of" imply that the slate is already decided and the committee is simply announcing who is going to do what. Instead, language such as "Our committee is proposing the following slate for your consideration" puts the situation in its proper perspective.

It is good practice to present a complete slate at one time. This indicates that careful consideration has gone into the overall picture and that thought has gone into balancing different positions appropriately. While it may be okay to bring a slate still in need of a few committee members to fill out what is already a sound committee, bringing a slate with everyone except, for instance, the clerk, indicates problems, and Friends should hesitate to approve such an incomplete slate.

Difficulties Finding People to Serve

> Sometimes it may seem impossible to find someone to serve. Nominations committees should not hesitate to bring their problem back to the meeting to ask for both guidance and practical help.
>
> (Britain Yearly Meeting *Faith and Practice*, 3.24g)

There may be times when a position on a committee goes unfilled if people are scarce. However, if certain positions become routinely difficult to fill, the committee should bring this to the meeting's attention. It may indicate that a committee or function is no longer a priority for the meeting. If there are ongoing problems in filling a number of positions, it may indicate wider problems within the meeting that need to be addressed.

If Things Go Wrong

As a member of a Nominating Committee, the last thing you want to have happen is to present a slate to the business meeting and have a Friend on the slate rise and say, "I didn't agree to do that!" Unpleasant as that might be, it is even more awkward to be a Friend sitting in business meeting and hear one's name read unexpectedly. What is one to do?

It is the nominee's responsibility to set the record straight. Hopefully, one can do it gracefully by rising and saying something like, "I believe I heard my name suggested as a member of the such-and-such committee. No one has asked me to serve on that committee." or "I have not agreed to serve on that committee" or "I told Sarah that I was unable to serve on that committee," depending on the case. You are likely to be asked on the spot if you are willing to serve. Do not hesitate to ask for time to consider it.

If you become aware after a slate is approved that someone was not asked or had not agreed to serve, it is your responsibility to bring this to the attention of a member of the Nominating Committee. That member should notify the rest of the Nominating Committee, and someone should be designated to talk to the Friend to apologize and ask whether he or she is willing and able to serve. If not, it is the Nominating Committee's responsibility to find a replacement, to work with the meeting's clerk to get the new person's appointment approved, and to notify the clerk of the affected committee.

Ending an Appointment

> Despite being made prayerfully appointments do not always turn out as planned. It is at the discretion of a meeting to end an appointment at any time if it is necessary to do so. Loving and tender care will be essential. An appointed Friend who finds the service inappropriate should be released.
>
> (Britain Yearly Meeting *Faith and Practice*, 3.25)

Sometimes Friends who have taken on a position find themselves unable to carry out its responsibilities. This may be because the service itself turns out to be inappropriate, because there are responsibilities involved the Friend was not aware of and cannot fulfill, because the Friend underestimated the effort required, or because the Friend's life circumstances change. When this happens, the individual can consult with the committee clerk and other Friends and, if they agree that the service is inappropriate or can no longer be done, resign from the position. It is more important that the job be done than that it be done by any particular person. Friends who find themselves unable to serve for any reason should act in the best interests of the group rather than out of a sense of guilt.

Chapter 10: Membership and Marriage

Basic Process

The process used for applications for both membership and marriage follows the same basic outline:

- The applicant(s) write a letter to the meeting requesting membership or to be married under the care of the meeting.
- The meeting sets up a clearness committee to meet with the applicant(s).
- The applicant(s) and clearness committee meet together.
- The committee reports to the meeting with a recommendation.
- The meeting makes a decision.

In some places, Ministry and Counsel sets up the clearness committee and/or receives its report rather than the business meeting as a whole. In the case of marriage, if the meeting decides to take the marriage under its care, it proceeds to set up a new committee to oversee the wedding.

Membership

The History and Meaning of Membership

> For our first 90 years, there was no formal membership process and no recorded lists of members. One became a Quaker not by meeting with a clearness committee, but by being convinced of the Truth through an experience of the transforming Power of God. This in turn led to a transformed life.
>
> (Thomas Gates, *Members One of Another: The Dynamics of Membership in Quaker Meeting*, p. 19)

> As England moved into the industrial age, social services were still administered by a person's religious denomination. Conscious of the consequences of suffering, Friends took special care of their members. One result of this care and concern for their members was that many, with no other involvement in the movement, claimed

> to be Friends. To counter this drain on Friends' limited resources, formal membership was recognized in 1737, to be granted only by the applicant's monthly meeting. At the time birthright membership was instituted to protect the children of needy Quaker parents.
>
> (Philadelphia Yearly Meeting, *A Quaker Path*)

Through the years of Quietism, when Quakers stressed their differences from the larger society, practically all people who participated in Quaker meetings were members. The exceptions were the occasional non-Quaker visitor and blacks, who were originally brought to meeting as slaves and, after Quakers had freed their slaves, encouraged to attend meeting for worship but usually made to sit apart. It was not until the 1780s that Friends decided to receive black members.[86]

The later years of Quietism were marked by increasing numbers of Friends being disowned by their meetings. Sandra Cronk explains this as follows:

> A forced change of behavior in the offender is no change at all. Yet the church was clear that it did expect to see an amendment of behavior. If this change was not forthcoming after a suitable time, working through all the avenues of caring outlined in Matthew 18, the meeting felt it had no choice but to recognize that the relationship of love and trust with the recalcitrant person was non-existent. . . . In such situations the meeting disowned the party involved. The disownment was understood not as the intention to cut one off from relationship with the community. The disowned one could still attend meeting for worship; social discourse was not interrupted. Disownment was the recognition that a fundamental covenantal commitment was already severed.
>
> (Sandra L. Cronk, *Gospel Order*, p. 30)

With the passing of Quietism and gradual emergence of Quakers into mainstream society, disownment became rare.

What Does it Mean to be a Quaker?

Because Quakers do not have a creed, it is sometimes difficult to pin down what membership means and what standards of

[86] Thomas D. Hamm, *The Quakers in America*, p. 35

behavior are expected. A creed is a set of beliefs that a spiritual community takes as normative, and which new members are expected to adhere to. Quakers throughout their history have rejected the very idea of agreeing on an authoritative set of beliefs—a creed—for several reasons: words, however inspired, are inadequate to express the full reality of the Divine; as we continue to receive new revelations from God, our understanding of the Divine changes and expands; ultimately, it is not what we think about—believe about—the Ultimate, but our individual and collective experience of the Divine working upon us and through us that matters, and this experience gives us not belief, but knowledge, of the Spirit.

> The Religious Society of Friends is a community of faith based on experience of a transforming power named many ways: the Inner Light, the Spirit of Christ, the Guide, the Living God, the Divine Presence. Membership includes openness to an ongoing relationship with God and willingness to live one's life according to the leadings of the Spirit as affirmed by the community of faith.
>
> (Philadelphia Yearly Meeting *Faith and Practice*, p. 34)

Practical results of becoming a member may be eligibility to serve in certain capacities, the expectation of participation and financial support of the meeting, and the expectation of spiritual and practical assistance from the meeting.

A problem that plagues Liberal Friends is the unconscious use of some testimonies as if they are creeds.

> Many new members are attracted to Friends because they resonate with the testimonies. . . . While this kind of attraction is not necessarily bad, the danger is that these testimonies come to be held as ends in themselves—and thus become creeds. Testimonies embraced as ideals are without spiritual grounding. They may be "good" notions but they remain mere notions. This danger is real because often Friends do not do well at making it clear to others that their testimonies are the *fruits* of their spiritual foundation, not the foundation itself. We are not Quakers because we have embraced the idea of pacifism or simple living or equal regard for both sexes. We are Quakers because we have encountered something within that convinces us that we can be and should be at peace,

> live simply, be loving toward all or live any other witness that may arise from this experience.
>
> (Robert Griswold, *Creeds and Quakers: What's Belief Got To Do With It?*, p. 17)

For many Liberal Friends, for instance, it is unthinkable that one can be a Quaker but not a pacifist. In some places, there is an expectation that all participants in a meeting engage in activism. Friends who are not led to activism or who are not so keen on pacifism are regarded as not up to snuff. Pacifist attitudes and activism become de facto criteria for who is a "real" Quaker.

At the same time, Pastoral Friends in North America have experienced an influx of Christians from other Protestant denominations, who attend a Quaker church because it is local. Pastoral Friends may also have been influenced by other Christian and Evangelical influences. The things that make Quakers distinctive from other Protestant denominations have often not been communicated well to newcomers. With a scarcity of Quaker pastors, ministers from other backgrounds have sometimes been hired. Over time, many Quaker practices have been diluted or lost, including meaningful open worship (worship based in silence), traditional testimonies, and the spiritual underpinning for Quaker business process.

Many Pastoral Friends believe that, to be Quaker, a meeting must be a place where "Jesus Christ is known, loved, and obeyed as Teacher and Lord."[87] Correct beliefs and certain social standards are championed. Some take beliefs such as certain details of orthodox Christian tenets on salvation or sanctification as the basis for accepting or rejecting others. Some have adopted Biblical literalism. Some have taken up the Quietist tendency of trying to keep apart from others with different beliefs and standards of behavior so as to avoid "contamination" from worldly pressures that might tempt them or their children to lose sight of the path to salvation. Within monthly meetings, yearly meetings, and

[87] From FUM's statement of purpose, posted on their website, February 2011

Friends United Meeting, such attitudes coupled with moves to dissolve dissenting meetings and to revoke a minister's recording have caused internal dissension. There is movement in some FUM yearly meetings to heal these dissensions.

In 1991, FUM created an enduring source of tension when it adopted a policy for employees and volunteers that states in part:

> Friends United Meeting holds to the traditional Friends testimonies of peace (nonviolence), simplicity, truth speaking, community, gender and racial equality, chastity, and fidelity in marriage. It is expected that the lifestyle of all staff and volunteer appointees of Friends United Meeting will be in accordance with these testimonies.
>
> Friends United Meeting affirms the civil rights of all people. Staff and volunteer appointments are made without regard to sexual orientation. It is expected that sexual intercourse should be confined to marriage, understood to be between one man and one woman.
>
> (FUM General Board Executive Committee Minute 91 GBEX 18)

This has been seen by many Liberal Friends as discriminating against gays and lesbians. In recent years, some monthly meetings have dropped their membership in FUM, and of the five yearly meetings that were dually affiliated with FGC and FUM, several have dropped or amended their FUM affiliation.

Do Quakers across the spectrum have any common grounds other than a shared history and remnants of common practices, foremost among these being organizational and business practices? History and experience point to working together on common projects, getting to know one another well enough to get past preconceptions and prejudices, and especially the group dynamics when young adult Quakers from across the spectrum get together to be energizing and bring all present to an appreciation of some core experiences: guidance from the Spirit, however named; the spiritual growth that comes from a community affirming leadings and concerns and naming gifts; and the difficult but potentially transformative experience of holding one another accountable—of demanding both individual and communal integrity.

Membership in Liberal Meetings

During the Civil Rights Movement and the Vietnam War, large numbers of activists were attracted to Liberal Friends and began attending meetings. Others also found a spiritual home with Friends. Meetings tended to adopt a hands-off approach to the question of when active attenders might become members, waiting for attenders to initiate the process. As more attenders became longtime and active participants in meetings, less and less functional distinction was made between members and attenders. In many Liberal meetings, faithful attenders are now treated little differently from members, participating fully in business meeting and holding positions of responsibility in the meeting. This has led to questions in some places about what, if anything, membership means. Many Liberal books of Faith and Practice are unhelpful on this topic. The meaning of membership among Liberal Friends is currently muddy and sometimes controversial, and questions have been raised as to whether membership is still relevant or should be dropped.

Meetings with a wide range of understandings of membership may avoid dealing with the issue by setting up clearness committees for applicants that operate without guidelines. Such committees seldom turn any applicant down; to do so would mean grappling with some of the underlying issues. The de facto criterion for membership can become simply compatibility with the existing group. This is unhealthy for the meeting. It is better to bring issues out into the open and to work toward a sense of the meeting.

Tallahassee Meeting in Florida has grappled with the meaning of membership. Part of the resulting membership minute reads as follows:

> What does it mean to be a member of our meeting?
>
> Membership is the outward sign of an inner experience of the Living God, the Inner Light, and of unity with the other members of a living body. Membership expresses that this Friend stands in solidarity with Friend's historic testimonies and constitutes a commitment to enter wholeheartedly into the spiritual and corporate activities of the meeting and to assume responsibility for both service

and support, as way opens.

Membership is a commitment on the part of the member to strive to follow God's leadings as they are revealed through individual worship and corporate discernment and of the meeting to support the member on his or her spiritual and personal journey. Membership does not imply the achievement of a certain standard of goodness. We are all learners and seekers.

(Jan Greene and Marty Walton, *Fostering Vital Friends Meetings: Part II*)

Howard Brinton, in his *Guide to Quaker Practice*, suggested that qualifications for membership be based on practice rather than belief, which makes sense for a group that looks to experience rather than creeds:

The customary procedures of the Society of Friends might be compared to the typical procedures of scientists. Scientific societies admit to their membership only those who are qualified to use, and willing to use, the scientific method. The basis of the test is not facts arrived at but the method used. Scientists may disagree on facts, but they do not disagree on method. Similarly, the Society of Friends accepts into membership a person who is willing to follow the Quaker method regardless of where it may lead.

(Howard Brinton, *Guide to Quaker Practice*, p. 14)

New England Yearly Meeting also points to experience as a basic criterion for membership:

Friends have developed a variety of standards for membership in the different yearly meetings, but these standards have all begun with the understanding that membership is founded on the experience of God's presence in our own lives.

(New England Yearly Meeting *Faith and Practice*, p.127)

Britain Yearly Meeting goes further and lists some fundamental elements of Quakerism members should ascribe to:

Membership is a way of saying to the meeting that you feel at home, and in the right place. Membership is also a way of saying to the meeting, and to the world, that you accept at least the fundamental elements of being a Quaker: the understanding of divine guidance, the manner of corporate worship and the ordering of the meeting's business, the practical expression of inward convictions and the equality of all before God.

(Britain Yearly Meeting *Faith and Practice*, 11.01)

This emphasis on what one does and on an underlying experience of the Divine provide useful guidelines for looking at membership. Patricia Loring further suggests that membership is a formal recognition of being part of a spiritual community:

Quite a few of us hang back from applying for membership from a sense of unworthiness. In my own case, I know I had a vague sense that I must somehow make the entire spiritual journey from self-centeredness to God-centeredness . . . before I could qualify as a member of the Religious Society of Friends. . . .

What was missing in my experience, of course, is missing in most modern meetings. There is rarely a clearly articulated sense that spiritual maturing or transformation is a life-long process. It is not mentioned that membership is simply a rite of passage in that process, the moment of adult declaration that this is the church structure, this is the spiritual community within which we feel called to live out the process of our spiritual maturing. . . .

(Patricia Loring, *Listening Spirituality, Volume II: Corporate Spiritual Practice Among Friends*, pp. 44-45)

Membership in Conservative, Pastoral, and Evangelical Meetings

The meaning of membership is generally not an issue among the other branches of Friends. North Carolina Yearly Meeting (Conservative) offers the following guidelines on membership in its *Faith and Practice*:

Persons may be accepted into membership who are willing to listen for and give expression in their lives to the promptings of the Inner Spirit in all areas of personal discipline and service to others. Some applicants may not yet profess complete adherence to all Friends doctrines and testimonies, but will indicate a readiness to wait upon the Lord and to seek divine guidance in those areas where they may not yet be convinced that the Quaker way of life is right... We insist that all members seek to live by the principles set forth in this book. . . .

(North Carolina [Conservative] *Faith and Practice*, p. 23)

Pastoral yearly meetings are generally explicit about expecting members to be Christian, and their disciplines usually contain a statement of "essential truths," the text of the Richmond Declaration, and an extract from George Fox's letter to the Governor of Barbados in 1671, in which he goes into detail on the Christian tenets generally held by Friends and others at the time. There is a tradition among Pastoral Friends that only members may speak in business meeting.

Evangelical Friends are, of course, Christian. EFCI's home web page declares: "We are drawn together through our clear committment to Jesus Christ and a common desire to change our local and international worlds for Christ." (www.evangelicalfriends.org, February 2011) Evangelical Friends Church—Eastern Region (the equivalent of a yearly meeting) lists a set of purposes and beliefs held in common by Evangelical Friends (www.efcer.org/7).

Children's Membership

During the Quietist period of Quaker history, when Quakers strove to maintain their distinctives by living apart from the larger society, more Quakers were born into the Religious Society than were convinced as adults. Children born and brought up as Quakers were given automatic membership status at their birth, giving rise to the description "birthright Friend."

As fewer Quakers are brought up Quaker, and as Quakers no longer live in largely Quaker communities, the idea of automatic membership has lost favor. Yearly meetings and sometimes different monthly meetings within yearly meetings differ in how they handle children's membership. Some still record birthright membership when both parents are members. Some allow children to be recorded as associate or junior members at the request of the parents when one or both are members. Others don't have any designation for membership for children. Associate members may be either transferred to full membership status at their request after they have reached an age of decision and are familiar with Friends' principles or they may go through the full process of becoming a member.

Meetings are often faced with the question of what to do when children who grew up in the meeting have moved away. When should they stop listing absent or former youth members? As with adult members who are no longer active, a good procedure is to first try to contact the individuals and find out if they are active among Friends elsewhere. The meeting may feel free to drop youth memberships from their rolls if there has been no contact for five years.

Applying for Membership

The Process

The formal process of becoming a member of a monthly meeting consists of writing a letter to the clerk, meeting with a clearness committee, and acceptance by the business meeting. In joining a monthly meeting, the person also becomes a member of the larger groups the monthly meeting belongs to: the regional meeting, if any; the yearly meeting; as well as the Religious Society of Friends or Friends Church.

Many books of Faith and Practice give guidance on applying for membership in a monthly meeting. Applicants for membership are instructed to address a letter to the monthly meeting stating why they feel drawn into the fellowship of the Religious Society of Friends, and indicating that they are in unity with its principles and testimonies. In some meetings, letters go to the clerk, while in others, they go to Ministry and Counsel.

Though there are variations regarding whether certain actions are taken by Ministry and Counsel or the business meeting, the following steps outline the actions to be taken when responding to an application letter. The exact sequence of events varies depending on when the application letter arrives, when business meetings are held, when Ministry and Counsel meets, and when the clearness committee meets and reports back.

Initial response

- The clerk or a member of Ministry and Counsel lets the applicant know that the letter has been received and explains what the rest of the process is.
- The person's application for membership is announced in business meeting. The letter of application is read aloud.

Clearness process

- A clearness committee is set up. If no further action has taken place by the next business meeting, report that a clearness committee composed of Friends A, B, C, etc., has been set up.
- The convener of the clearness committee schedules a meeting. Traditionally, the meeting is held in the applicant's home, which works well, as one learns a lot about a person simply by being in their home.
- The convener of the clearness committee suggests appropriate readings and preparation to the applicant and members of the clearness committee. This often consists of reading pertinent sections of Faith and Practice along with considering a set of queries that suggest pertinent topics to discuss.
- The clearness committee meets with the applicant. This is a time both to inquire about the applicant and for the applicant to ask questions. In most situations, one meeting is sufficient, but more may be held if needed.

Reporting, decision, and follow up

- The clearness committee reports to business meeting or in some meetings to Ministry and Counsel, in which case Ministry and Counsel reports to the business meeting. In some meetings, the applicant is asked to leave the room while the matter is being considered (see below on "Having the Applicant Leave the Room"). The report from the clearness committee, either oral or written, should contain the following elements:
  —The names of those who served on the committee.
  —Where and when the meeting was held.
  —A brief description of the meeting's general tenor and possibly things shared by the applicant.

—Pertinent information on the applicant: religious background, other memberships, familiarity with Friends worship and business, etc.
—Issues taken into consideration—for instance, support from the applicant's family.
—The committee's recommendation.

- The business meeting comes to a decision.
- If the meeting approves membership, it arranges for an appropriate welcome of the new member.
- The recorder or statistician obtains the required information from the new member and adds the information to the meeting's records.

Having the Applicant Leave the Room

If applicants attend the business meeting where a decision is to be made, some meetings ask them to leave the room while the matter is discussed. Meetings should set a policy on this, apply it uniformly to all applicants, and let applicants know in advance what to expect. Some yearly meetings go further and ask any persons present who are not members to leave.

> When sensitive matters, such as membership, are before the meeting, non-members are usually asked to leave the room temporarily in order to protect the privacy of individuals and ensure that the deep discernment required is undertaken by experienced Friends. It is recognised that membership decisions are the responsibility of members.
>
> (Australia Yearly Meeting, "Quaker Business Method: The Practice of Group Discernment")

Guidelines for Appointing Members to a Clearness Committee

- For most meetings, it works best to have Ministry and Counsel set up the clearness committee. A seasoned Friend with experience serving on clearness committees for membership should be named as convener; this may be a member of Ministry and Counsel.

- Members of a clearness committee for membership should themselves be members of the meeting.
- Some members of the committee may be Friends requested by the applicant because they know and feel comfortable with them; those setting up the committee have no obligation to include any of the requested Friends, however.

The Clearness Meeting

> The visit should take place in an atmosphere of openness and caring so that both the committee members and the applicant feel comfortable in exploring fundamental questions of religious belief and practice and the responsibilities involved in membership of the Society.
>
> (Philadelphia Yearly Meeting *Faith and Practice,* Our Meeting Community, Membership)

The clearness process used when someone applies for membership presents an opportunity for deep sharing and building a relationship with the applicant. Members of the committee are advised to take their responsibilities seriously and to go deeply enough with applicants to be able to be clear about their suitability as members. Members of the clearness committee can share deeply of their own journeys and understandings.

Even in cases where applicants are longtime participants and there is no real question about whether they will be accepted, Friends should take the opportunity to explore applicants' spiritual journeys, current understandings of Quakerism, and senses of how to live as Quakers. Something is lost if the clearness meeting is simply an occasion for socializing and congratulations.

> This is a challenging but critically important task for our membership clearness committees. Too often, these committees are content to relate to a prospective member only on the . . . level of belonging and acceptance, when in reality the individual may be well beyond that in her own spiritual development. As a consequence, the prospective member, while wanting to feel that joining the meeting is a significant life event, can sometimes experience the clearness process as perfunctory and superficial. The meeting has then missed an important opportunity to help that new member toward growth.
>
> (Thomas Gates, *Members One of Another*, p. 37)

Possible Topics to Discuss

Several books of discipline contain lists of questions and topics to address during a clearness meeting, notably those of New England, Philadelphia, and Baltimore Yearly Meetings. The following are offered as suggestions. Not all the topics are pertinent to every applicant. A committee may wish to select some of these to discuss and may want to add some of their own.

- Ask about the spiritual journey of the applicant.
- How familiar is the applicant with Friends' beliefs and practices? Are there some in particular which attracted the applicant to Friends? Are there some he or she finds puzzling or disturbing?
- Discuss the applicant's familiarity with Friends decision making processes. Has the applicant attended meetings for business?
- Inquire as to other religious affiliations and discuss whether they are to be terminated or continued.
- Carefully explain the method and spirit in which Friends meetings for worship and for business are conducted, together with such responsibilities implied by membership as faithful attendance at meetings for worship and business, service on committees, a willingness to share a just portion of the financial support of the meeting, and participation in larger Friends' groups. Explain the relationship between the monthly, regional, and yearly meeting. Describe the range of beliefs present in the meeting and yearly meeting.
- Encourage the applicant to ask questions.

The Two Aspects of Clearness

There are two aspects to the clearness to be looked for when considering an application for membership:

- Is the applicant ready for membership?
- Is the meeting ready to accept this individual into membership?

It is essential that those desiring to join the meeting have regularly attended meetings for worship and have attended some meetings for business.[88] There are times when the committee

[88] Baltimore Yearly Meeting *Faith and Practice*, p. 49

discerns that an applicant does not know enough or has not been involved long enough to have an understanding of what joining the meeting means. In this situation, it is appropriate to recommend that the meeting postpone a decision. The committee should outline specific requirements or recommendations to help the applicant gain such an understanding. The meeting and the applicant should come to a mutual understanding of what will trigger a review of the application for membership. This is usually a length of time or the degree of progress reported by the applicant.

Sometimes an applicant is clear in understanding but is not willing to participate in Quaker process—that is, refuses to attend meetings for business, does not admit that being a member means that the meeting has any authority or responsibility for him or her, or otherwise appears to welcome the rights of members but not the responsibilities. In such a case, it is appropriate for the committee to recommend either that the applicant not be accepted into membership or to postpone the decision while the applicant is labored with. The reasons for such a recommendation should be stated truthfully, clearly, and lovingly. It may be better and easier on everyone's nerves to turn the individual down in a loving fashion than to hold out the hope of membership in return for good behavior, which hints at a lack of integrity. Such a recommendation needs to be presented to the business meeting with an attitude of loving concern for the applicant as well as for the meeting. It helps if the meeting has already considered issues around membership and come to a common understanding before a particular case arises. The reasons for turning down the application should be explicitly stated and explained to the applicant.

There may also be times when the applicant is ready for membership, but the meeting is not ready to accept the individual. There may be questions about the individual's past behavior, familiarity with the meeting, or other unresolved issues.

Recommendations

There are three possible recommendations the clearness committee can make:

- Accept the person into membership.
- Do not accept the person into membership.
- Postpone a decision until after certain requirements or suggestions have been met.

Usually, of course, applicants are accepted. In cases where the applicant is insufficiently familiar with Friends worship and business to have a clear understanding of what membership means, the committee should recommend postponing a decision with the understanding that particular actions will be taken by the applicant. This might be a course of reading, attending particular meeting events or conferences, or other activities designed to bring the applicant closer to Friends. It is best to either set a specific time interval for reviewing the application or make the applicant responsible for re-applying when he or she feels ready.

When an application is reviewed, substantial progress would indicate that the person may be ready for membership. The passage of time with no change on the part of the applicant would indicate that the person should not be accepted into membership. In such a case, it is best to recommend that the application be turned down while letting the applicant know that if things change he or she can apply again in the future.

If there have been previous problems with the individual's behavior, the committee may either postpone a decision or recommend that she or he not be taken into membership. Friends are advised not to accept into membership someone who is likely to be a problem. It is helpful to identify the particular behaviors that are objectionable. If the person is in need of therapy, the meeting can suggest that they seek it. This may strike some Friends as harsh, but it is many Friends' sorrowful experience that dealing firmly with a person who is a sexual predator or who consistently disrupts worship is better *for that person* than allowing continued destructive behavior. An applicant who has been turned down can apply again in the future.

Welcome

In most meetings, the membership process ends with some form of welcome to the new member. This could be a whole meeting gathering after regularly scheduled worship, two or three Friends getting together with the new member, or whatever works for the meeting and the new member. New members are often given a year's subscription to *Friends Journal* or *Quaker Life* or a copy of *Faith and Practice.*

Membership Procedures of Chapel Hill Meeting

Chapel Hill Meeting in North Carolina, which is affiliated with Piedmont Friends Fellowship, uses a more careful process than usual. Extra steps include:[89]

- Members of the clearness committee usually meet once or more without the applicant to clarify with one another their perceptions of clearness, the meaning of membership, and any concerns they might want to pursue in some depth. This is sometimes done just prior to the first meeting with the person requesting membership and also afterward to reflect with one another, share possible reservations, and consider any need for further meetings.
- The clearness committee will meet several times with the person requesting membership to explore the meaning of membership, the commitments involved, and any other issues which may seem relevant.
- The convener of the clearness committee is responsible for presenting a short biography of the new member for publication in the newsletter and introducing him or her to the next convenient meeting for worship. The clerk is responsible for ensuring that tokens of acceptance/recognition (e.g., subscription to *Friends Journal*) are presented to the new member.
- Members of both the clearness and welcoming committees generally have a continuing responsibility for keeping in touch with the new member, reflecting the meeting's ongoing concern for his or her welfare.

---

[89] Jan Greene and Marty Walton, *Fostering Vital Friends Meetings: Part II*

Ongoing Nurture of Members

Baltimore Yearly Meeting's *Faith and Practice* recommends that the meeting should arrange "for particular Friends to accept a continuing responsibility to embody the meeting's ongoing concern for the welfare of the new member."[90] A few meetings, like Chapel Hill, have formalized additional ways of seeing that new members get ongoing nurture and are offered opportunities to become knit into the community. In Sandy Spring Friends Meeting (Baltimore Yearly Meeting), new members are given a "Welcome and Nurture Committee," which is responsible for an initial welcoming visit, ongoing contact for an indefinite period of time, and seeing that the new member fills out information for the meeting's recorder.

Some ways of offering nurture to new members include:

- Discuss the responsibilities of membership, including financial support, committee membership, and meeting for business.
- Give them a subscription or invite them to subscribe to an appropriate Quaker magazine.
- Give them printed information about the meeting, such as a directory of members and attenders, a recent newsletter, a list of current committee members, and the meeting's budget.
- Give them newsletters from the yearly meeting and FGC, FUM, or EFCI.
- Give them a list of suggested introductory readings about Friends.
- Give them a copy of Faith and Practice.
- Make them aware of all the activities in the meeting: meetings for business, memorials, and weddings; religious education for children and adults; social gatherings such as Friendly Eights[91]; and monthly meeting committees.

---

90 Baltimore Yearly Meeting *Faith and Practice*, pp. 49-50

91 Friendly Eights are groups of (approximately) eight Friends formed from all those in the meeting who are interested to meet for a meal and fellowship, usually once a month for a year or during the school year.

- Make them aware of yearly meeting sessions and Quaker conferences and retreats.
- Make them aware of opportunities with Quaker organizations such as AFSC and FCNL.
- Make them aware of Quaker organizations they may wish to associate with such as the Fellowship of Friends of African Descent or the Fellowship of Quakers in the Arts.

Sojourning Membership

When Friends live away from their home meeting temporarily, they may ask their home meeting to write a minute requesting sojourning member status for them with the meeting they are attending. A different situation arises when a Friend moves and becomes active in a new meeting while maintaining membership in their "home" meeting. Some Friends feel bound to the meeting they left behind by a sense of loyalty, a sense of its being "home," and a wish to stay connected with it. Asking for sojourning member status at least acknowledges this reality of dual loyalties.

It is good practice for Friends who are ready to take on a responsible position in a new meeting—clerking a committee, serving as an officer, or the like—to transfer their membership there. Keeping connected to a former meeting can be as simple as subscribing to its newsletter.

When Members Move Away: Transferring Membership

It is recommended that members who move and can no longer participate in the life of a meeting look for a new meeting. When one is found, the Friends can request that their memberships be transferred to the new meeting. Here are the steps:

- The Friends send a letter to the meeting in which they hold membership asking that their memberships be transferred to the new meeting. It is helpful if they provide the correct name and mailing address for the new meeting.
- When the old meeting approves, the clerk issues a transfer

of membership, either using a certificate for that purpose or writing a letter to the new meeting.

- At the new meeting, Ministry and Counsel looks into the situation—are the new Friends attending meeting and becoming part of the meeting's life? Are there any problems?
- If the committee reports that it has found all to be well, the new meeting accepts the transfer at its next business meeting and records the Friends as members of that meeting.
- The new meeting notifies the old meeting that it has accepted the transfers. Only at this point does the old meeting remove the Friends from its membership rolls.
- It is good for the new meeting to welcome the new members in some fashion.

Couples or entire families can go through this process together using one letter of request. The membership status of children should first be discussed with the new meeting, as meetings differ on how they handle children's membership.

Transferred memberships are almost always accepted. An exception is when the Friend is unknown to the new meeting. If no one is aware that such a person has come among them, the committee handling the matter may either recommend that the transfer be rejected or may contact the home meeting and ask that one of their members contact the Friend and find out what is going on before the committee brings a recommendation to business meeting. Rarely, a new meeting may experience problems with a Friend who is requesting a transfer. The meeting has no obligation to accept the membership, but needs to enter into a careful process of discernment with the Friend and the home meeting so that whatever decision is made is done with a regard for Truth and everyone's dignity.

Terminating Membership

Resignation

If a member wishes to resign, she or he should write a letter to the meeting stating so. It is advised that the meeting, if possible, appoint a committee to visit in love and inquire into the cause.

If the Friend still desires to terminate membership, the request is brought to business meeting. If Friends concur, they issue a minute allowing the request and send a copy to the person.

Inactivity

It is a duty of a monthly meeting to keep in touch with its members. It is good practice for a meeting to send a letter once a year to members who live at a distance indicating the meeting's kindly interest and inquiring into their religious life and activities. Members who live locally but no longer participate in the life of the meeting and show no interest in it should be labored with by members of Ministry and Counsel or their equivalent. Some yearly meetings recommend that after a period of five years, meetings may drop inactive Friends from the list of members and, if possible, notify them of the action.

Disownment

History

Disownment began during the era of persecution in the late 1600s as a means of clarifying what actions were truly Quaker. If a person persistently engaged in behavior inappropriate for a Quaker and refused to make a public statement acknowledging the error of this conduct, Friends issued a statement to the effect that the offender should not be considered a Friend.

Disownment again became an issue in the mid-18th century, when standards of behavior suitable for Quakers were strictly enforced. Termination of membership by action of the monthly meeting might occur in response to continuing unacceptable behavior (also called "being read out of meeting" or "being put out of meeting"). Disowned Friends could continue to attend meeting for worship but were barred from business meetings, which at the time were open only to members. After the Civil War, among Orthodox Friends some members were disowned for incorrect belief rather than for unsuitable behavior. The practice of disownment almost died out among Friends in the latter half of the 1900s except among Conservative Friends.

There was a brief spark of interest when Richard Nixon was

President of the U.S. His home meeting, East Whittier Friends Church, received minutes from more than 200 meetings asking them to disown Nixon. East Whittier Friends declined. Nixon remained on their membership rolls.

Current Practice

In recent years, a few members have been disowned by their meetings when it became known that they had molested a child or for other unacceptable behavior. While it is very rare, if a meeting is in a position of considering reading a Friend out of meeting, it behooves the meeting to follow a careful process, as described below.

> Those whose conduct or publicly expressed views repeatedly deny Friends' principles should be labored with lovingly and patiently for as long as there is reasonable hope of restoring unity with the fellowship. No judgment should be placed hastily nor in the spirit of condemnation. Monthly meetings, however, have the authority to record a minute of disunity with the person's actions or in exceptional circumstances to terminate membership.
>
> After a formal complaint that a member's conduct is not in harmony with Friends' principles is made, approved and entered into the minutes of the monthly meeting, such member should not sit in business meetings until the case is settled. The member should be promptly notified of the charges in writing and given an opportunity to present his or her case to the meeting. The monthly meeting should assure itself that all possible steps to aid the member's return to unity with the meeting have been taken, remembering that all persons are subject to error and that love and forgiveness may restore unity. In all cases where the monthly meeting believes that terminating membership of an individual is the only remaining alternative, such member should be notified of the impending action, if possible, before final action is taken. If the final judgment of the meeting is disownment, a copy of the minute should be delivered to the individual along with notification of the right to appeal. One whose membership has been discontinued and who desires to be reinstated may be received into membership in accordance with the procedure for admitting new members.
>
> (Ohio Valley Yearly Meeting *Faith and Practice*, p. 46)

Disownment is an acknowledgement of a broken relationship between the individual and the meeting.

> [A monthly meeting may disown a member] when in the judgment of the monthly meeting further affiliation of a member is hurtful to the spiritual life of the meeting. Such disciplinary disownment is a most grave step and shall be taken only after prolonged prayer and loving attempt to remedy the situation.
>
> (North Carolina Yearly Meeting [Conservative] *Faith and Practice*, p. 25)

Marriage

History

In the early years of Quakerism, only marriages performed in the state church were recognized as legal. Quakers instead developed a marriage ceremony based in silent worship. As an attempt to provide a legal footing for the procedure, Friends developed a quasi-legal document, the Quaker marriage certificate. The elements of these early marriages—a meeting for worship; simple vows spoken directly by the bride and groom to one another with no intermediary or person to prompt them; and a certificate that described the persons and the proceeding in careful detail and signed by a number of witnesses—remain the format for traditional Quaker weddings today.

Tom Hamm describes the normal course of a marriage under the care of a meeting during Quietism:

> Until the late nineteenth century, in order to marry, Quaker couples had to have the approval of their monthly meeting. That process began when the couple appeared before both the men's and the women's monthly meetings and "gave in" their intention. Committees of men and women were then appointed to be sure that the couple were "clear" of commitments to others and parental consent; they did not judge whether they were "right" for each other. At the next monthly meeting, approval would be given and the couple "passed meeting" and were at liberty to marry, almost always at the conclusion of a midweek meeting for worship within the next month.
>
> (Thomas D. Hamm, *The Quakers in America*, p. 195)

The Quaker Wedding Ceremony

> The Friends marriage ceremony reflects our belief that the marriage contract is made by the couple themselves, completed and blessed by God.
>
> (Ohio Yearly Meeting *Faith and Practice*, p. 33)

Weddings may take place during a regularly scheduled meeting for worship, but are usually held at a specially appointed time. It is customary for as many members of the meeting as possible to be present; the event is open to all. Meeting members as well as family and friends of the couple attend. After those attending are seated, the oversight committee and the wedding company enter and take their seats. Usually, the couple sits on the front bench that faces the meeting, any attendants sit beside them, and the members of the oversight committee sit behind them. Often a member of the meeting will stand and explain the procedure which will follow for the benefit of family and guests unfamiliar with Quaker worship. The meeting then settles into worship. After an appropriate interval, the couple stand and take each other by the hand, facing each other. In turn, each recites to the other the vows, using words to this effect:

> In the presence of God, and before these our Friends, I take thee, _____, to be my [wife/husband/partner], promising, with divine assistance, to be unto thee a loving and faithful [husband/wife/partner], as long as we both shall live.

The declaration should be made in the language spoken generally in the place. It may also be given in another language when appropriate. If there are rings, they are exchanged. The couple resume their seats.

The Quaker wedding certificate on its table is placed before them by pre-arranged persons and the couple sign it. The entire certificate, including the signatures, is read aloud by the appointed person. The table and certificate are then moved aside.

The meeting settles again into worship, during which those moved to speak may do so, until the meeting is closed by the designated person.

The wedding company withdraws or forms a receiving line.

All those present sign the certificate under the supervision of a designated person, reserving particular spaces, if desired, for the signatures of family or members of the wedding party. Children able to write their names are encouraged to do so. Parents of small children may write those children's names.

Variations on the Vows

Slight changes in the wording used include:

- In the presence of God, and before these our Friends, I commit myself to you, ______, promising, with divine assistance, to be unto you loving and faithful, as long as we both shall live.
- Friends, I take this my friend [name] to be my [wife/husband], promising, through Divine assistance, to be unto [her/him] a loving and faithful [husband/wife], so long as we both on Earth shall live.

Any words agreeable to the couple and the committee of oversight can be used.

The Process of Getting Married Under the Care of a Meeting

> When a couple feels called into such a covenant relationship, they seek clearness with their meeting. When the meeting finds clearness in the couple, and clearness within the meeting to take their relationship under the care of the Meeting, a meeting for Worship is specially called in which the couple publicly affirm and celebrate their lifetime commitment to one another.
>
> (North Pacific Yearly Meeting *Faith and Practice*, p. 68)

Many books of Faith and Practice give guidance on marriage under the care of a monthly meeting. Though there are slight variations, the following steps are followed by most meetings.

- The couple writes a letter to the meeting, usually addressed to the clerk. Both sign the letter. It is expected that at least one is a member or regular attender of the meeting. If the couple has a wedding date in mind, it should be far enough in the future to allow the clearness process to occur without the pressure of time.

- The clerk or a member of Ministry and Counsel lets the couple know that the letter has been received and explains what the rest of the process is.
- A clearness committee is appointed. The convener of the clearness committee schedules the meeting for clearness and suggests appropriate readings and preparations to the applicants and members of the clearness committee. This often consists of reading pertinent sections of Faith and Practice along with considering a set of queries that address pertinent topics to discuss. A short book such as Tom Mullen's *A Very Good Marriage* may be recommended.
- The clearness committee meets with the couple in a spirit of loving concern.
- The clearness committee reports to the meeting. The report may be oral or written, and should include the following:
  —When the committee met with the couple (date and place).
  —A one-paragraph summary of the committee's experience at the meeting.
  —The committee's judgment of the readiness of the couple for marriage, including issues taken into consideration, for instance, support from family and friends for the marriage, legal requirements, or any existing children.
  —The relationship of the couple with the meeting—whether they are members of the Religious Society of Friends, how long they've been attending, how active they are.
  —Recommendation.
- The meeting makes a decision.

If the meeting approves taking the marriage under its care, it appoints an oversight or arrangements committee. Often, some of the members of this committee are suggested by the couple. In some places, the members of this committee are the same as those on the clearness committee. The committee works with the couple to ensure that the couple's desires are met regarding the ceremony and that it is accomplished with simplicity, dignity, and reverence. They make sure that legal requirements are met. Usually, members of the oversight committee sit on the bench behind the couple during the wedding. After the wedding, the oversight committee reports to the monthly meeting concerning the accomplishment of the marriage in good order.

The Marriage Clearness Meeting

> The committee should help the couple explore questions and areas of their relationship which they perhaps had not considered. Such a procedure is intended to enable the couple to understand as fully as possible the new relationship into which they may enter, as well as to identify their own expectations and capacities.
>
> (Ohio Valley Yearly Meeting *Faith and Practice*, p. 55)

> We are called to help the couple think through and envision what is involved in building a lasting and fulfilling relationship.
>
> (Elizabeth Watson, *Clearness for Marriage*, pp. 1-2)

In order to make a recommendation on behalf of the meeting, committee members should be members of the meeting. There are three aspects to the clearness to be looked for when considering an application for marriage under the care of the meeting:

- Is the couple clear of any prior commitments?
- Is the couple ready for marriage?
- Is the meeting ready to accept responsibility for this marriage? Questions committee members may wish to consider are:
- How long have the couple known each other? How well do they know each other?
- Do they know each others' families and friends? Are they compatible?
- Are there any objections to the marriage from family, friends, or existing children?
- Are they in general agreement on hot topics such as money, children, and the role of each partner within the marriage?
- Are they in agreement about the place of any existing children in their lives?
- How do they resolve conflicts? (If they say they don't have any, this may indicate an area for further exploration.)

If members of the committee have doubts about the couple's

readiness or find themselves uneasy with the couple's dynamics or possibilities of abuse or addiction, it may be appropriate to recommend to the couple that they work on the relationship before meeting again with the committee. The committee should identify the sources of concern and suggest appropriate actions such as attending counseling, discussing particular issues, or meeting each other's family and friends.

Sometimes a committee feels comfortable with a couple's readiness for marriage but there are questions about whether the meeting is ready to accept responsibility for this marriage. This may be because:

- The couple is new to Quakerism.
- The couple is new to the meeting.
- The couple is about to move away.
- The proposed wedding date does not allow enough time for the meeting to fulfill its responsibilities.

In this situation, the committee can explore with the couple whether holding a Quaker-style wedding would be satisfactory. This could be held in the meetinghouse in the traditional manner of Friends. The difference would be that a minister with the legal authority to perform marriages in that state might need to be present to fulfill the legal requirements. This can be done in an unobtrusive manner.

In the case of a couple with longstanding ties to Quakerism but not to the meeting they apply to, the committee can help the couple explore whether their previous meeting or meetings could take the marriage under their care. With the cooperation of a home meeting, the wedding could still take place in the new meeting's area, or it could be done under the joint care of the two meetings.

Questions to be Considered

The covenant of marriage is solemn in its obligation and fundamental in its social significance. Therefore, the couple considering marriage under the care of a Friends meeting should discuss honestly and frankly with each other the duties and responsibilities assumed in marriage and in establishing a home.

(Baltimore Yearly Meeting *Faith and Practice*, Appendix F)

The Human Relations Committee of Ohio Yearly Meeting (Conservative) issued a short pamphlet, *Growing in Marriage*, which presented "a few of the questions which should be thoughtfully answered individually and as a couple when marriage is being considered":

- What are your priorities is life?
- What are your basic values, goals and beliefs? Are they similar?
- What are your expectations of marriage? To what degree is your decision to marry based on: intense feelings? careful, thoughtful and prayerful consideration and mutual discussion? physical attraction? practical convenience? fulfilling the expectations of others? rebelling against the expectations of others?
- Do you both see marriage as a sacred and life-long relationship?
- Will the relationship allow and encourage individual as well as collective spiritual, intellectual and social growth?
- How do you plan to seek the Divine assistance you will invoke in your marriage vows?
- How well do you know yourself and your partner? Are current differences accepted?
- Do you try to be in touch with your partner's feelings and needs? Can you communicate your own? Are you able to be honest with each other?
- Are you able to ask for and give support during difficult periods?
- How do you resolve conflict? What do you do when you are angry?
- Is there a general willingness to share: possessions, friends, housework?
- What will your household roles be? Who makes financial and other major decisions? Will you need to balance two careers?

(Human Relations Committee, Ohio Yearly Meeting [Conservative], *Growing in Marriage*, pp. 1-2)

Baltimore Yearly Meeting's discipline has an extensive list of questions for the couple to consider before applying to the meeting for marriage under its care. Alternately, these could form the basis of a clearness meeting.[92] For a copy, see the Sample Forms.

Recommendations

There are three possible recommendations the clearness committee can make:

- Take the marriage under the care of the meeting (or jointly with another meeting).
- Do not take the marriage under the care of the meeting.
- Ask the couple to wait for a specified period of time and then re-apply.

In cases where the committee is doubtful of the viability of the relationship or when one or both of the couple are insufficiently familiar with Friends' worship and business, the committee might recommend postponing a decision. In one known case, a couple who were asked to wait six months realized by the end of that time that they shouldn't marry. Most couples, however, are unwilling to wait and turn elsewhere or ask for a Quaker-style wedding that is not under the care of the meeting.

Preparations, Responsibilities of the Couple, and the Oversight Committee

At some point, the oversight committee and the couple should go over:

- The details of the procedures for a Quaker wedding.
- The Quaker marriage certificate, its purpose, wording, and procurement.
- The wording of the vows they will exchange.
- The date and time of the wedding.
- Legal requirements: how to secure a marriage license and to meet any other legal requirements in a timely fashion.

[92] Baltimore Yearly Meeting *Faith and Practice*, Appendix F

Further suggestions for preparing for a wedding and the various responsibilities of the couple and the oversight committee can be found with the Sample Forms.

Meeting Responsibility to Sustain Marriages

> The meeting not only is asked to allow the wedding and see to its good order, but also to care for and share in the marriage and help in its success with advice and counsel.
>
> (Ohio Valley Yearly Meeting *Faith and Practice*, p. 54)

Meetings vary widely in whether and how they support marriages. One way of consciously supporting relationships within a meeting is through encouraging or enabling couples to participate in a couples enrichment workshop. FGC has developed a pool of Quaker leaders and sponsors workshops. Meetings interested in providing a workshop in their area can contact FGC.

Divorce

> The life of the meeting community should sustain and enrich marriages through worship, marriage and family programs, and counseling. In the event that a couple experiences marital difficulties or contemplates separation or divorce, the meeting should make available to them whatever of its resources may be helpful.
>
> (New England Yearly Meeting *Faith and Practice*, p. 257)

Quakers have generally held similar views on divorce as those with comparable theology in other denominations. Until the late 19th century, Quakers of all persuasions made divorce a ground for disownment. Well into the 20th century, they disapproved of divorce, and it was understood that no divorced person could be a recorded minister. Today, some Evangelical Friends still hold to older views; other Friends are more accepting of divorce. No yearly meeting makes divorce in itself a ground for loss of membership, but Pastoral Friends may not accept pastors who have been divorced. Most Liberal Friends are distressed by divorce and may feel called on to offer the support of the meeting to both parties.

Meetings can offer to set up a clearness committee to help a couple experiencing difficulties. The committee can counsel them in preserving the marriage or to help keep the divorce process as amicable as possible. Members of such a committee can also help the meeting from taking sides.

References

Glossary

> It is important for Friends to speak plainly and clearly concerning their faith and practice, but at times the use of traditional Quaker phrases and terms seems to make this somewhat difficult. As more people come into the Religious Society of Friends it is helpful to be clear about the words that have unique meaning to Friends.
>
> ("Seasoned Friends" Study Guide)

Quakers have developed an entire vocabulary to describe common experiences. This is a list of some of the terms used in Quaker practice. Some are only used by a particular branch of Friends or in a particular geographic region. Some are traditional but have fallen out of use. Some are new. Many have other meanings in the secular world.

There is more information on many of these words and phrases in the text. Please check the index or an appropriate section of the book.

Acting—An "acting clerk" or "acting recording clerk," etc., denotes a Friend who is filling in for the appointed person for this occasion.

Ad hoc—Latin: "to the purpose." An ad hoc committee is created for a particular short-term purpose, and the committee ceases to exist when its work is done.

Advancement—(1) In the context of a meeting: growth in numbers; growth in strength; development. (2) In the context of a nonprofit organization: raising money.

Advices—Principles for the guidance of the meeting and its members.

Affiliation—There are three large umbrella organizations that yearly meetings can affiliate with: Friends General Conference (primarily U.S. and Canada); Friends United Meeting; and

Evangelical Friends Church International. Yearly meetings in North America which are "unaffiliated" with any of these are called Independent.

Affirm—Following Jesus' directive, "Swear not at all" (Matthew 5:34), Quakers since earliest times have refused to swear on the Bible in court or take an oath of loyalty. Instead, they "affirm" their testimony. This is now accepted in U.S., Canadian, and British law, but many court officers aren't aware of it. Refusing to take oaths was one of the things that got early Friends thrown into jail frequently. They adopted this witness on two grounds: it implied a double standard of truth, while Quakers asserted that Christians should tell the truth under all circumstances; and it was based on Scripture.

After the manner of Friends—The way Quakers do things.

Allowed meeting—(1) A worship group that is under the care of a monthly meeting. Also called an Indulged Meeting. The terms "allowed" and "indulged" have mostly been replaced by "worship group." (2) Sometimes applied to Friends from various meetings who gather at a common vacation site, or to the occasional use of a historic Friends meetinghouse.

Alternatives to Violence Project (AVP)—A program begun in 1975 through the collaboration of prison inmates and Friends in New York Yearly Meeting. Originally a program for prisoners consisting of a series of experiential workshops that taught people how to create successful personal interactions and transform violent situations, it has been used successfully in many other settings. AVP is now a worldwide association of volunteer groups offering workshops in conflict resolution, responses to violence, and personal growth.

American Friends Service Committee (AFSC)—An organization formed in 1917 to train and equip Quaker conscientious objectors to perform war relief and reconstruction work in Europe during World War I. It currently does relief and social justice work around the world. While supported by several branches of Friends, it is also supported and partly staffed by non-Quakers.

Anchor Committee—Oversight committee for an individual

Friend's ongoing Spirit-led work or ministry. Also called a "committee for support and guidance" or other descriptive name.

Annual sessions—A yearly meeting's annual gathering to worship and conduct business.

Appointed meeting—A specially called meeting for worship, originally for the purpose of hearing a visiting minister. It is currently used to refer to an occasional meeting held in a meetinghouse that is usually closed.

Apology—In theology, a defense of a story or belief. Apologies have been part of the Christian tradition since at least the fourth century. Robert Barclay wrote a systematic explanation of Quaker beliefs which appeared in Latin in 1676 and in English in 1678, titled *An Apology for the True Christian Divinity Being an Explanation and Vindication of the Principles and Doctrines of the People Called Quakers*. It is referred to as Barclay's *Apology*.

Associate member—A status used by some meetings for children. In some places called a Junior Member.

Attender—One who attends and participates in meeting activities but has not become a member.

Baptism—Almost all Quakers reject water baptism along with other outward sacraments. Early Friends insisted that the only true baptism was that of the Holy Spirit. In defense of this position, they quoted John the Baptist: "I indeed baptize you with water unto repentance: but he that cometh after me is mightier than I, whose shoes I am not worthy to bear: he shall baptize you with the Holy Ghost, and with fire." (Matthew 3:11)

Barclay Press—Publishes books, pamphlets, religious education materials, and periodicals of interest to Evangelical Friends. Based in Newberg, Oregon.

Beanite—An independent branch of Quakers unintentionally started by Quaker ministers Joel and Hannah Bean in San José, California, in the 1880s. Also the three yearly meetings in the western U.S. that spring from that tradition: Pacific, North Pacific, and Intermountain (though Intermountain

YM is now affiliated with FGC).

Being eldered—See "eldering."

Ben Lomond—A Quaker retreat center in Ben Lomond, California, reporting to College Park Quarterly Meeting.

Birthright—Originally, a child accorded membership because the parents were Quaker. Almost all yearly meetings have now dropped automatic membership at birth, but Friends still use the term to refer to Friends who grew up in a Quaker family.

Book of Discipline—An earlier name for a book of Faith and Practice. Some yearly meetings still use the term, often in combination with "Faith and Practice."

Break meeting—Term used for ending a meeting for worship when a designated Friend shakes hands with a person next to him or her. Following this all shake hands with their neighbors.

A Brief Synopsis of the Principles and Testimonies of the Religious Society of Friends—A statement of faith adopted in 1912 by a representative body of Conservative yearly meetings, which was subsequently approved by all the constituent yearly meetings at the time: New England, Canada, Ohio, Western (in Indiana), Iowa, Kansas, and North Carolina. It runs to almost 7,000 words. The text can be found on the internet.

Britain Yearly Meeting—Until 1995, known as London Yearly Meeting. It includes Friends in Scotland, England, and Wales.

Branch—Quakers in North America experienced a series of schisms and separations between 1827 and 1956, resulting in separate bodies of Friends with differing theologies and practices. In addition to major branches of Friends, any number of small groups have broken off over the years. Some of these small groups have died out, while others continue. There are Liberal, Conservative, Pastoral, and Evangelical meetings in various places throughout the world.

Bring forward—To present an item of business or share a concern or suggestion.

Business meeting—See "meeting for business."

Business process—See "Quaker process."

Called meeting—A business meeting called to address a particular concern or item of business at a time other than the usual one. Also referred to as a "called session."

The Canadian Friend—The magazine of Canadian Yearly Meeting.

Canadian Friends Service Committee (CFSC)—A service organization of Canadian Yearly Meeting.

Casa de los Amigos—A center for peace and international understanding in Mexico City, Mexico.

Center or **Center down**—A process of stilling our bodies, minds, and spirits and focusing on the presence of God within.

Certificate of transfer—A traditional form or letter a monthly meeting issues to transfer a Friend's membership from one meeting to another. Also called a Certificate of Removal. Largely replaced among Liberal Friends with a less formal letter.

Certificate of removal—Same as "certificate of transfer."

Church—(1) The people of Christ rather than a building. (2) Some Pastoral Friends refer to their local congregation and building as a church rather than a meeting.

Christ Within—See "Inner Light."

Christ—(1) The eternal Light as presented in the beginning of the Gospel of John (1:6-9) and in Colossians 1:12. An early Quaker understanding of Christ as universal and timeless, who spoke to ancient peoples and continues to inform and guide those today who hear and follow, whether or not they are Christian or have ever heard of Jesus. Emphasized by Liberal Friends. (2) Jesus of Nazareth, the historical Messiah whose willing death and subsequent resurrection brought all people into a new covenant with God. Emphasized by Evangelical Friends.

Historical schisms among Friends were fomented in part from differing emphases on these understandings of Christ, which were for early Friends and some Friends today inseparable.

Clearness—A sense of rightness about a certain decision or action; confidence that an action is consistent with the Divine will.

Clearness committees—Clearness committees that are used for applications for marriage and membership assess applicants' clarity to join or be married under the care of the meeting as well as the committee's clarity in recommending or rejecting the application. Clearness committees to help individuals in personal discernment seek to help the person find clarity in understanding God's will.

Clerk—(1) *noun* The person who facilitates a meeting for business. Also called the presiding clerk or presiding officer. *Parallel secular terms:* chairman, president. (2) *verb* The act of guiding a business meeting.

Clerk, please—A stock phrase used in business meeting to notify the clerk that one feels that one has something to contribute. Some clerks or groups prefer Friends to raise a hand until acknowledged by the clerk.

Comfortable—Saying that one is comfortable signifies that one is in unity with the decision being proposed. See also Easy.

Collection—Among Conservative Friends, a gathering; the separate selves are "collected" into a body.

Communion—For Quakers, communion is being in communication with the Divine, especially in a meeting for worship.

Concern—An ethical issue one feels called by God to act on. It is distinct from a human care or worry.

Consensus—An acceptable agreement reached through cooperative discussion. For a period of time, some Friends used "consensus" to describe Quaker decision making process. Now called "sense of the meeting."

Conscientious objection—A principled refusal to participate in certain social or political practices. Early Friends had conscientious objections to taking oaths, paying tithes, and any action required by authorities that they believed to be unjust. It is commonly applied today to the refusal to undertake military service or pay war taxes.

Conscientious Objector (C.O.)—Shorthand for "conscientious objector to war." Someone who refuses to participate in war or related activities on grounds of conscience or in living according to divine will.

Conservative Friends—Quakers in the Wilburite tradition and others who have kept to many traditional quietist Quaker practices. Not a political description.

Continuing Revelation—The belief that God still speaks to people directly.

Convener—(1) Member of a committee, usually the first person named, who is asked to convene its first meeting. (2) A person in a worship group who helps organize when and where Friends meet and facilitates any other decisions the group makes. This person usually also serves as the contact person for communication with the monthly meeting the group is under the care of (if any) as well as other Quaker bodies.

Convicted—A strong sense of the wrongness of one's actions and way of life. Used by early Friends to describe their initial encounters with the Inner Light.

Convinced—Having accepted a new truth.

Convinced Friend—A convert to Quakerism.

Co-opt—Some committees are authorized to recruit others to serve on the committee without going through the usual nominating process. Co-opting may be temporary or for a given term of office.

Corporate—Of the meeting as a whole.

Corporate Leading—Divine guidance received by a group or meeting.

Covered Meeting—A meeting in which those present sense real spiritual power and influence. Also called a gathered meeting, though Conservative Friends make a distinction between the two.

Creaturely Activity—*archaic* Activity outside of true spirituality; worldly.

Discernment—Coming to identify the Truth by prayerfully sifting through one's impressions while listening for Divine guidance.

Discipline—Until the 20th century, the common term for the body of rules and customs by which Friends governed their meetings and lives and the book in which they were written down. The book is now more commonly called Faith and Practice.

Disownment—An acknowledgement of an existing state of broken relationship between an individual and the worshipping community in which the meeting terminates the individual's membership.

Divine guidance—Promptings from the Spirit to an individual or group that guide their actions or decisions. Quakers are to seek divine guidance in all their doings.

Earlham—(1) Home of the Gurney family near Norwich in East Anglia, England. (2) A Quaker college in Richmond, Indiana, established in 1859.

Earlham School of Religion (ESR)—A Quaker seminary in Richmond, Indiana, associated with Earlham College. It serves all branches of Friends, though draws its students primarily from FUM meetings.

Easy—Saying one is easy or that one feels easy signifies that one is in unity with the decision being proposed.

Elders—Friends of any age with gifts of spiritual nurture. In meetings where elders are named, they have care for the meeting for worship and the spiritual life of the meeting. In meetings where they are not formally recognized, the term is used to refer to spiritually sensitive Friends who name and foster gifts and nurture the spiritual growth of others.

Eldering—(1) The exercise of spiritual leadership either to support and encourage members or attenders in their ministry or to question or discourage an individual whose behavior is deemed inappropriate. Eldering should always be grounded in love and concern. (2) For much of the 20th century, "being eldered" had the negative connotation of being admonished or criticized.

Endorsing a travel minute—An endorsement is a note about a visit from a traveling Friend. Travel minutes are usually endorsed by the clerk of each group with which the Friend meets.

Epistle—A letter from a yearly meeting or other body of Friends to other bodies of Friends. Such letters are sent from a Friends meeting, organization, or gathering to testify to God's work in their midst. Typically, yearly meetings issue an epistle "to Friends everywhere" at their annual sessions, though in fact these may be sent only to Friends in the same branch.

Evangelical Friends—(1) Among Friends worldwide, most would consider themselves to be evangelical; that is, they seek to spread the Christian Gospel. Pastoral Friends are generally evangelical. (2) A branch of Friends whose central organization is Evangelical Friends Church International (EFCI) (previously known as Evangelical Friends International or EFI, and before that as Evangelical Friends Alliance or EFA).

Ex officio—Latin for "by virtue of official position." To serve on a committee ex officio means that whoever holds a particular office is automatically a member of the committee. For instance, treasurers are ex officio members of Finance Committees.

Exercise—1) A minute of exercise is one that states where the meeting is at a given moment when there is as yet no clarity to act. 2) *mostly archaic* A deep concern which a person feels under compulsion of the Spirit to bring to a meeting for worship or business and the subsequent exploration of the concern. 3) Historically in Philadelphia Yearly Meeting and other places, a written summary of vocal ministry and spiritual concerns expressed during yearly meeting sessions was called a minute of exercise. More recently in Philadelphia Yearly Meeting, it is used to refer to an expression of a clerk's insights and concerns at the close of any meeting for business. Some yearly meetings record the exercise of the Spirit (vocal ministry) during annual sessions.

Exercises—Vocal ministry and prayer in a meeting for worship or business.

Experiential Religion—A religion in which personal spiritual experience is the foundation for belief and practice. The word "experimental" was used by early Friends with this meaning. The experiential basis for Quakerism distinguishes it from most other religious bodies.

Facing Benches—In older Friends meetinghouses, rising tiers of benches face the body of the meeting. Traditionally, ministers and elders sat on the facing benches so if they spoke they might be more easily heard. Also called the gallery or the ministers' gallery. Many meetings now use different seating arrangements.

Faith and Practice—A book that includes the business practices, doctrine, advices, and queries of a yearly meeting; some include quotations from Friends over the centuries. Also called a "Book of Discipline".

Fellowship of Reconciliation (FOR)—An organization founded in 1914 by an interfaith group of European Christians to find ways to end war. A branch was founded in 1915 in the United States. Currently an interfaith and international movement with branches and groups in over 40 countries and on every continent. Many Quakers have been involved throughout its history.

FGC Bookstore—See QuakerBooks of FGC.

First Day—Sunday, the first day of the week; see "plain speech."

First-day school—Sunday School. Introduced among Friends in the mid-nineteenth century.

Five Years Meeting—An association of Orthodox yearly meetings started in 1902 that originally met every five years. In 1966, it began meeting every three years and changed its name to Friends United Meeting.

Friend speaks my mind—See "This Friend speaks my mind."

Friendly Adult Presence (FAP)—An adult who provides oversight and help in Quaker teen or youth activities.

The Friend—A weekly independent Quaker magazine published in London, England.

Friends—Members of the Religious Society of Friends. The term "Friends" or "Friends in the Truth" was used as early as 1652.

Friends Bulletin—See "*Western Friend.*"

Friends Church—(1) A pastoral meeting. (2) Evangelical Friends Church International.

Friends Committee on National Legislation (FCNL)—A national Quaker lobbying group in the United States founded in 1943. Its board represents many yearly meetings. It consults monthly meetings throughout the United States annually.

Friends Committee on Unity with Nature (FCUN)—The former name of Quaker Earthcare Witness (QEW).

Friends General Conference (FGC)—A service organization and fellowship for Liberal Friends mostly in the U.S. and Canada.

Friends for Lesbian, Gay, Bisexual, Transgender, and Queer Concerns (FLGBTQC)—A North American spiritual community of gay, bisexual, and otherly-gendered Friends. It sponsors two annual gatherings, one in midwinter and one at FGC's annual Gathering. Formerly FLGC.

Friends Journal—An independent monthly magazine based in Philadelphia. Commonly associated with FGC and other unprogrammed Friends, it has readership in every yearly meeting in North America and in forty-two other countries, serving Friends across the branches of Quakerism.

Friends meeting—(1) A monthly meeting. (2) Any regularly held meeting for worship.

Friends Service Council (FSC)—Former name for the service organization for British Friends. The FSC and Friends Peace and International Relations Committee merged in 1978 to form Quaker Peace and Service, which was renamed Quaker Peace and Social Witness in 2000.

Friends United Press—A book publisher run by FUM.

Friends United Meeting (FUM)—A worldwide confederation of yearly meetings that are mostly pastoral. The central offices are in Richmond, Indiana.

Friends World Committee for Consultation (FWCC)—An international organization that sponsors gatherings and encourages consultation among all the branches of Friends. It has regional offices throughout the world.

Gallery—(1) See Facing Benches. (2) Most 18th century meetinghouses in the U.S. were two stories high, and a second-story gallery was built around the three sides of the room that were not over the facing benches.

Gathered meeting—A meeting in which those present sense real spiritual power and influence. Also called a covered meeting, though Conservative Friends make a distinction between the two.

The Gathering—A weeklong conference held by FGC somewhere in the U.S. or Canada every summer during the week that includes the fourth of July. The location moves every year.

General meeting—(1) Until around 1900, a public gathering to present Quaker leaders and speakers to non-Friends. (2) A regional gathering. (3) In the U.S. in the late 19th century, a revival meeting. (4) A name for meetings of Friends which later came to be called Yearly Meetings.

Good order—The procedures for Friends business, witness, and personal interactions that are in line with divine order. Also called "right order" or "rightly ordered" or "gospel order."

Good practice—"It is good practice" means "it has been found to work well."

Gospel ministry—Vocal ministry that comes not from oneself, but through oneself from the Spirit.

Gospel Order—(1) Patterns of faithful living. Gospel Order unites the inward life of prayer and worship, the daily life of caring and accountability in the meeting community, and prophetic witness in the world. The exact patterns may change to fit new times or situations. Used widely by the first generation of Friends. The term is coming into renewed use. (2) Organizing the Church according to divine order, for instance, the common Quaker structure of monthly, regional, and yearly meetings.

Great Separation—The first major schism in U.S. Quakerism, it began in Philadelphia Yearly Meeting in 1827. Also called the Hicksite-Orthodox Separation.

Guidance—See "divine guidance."

Gurneyites—In the early 1840s, Orthodox Friends in the United States split between evangelicals who stood with Joseph John Gurney, a Quaker evangelist from England, and those who stood with John Wilbur, who wanted to maintain traditional Quakerism. Starting in the late 19th century, many Gurneyite Quakers adopted the use of paid pastors, planned sermons, hymns, and other common elements of other Protestant worship services. Gurneyites were the forerunners of most of FUM and all of EFCI.

Half year's meeting—A regional meeting that gathers twice a year. Also called half yearly meeting.

Hat honor—*archaic* The expectation in mid-1600s society that social inferiors would take their hat off to their superiors. In England, violation of this custom by Quaker men who believed that all were equal in the sight of God often led to imprisonment.

Head of meeting—*archaic* During Quietism, the oldest Friend who sat on the facing bench. When meeting for worship was concluded, he or she shook hands with a neighbor to break meeting.

Hedge—During the Quietist period, such features of Quaker practice as plain dress served to mark off Quaker society from the rest of the world and maintain a clear separation—as Friends sometimes put it, they formed a "hedge" around Quaker society. This was seen as a good thing, so that Quakers would not be tempted by the seeming delights of the larger society.

Hicksite-Orthodox Separation—See "Great Separation."

Hicksites—The smaller group to emerge from the separation of 1827–1828, characterized by theological openness and opposition to what they saw as Orthodox abuse of power. Named for Elias Hicks, a recorded minister from Long Island. See Great Separation.

Hold in the Light—Be a channel for God's healing love for an individual or group of people.

Holiness Friends—A flavor of Quakerism that arose in the first part of the 20th century, influenced by Wesleyan holiness revivals sweeping the U.S. Holiness doctrines were especially influential among California, Oregon, Kansas, Iowa, Indiana, New York, and North Carolina Friends.

Ibid.—Common abbreviation for ibidem, a Latin term meaning literally "in the same place." Used in footnotes and bibliographies to refer to the book, chapter, article, or page cited just before.

In the face of the meeting—During meeting for business, in front of everyone. One may read a report in the face of the meeting. To take minutes in the face of the meeting means to write and approve minutes as the business is conducted.

In one's own strength—Attempting to do work without divine input or power; the implication is that the work cannot be done without the Spirit.

Independent Meeting—(1) A monthly meeting that is not affiliated with a yearly meeting. (2) In the U.S., a yearly meeting that is not affiliated with any of the Quaker umbrella organizations—FUM, FGC, or EFCI. (3) A Beanite meeting.

Independent meeting movement—(1) Beanite Friends. (2) A movement which began in the U.S. in the 1920s and '30s and is still going strong. Independent meetings are formed by Friends originally from several yearly meetings or arise spontaneously from a group of people with no Quaker background. They are not set up by one particular monthly or yearly meeting, though they often come into formal relations with other meetings.

Indulged meeting—See "allowed meeting."

Inner Light—The direct, unmediated experience of the Divine. It shows us our motivations and true selves, corrects us, guides us, and leads us. It also gives us strength to act on its guidance. Also called the Inward Light, the Light Within, the Christ Within, the Guide, the Light of Christ, the Spirit, the Spirit of Truth, the Holy Spirit, the Seed, the Inward Teacher, that of God in every person, etc. Evangelical Friends see it as the influence of the Holy Spirit, showing our need for the Savior, Jesus Christ.

Integrity—One of the basic practical principles or testimonies of Friends. It calls Friends to both a wholeness and harmony of the various aspects of their lives and truthfulness in whatever they say and do.

Interim Meeting—Term in some yearly meetings for a representative meeting that conducts business on behalf of the yearly meeting between its annual sessions.

Inward Light—See "Inner Light."

Intervisitation—Visits between monthly meetings or yearly meetings. Some yearly meetings have set up programs to facilitate members and attenders of meetings visiting other meetings within the yearly meeting or to visit other yearly meetings.

Journal—An autobiographical record of a Friend's activities and spiritual journey. Often written anticipating that it would be published, so not a private diary. Writing a journal was traditional among Friends ministers for the first 200 or more years of the Religious Society's history, and they were often written after the fact. The best known are those by George Fox and John Woolman, but many others have been preserved and some of those have been published.

Junior member—See Associate member.

Labor with—An effort by one or more Friends to engage with others on a matter they disagree about in order to come to unity.

The Lamb's War—The English Civil War of 1642-49 brought out hopes among the winning Parliamentarians, Puritans, and workers, for a new social and church order, a "New England" under the direct rule of Christ. It used the imagery of Christ as a lamb in the Book of Revelation. As it became clear that human beings and government structures were only outwardly transformed, George Fox and James Naylor, whose best tract was called *The Lamb's War*, spoke of a worldwide conquest of humanity inwardly and outwardly by the Spirit. The Quaker movement and each Friend were enlisted in this struggle. Hence, "The Lamb's War" is identified with the struggle between good and evil.

Lay down—To discontinue or dissolve.

Lay over—To postpone a decision or item of business to a future business meeting.

Leading or Being led—An impulse from the Spirit that guides one to an act or decision.

Letter of introduction—A letter usually written by the clerk for a Friend who will be visiting other meetings in the course of his or her secular travels, but who is not traveling under a concern. Compare to Travel minute.

Liberal Friends—A general term for Friends who practice unprogrammed worship but are not part of the Conservative branch of Friends. (In this context, the terms "Liberal" and "Conservative" have theological and social, but not political, meanings.) Historically, Liberal Friends come out of the Hicksite, Beanite, or Independent meeting movement. Also called "liberal unprogrammed" or "FGC" Friends, whether or not they are actually affiliated with FGC.

Liberate—To set a Friend free for religious service such as traveling among Friends. This may include the meeting's taking on responsibility for the Friend's family or business or for financial support of their work. Also referred to as "releasing a Friend."

Lift up—To emphasize or make explicit a particular point or concern.

Light—A description for God/Christ/Spirit when experienced as giving clarity, revelation, and/or revealing the true state of things. Also referred to as the Word of God, the Way, the Truth, and the Life, the Eternal Christ, etc. See John 1:4-9 for the scriptural basis for the use of Light as a metaphor for Christ. Also called "Light of Christ." See also Inner Light.

Light within—See Inner Light.

Listen in tongues or **Listen under**—Seeking to discern what is "under" the words, emotions, and conflicts that others are expressing. Listening to the heart and intent of another person rather than just the language used. The assumption is that under these things is to be found the person's truth, ready to be uncovered and understood. "Listening in tongues" presents a parallel to the "speaking in tongues" that occurred at Pentecost. It is a relatively new term among Friends.

Listening meeting—See Threshing meeting.

Listening spirituality—The title of two books by Patricia Loring, and by extension an understanding of listening for the divine will as central to the practice of Friends.

London Yearly Meeting—London Yearly Meeting has met annually since 1668. In the cause of truth and inclusion, in 1995 it changed its name to Britain Yearly Meeting. It includes Friends in Scotland, England, and Wales.

Marry out of meeting—Marry a person who is not a member of the Religious Society of Friends. During the Quietist period, this was grounds for disownment.

Meeting—Used by itself, "meeting" refers to both an event, such as a business meeting or meeting for worship, and to an institution that others would call a church. It is also found in many phrases beginning with "meeting for . . ." such as "meeting for business" and "meeting for healing." Sometimes used with comical intent, such as "meeting for eating" (potluck) or "meeting for sleeping."

Meeting for business—An appointed gathering to make corporate decisions under the leading of the Spirit. Also called "monthly meeting," "business meeting," and "meeting for worship with attention to business." Some Friends object to this latter term as inaccurate (because their experience is that business meeting is not the same as worship) or simply as clumsy.

Meeting for healing—A gathering for Friends to bring God's Light to bear on the physical, spiritual, and/or psychological brokenness of participants or others, with the aim of allowing God to use Friends present as channels for healing. Usually led by one or more Friends with a gift for healing.

Meeting for sufferings—(1) A committee to support and care for members and their families who suffer because of their commitment to Friends principles (more in use in the early days of Quakerism). (2) Currently in Britain Yearly Meeting, Meeting for Sufferings is the name of a representative committee that acts in a deliberative and executive manner when the Yearly Meeting is not in session.

Meeting for worship—What other denominations call a church service. For unprogrammed Friends, it is a gathering of a group of individuals in quiet waiting upon the enlightening and empowering presence of the Divine. For Pastoral Friends, it may include hymns, a sermon, readings, and a collection. Most Pastoral Friends include a period of silent waiting on the Lord, called "open worship." Today, typically held for an hour on Sunday mornings. In earlier times, meetings for worship might last considerably longer—until the elders discerned that the group was done worshiping—and midweek worship was common.

Meetinghouse—For Friends, the church is the people of Christ rather than a building. Early Friends derisively called the Anglican church buildings of their day "steeplehouses." Friends, in common with others in the Puritan tradition, called their buildings "meetinghouses." The hallmark of a meetinghouse is extreme simplicity and the absence of any liturgical symbols.

Sometimes written as two words: meeting house.

A typical meetinghouse in the U.S. in the 1800s consisted of one large rectangular room. At the front was a ministers' gallery consisting of benches facing the rest of the room, often on a dais. The remaining benches were separated by a space or low wall. Men sat on one side, women on the other, and there were separate doors for men and women to enter the meeting room. Panels could be put into place to divide the room in two so that separate men's and women's business meetings could be held. They tended to be two stories high, but the second story consisted only of narrow galleries built around the three sides that were not over the ministers' gallery. A number of these buildings are still in use today.

Member—Someone who has formally joined a Friends meeting.

Memorial minute—A minute that contains a brief biography of a recently deceased Friend with special emphasis on his or her activities among Quakers.

Men's meeting—See Women's meeting.

Message—Words shared in meeting for worship. Hopefully, they are Divinely inspired. Also called "vocal ministry."

Mind the Light—*archaic* An admonition to attend to the Light Within for guidance in one's life. It urges both active obedience to divine leadings and careful nurturing of one's openness to the Light.

Minister—(1) *noun* All Friends; we are "ministers to one another." (2) *noun* A man or woman who has been recognized and recorded by a meeting as having a special gift of ministry, especially a gift of vocal ministry. (3) *noun* A person hired or functioning as a pastor of a Friends congregation. (4) *noun* A Friend who is called to travel under a concern. (5) *verb* To offer vocal ministry or other service.

Ministry—(1) Short-hand for "vocal ministry," that is, spoken messages during worship. (2) Any service that helps bring people closer to the Kingdom of God.

Minute—(1) *noun* A statement that captures the sense of the meeting — the decision, action, or witness taken by those at a given meeting for business. (2) *verb* To write a minute.

Minute of Exercise—See Exercise.

Minute of travel—See Travel minute.

Monthly meeting—(1) The basic Quaker business unit, which gathers monthly to conduct business; business meeting. (2) The people who make up the body of a monthly meeting for business.

Move forward—Make progress in understanding or reaching unity on an item in meeting for business.

Moved to speak—The feeling of being required by God to speak in a meeting for worship or business.

Nontheist—An umbrella term for a range of belief systems that reject traditional Christian concepts of God as "transcendent, personal, and supernatural." Came into use among Friends in the late 1900s.

Notion—*mostly archaic* A mistaken idea based on human reasoning or tradition; lacking spiritual insight.

On the floor of business meeting—During meeting for business. Often used to refer to unexpected actions, or matters that might otherwise have been brought up first in a committee or other body for seasoning.

Open worship—A period of traditional Quaker worship during which Friends may rise and speak, especially as one part of a programmed worship service.

Opening or Opened—Unexpected enlightenment or inspiration from God that reveals permanent or universal truths or meanings of Scripture. A common term in George Fox's writings describing an insight or revelation. See also Proceed as way opens.

Opportunity—During Quietism and still where traveling ministers visit, an occasion for the minister to speak in a public meeting, meet with local ministers and elders, visit members in their homes, or meet with a group of local Friends. These occasions provide an "opportunity" for the Spirit of God to move among the gathered group.

Orthodox—Early 19th century Friends in the U.S. who placed more emphasis on the authority of Scripture and the need for atonement than on direct experience of the Spirit. See

Great Separation.

Out of unity—*mostly archaic* Acting in a way not in harmony with Friends' principles and testimonies.

Overseer—Originally, a man or woman charged with reporting to monthly meetings violations of the discipline. In some unprogrammed yearly meetings today, a committee of overseers provides pastoral care in the meeting. Because of overtones of slavery, many meetings have dropped the term "overseer."

Pacifist—A person whose conscience or Divine leading renders him or her unable to participate in war or violence.

Pastor—The preferred term in Pastoral meetings for the minister.

Pastoral Meeting—A Quaker meeting that calls a Friend with spiritual gifts to live near the meeting and minister to it. The worship service centers on a sermon by the pastor. Usually the meeting provides financial support, though a few pastors are unpaid. Also called a Programmed Meeting.

Peace church—A Christian denomination that teaches that Jesus instructed his followers to forswear violence and killing. Christians were pacifists for the first three centuries, but when Constantine made Christianity the state religion of the Roman Empire, it became acceptable for Christians to enlist in the Roman military.

Like Quakers, other peace churches arose during the Protestant Reformation. The Mennonites and Church of the Brethren come out of the Anabaptist movement that arose in northern Europe in the 16th century, and various denominations with Anabaptist roots have pacifist tendencies or did at one time. The Amish, who broke off from the Mennonites, are pacifist but keep within their religious communities and do not engage with the outside world. Moravians in Europe are still a peace church. In the U.S. and Canada, Quakers, Mennonites, and Brethren have come together at various times to work together on peacebuilding.

Peace Testimony—The corporate commitment of Friends to pacifism and nonviolence.

Peaceable Kingdom—(1) "The wolf shall also dwell with the lamb, and the leopard shall lie down with the kid; and the calf and the young lion and the fatling together; and a little child shall lead them." Isaiah 11:6 (2) One of over 100 paintings by Quaker artist Edward Hicks (1780-1849) representing the Peaceable Kingdom, typically with a vignette of William Penn's treaty with the Indians in the background and animals, trees, and one or more children in the foreground.

Peculiar people—A self-description by early Friends. Originally, it meant "chosen" or "special," but it has continued to be used as a self-description meaning "strange" or "different."

Pendle Hill—(1) A hill in northern England from which George Fox envisioned "a great people to be gathered" in May of 1652. (2) A Quaker study center in Wallingford, Pennsylvania, near Philadelphia.

Permanent board—See Representative meeting.

Plain dress—The simple and unadorned garments traditionally worn by Friends as a witness to the equality of all people. They were originally the standard working clothes of the late 1600s, but over time other people's fashions changed and they became a distinctive costume. Wearing plain dress served into the 20th century as an outward symbol of being a Quaker. The wearing of plain dress has mostly died out among Friends except by some Conservative Friends, though in recent years some other Friends have felt called to this witness.

Plain speech or plain language—(1) Traditional Friends grammar using *thee*, *thy*, and *thine*. Originally, this was a witness to the equality of all people at a time when powerful people were addressed in the plural ("you"), but "thee" was used between equals. When English speakers began addressing everyone as "you," this practice lost its power as a witness, but remained in use into the 20th century as part of Friends tradition. It is still used among Conservative Friends in their minutes and reports, and by some Conservative Friends in their homes. Few use plain speech when speaking to non-Friends. In America, plain speech retained the grammar that was normal in Northern and Western England in the 17th century, such as "thee is," but was replaced in England by the biblical forms used in the south of England and by more educated leaders.

(2) Another characteristic of plain speech is calling the days of the week "First Day," "Second Day," etc., and calling the months "First Month," "Second Month," etc. These terms avoid the use of the names of pagan gods (Sun-god's Day, Moon-god's Day, the Month of Janus, etc.). This language continues to be used among Conservative Friends. The use of "First Day," etc., is also found today in some minutes of Quaker bodies that do not use these terms in speaking, and religious education for children is still widely referred to as First-day school.

(3) Friends traditionally have not used honorific titles such as Mr., Mrs., Dr., or Rev. as a testimony to equality, instead referring to people by their first and last names together, such as "Gertrude Brown."

Polity—Form of church government.

Popcorn meeting—A descriptive term for an unprogrammed meeting for worship in which many people pop up and speak, one after another, leaving insufficient time to consider what has been said.

Powell House—The retreat and conference center of New York Yearly Meeting.

Pre-business meeting—An innovation by Young Friends of North America, pre-business sessions were set up to go over upcoming business items with questions and answers and open discussion to help participants, many of whom were new each year, to gain an understanding of matters to be taken up formally during meetings for business.

Preparative meeting—(1) A group of Friends organized for worship and business under the care of a monthly meeting. In the U.S. and Canada, this usually refers to a body of Friends preparing to become a monthly meeting. (2) In Britain Yearly Meeting until recently, one of a group of meetings that gather weekly for worship and to "prepare" business to be brought before a joint business meeting. Since 2007, these have been called "local" meetings.

Presiding clerk—The person primarily responsible for facilitating a meeting for business. See Clerk.

Proceed as way opens—To begin a service or course of action in which only the first few steps can be undertaken as things currently stand, with the expectation that there will be a way around apparent barriers or guidance on how to proceed as one moves forward.

Process—See Quaker process.

Process minute—See Minute of exercise.

Programmed meeting—A meeting for worship with pre-planned elements, which may include a message, music, readings, a collection, etc., often conducted by a pastor. Traditionally it includes a period of open worship during which Friends from the body of the meeting may speak. Also called a pastoral meeting.

Quaker—The unofficial name of members of the Religious Society of Friends. There are two different stories of its origin. It was said by George Fox to have been first applied by Justice Bennet in 1650, "because I bade them tremble at the word of the Lord." (*Journal*, 1694 ed. p. 8). It was said by Robert Barclay to have been applied as a term of reproach because "sometimes the power of God will break forth into a whole meeting . . .. and thereby trembling and a motion of the body will be upon most if not upon all." (Mather, *Barclay in Brief*, p. 51) "Quaker" was in general use at the time as a term of derision for sects given to fits of shaking during religious fervor, much as the term "holy roller" is used today. The trembling in early Quaker meetings was often dramatic, but Friends found many prophets and others in the Bible who trembled, and eventually claimed the term "Quaker" as a nickname.

QuakerBooks of FGC—A bookstore run by Friends General Conference, which carries books and pamphlets published by FGC as well as many others of interest to Friends. The store can order any book they don't normally carry. It can be found online at www.quakerbooks.org.

Quaker Earthcare Witness (QEW)—A North American organization that focuses on issues of ecology and stewardship of the Earth; formerly Friends Committee on Unity with Nature (FCUN).

Quaker Hill—The location of the Quaker Hill Conference Center and the offices of FUM in Richmond, Indiana.

Quaker Life—A Quaker magazine published by FUM.

Quaker Monthly—A magazine published by Britain Yearly Meeting.

Quaker Peace and Social Witness—The current name for Canadian Yearly Meeting's service committee.

Quaker Press of FGC—A book and pamphlet publisher run by FGC.

Quaker process—Includes the practices typically used by Quakers to make corporate decisions, such as sense of the meeting and writing minutes, as well as typical ways the meeting community functions, such as the use of committees and clerks. The key is not the particular forms used but that they are undergirded by seeking God's will.

Quaker Quest—An outreach program developed by British Friends which has spread around the world. In North America, training and administration are done by FGC.

Quaker Star—The black and red star used unofficially as a symbol of Quaker service since the late 19th century, and officially adopted by the American Friends Service Committee in 1917. Since then it has been adopted by various Quaker organizations throughout the world. Each adopts a different graphic which appears in the center of the star, including several versions of a dove.

Quarterly meeting—Two or more monthly meetings in a geographic area that traditionally meet four times a year to conduct business. The area covered and the meetings within it are referred to as a "Quarter," for instance, Salem Quarter.

Queries—A set of questions based on Friends' practices and testimonies that are considered by meetings and individuals as a way of both guiding and examining individual and corporate lives and actions. As such, they are a means of self-examination. Traditionally, each yearly meeting develops a set of queries and advices and publishes them in its book of discipline (Faith and Practice). Not everything in the form of a question is a Query in this sense. See also Advices.

Quietism—In the period from approximately 1700 to 1826, Quakers functioned as a largely closed society with a distinctive culture. Plain dress and plain speech marked Quakers as separate from the rest of society. Friends strove to do as well as say nothing of spiritual importance without feeling it to be a leading by the Spirit. See also Hedge.

Raise up—Ask someone or a body of Friends to consider.

Read out of meeting—See Disownment.

Recorder—The person appointed by a meeting to maintain statistical information on the members of that meeting, including membership, births, deaths, and marriages. Called in some places a statistician.

Recording or **Recording a minister**—The recognition by a local or yearly meeting that an individual has a consistent, observable gift of vocal ministry. This person is given a minute or certificate of recording, normally after a process of clearness and a period of mentoring, which may involve study. This signifies to other Friends and to the world at large that this person's ministry is affirmed. Friends believe that ordination can only come from God; thus they record what God has ordained. Currently used mostly among Pastoral and Conservative meetings.

Recording clerk—The person appointed to take minutes at meetings for business.

Regional meeting—A group of monthly meetings within a geographic region. Regional meetings meet together at various intervals. Names such as "quarterly meeting" or "half yearly meeting" refer to the established intervals for specific regional meetings.

Released Friend—A Friend whose leading to carry out a particular course of action has met with approval from a meeting, which then releases the Friend from the usual obligations of a member. The meeting may also take on responsibility for the Friend's family or business or for financial support of his or her work to support the Friend in following the leading. Also referred to as a "liberated Friend."

Religious Society of Friends—The official name for Quakers. It includes all the branches of modern Quakerism except EFCI, which calls itself the Friends Church.

Representative meeting—A body made up partly of delegates or representatives from the constituent monthly meetings that conducts business on behalf of the yearly meeting between its annual sessions. In some yearly meetings, it is called an administrative council or permanent board.

Reunification—A movement that began in the 1920s to heal the Hicksite-Orthodox Schism (see Great Separation). It resulted in five unified yearly meetings, often with dual affiliation with FGC and FUM. The united yearly meetings are: Canadian, New York, New England, Baltimore, and Philadelphia.

Revival—In Christianity, a gathering intended to revive religious faith and bring about conversion, characterized by impassioned preaching and singing. Practiced by churches in the Evangelical Friends Church International branch of Quakerism.

Richmond Declaration of Faith—A statement of beliefs approved by a conference of Orthodox Friends in Richmond, Indiana, in September of 1887 in the hope that Orthodox Friends would come to unity on limiting pastoral ministry and excluding any need for physical "elements" in the sacraments. It has been widely accepted by many, but not all, Orthodox Friends, and has been an important document for Friends United Meeting. The full text runs close to 7,000 words (approximately 11 pages); it is often abbreviated when printed in books of discipline. Its orthodox stance on Scripture and Christology as well as the suspicion that it serves as a creed have made it a barrier to unity with non-FUM Quakers over the years. It is also from time to time a source of discord within FUM.

Right ordering—Doing things according to good order.

Right Sharing of World Resources (RSWR)—The RSWR mission is twofold: to work within the Religious Society of Friends to educate Quakers about the poverty of a life focused on materialism; and to share our economic wealth with partners who are burdened by economic poverty through financing small self-help projects in the developing world. Originally an agency of FWCC created during the Cold War, it became an independent program in 1999, and is headquartered in Richmond, Indiana.

Rightly held—Conducting business or holding worship according to continuing revelation and Friends accumulated wisdom as expressed in Quaker business procedures.

Rise of meeting—The end of a meeting for worship or business.

Sacrament—Most Christians believe that certain rites are outward and visible signs of inner spiritual grace. Friends believe in those personal inner spiritual experiences, but feel that the outward rituals may be empty. Rather than limiting sacraments to a select list, Friends feel that all of life's activities have sacred potential.

Schism—See Separation.

Set off—To establish a new meeting by dividing an existing one.

School of the Spirit—1) A ministry under the care of the Standing Committee on Worship and Care of Philadelphia Yearly Meeting. It offers retreats, workshops, and one- and two-year programs to deepen Friends' faithfulness. It has created a fellowship of those who have shared in its programs. 2) The traditional meetings of ministers and elders were sometimes referred to as a "school of the Spirit."

Scripture—The Bible.

Seasoned Friend—A Friend who has a deep understanding of Quaker process, lives a life of faith, and listens to and obeys the Inner Teacher.

Seasoning—Giving a matter attention over a period of time and by disparate Friends. Taking the time to seek the Light rather than moving into a matter hastily. Actively working to increase one's understanding and to discern God's will.

The Seed—(1) The Inner Light. (2) Isaac Penington, an early Friend, made a distinction between the Light and the Seed within us which responds to it and is within every person, but is buried until "ploughed up."

Seekers—Anyone searching for Truth. Historically, it referred to a group of people who were dissatisfied with the Church of

England of the mid-1600s and who waited upon God for new guidance. Many joined the Quaker movement and became "finders." Currently, it refers to people who are searching for spiritual truth and a faith community for whom Quakerism may have a strong appeal.

Semi-programmed meeting—A meeting that pre-plans some elements of its meeting for worship. It may be conducted by a pastor and may include a message, music, readings, etc. It also includes substantial periods of open worship based on silence during which Friends from the body of the meeting may speak. See also Programmed meeting.

Sense of the meeting—A decision that reflects what God wants, achieved through listening to the Spirit together during business meeting. Also called "unity. "

Separation—Schism; split. Quakers in the U.S. and Canada went through a number of splits between 1827 and 1956, leading to separate yearly meetings for the different groups, sometimes within the same geographic areas.

Settled—A meeting when the body of Friends has centered down.

Silent grace—Traditionally, Friends spend a short period of time before a meal in silent worship. Some hold hands around the table.

Silent worship—Shorthand for "worship held on the basis of silence." The worship is not expected to be entirely silent, as Friends may speak out of the silence as led by the Spirit. To emphasize that the basis of Friends' worship is not just a lack of noise, "stillness" may be a better description of the internal state desired in order to focus on that which is eternal rather than mental busy-ness.

Simplicity—(1) Living a life focused on that which is eternal. Moving toward simplicity involves getting rid of possessions or activities that distract one and incorporating into one's life things that support a life of obedience to the Spirit. (2) Living in a way that is ecologically sustainable, that is, limiting one's draw on natural resources and energy.

Sojourning Friends—Friends who are temporarily living in the vicinity of a monthly meeting other than where they hold membership who have received the status of "sojourning members." The Friends' financial responsibility and memberships remain with their home meeting.

Speak to one's condition—(1) Having someone accurately describe your spiritual state or mode of life, particularly when the other person doesn't know you. (2) The experience of receiving a message directly from God or through another person that helps with whatever you're struggling with.

Speak Truth to Power—The title of an AFSC pamphlet published in 1955 that proposed a new approach to the Cold War. The phrase came to Milton Mayer toward the end of the week in the summer of 1954 when the composing committee finished work on the document. At the time Mayer attributed the phrase to a 17th century Friend, but numerous searches have found no earlier use of the phrase. Over time, it has become almost a cliché. It is used far beyond Quaker circles, often by people who have no idea of its origins.

SPICE(S)—An acronym for a list of modern testimonies: Simplicity, Peace, Integrity, Community, Equality, (Stewardship).

Spirit—Used alone, it is a way of referring to the Divine while avoiding traditional terms. Used with "the," as in "the Spirit," it is a synonym for terms such as Spirit of God, Holy Spirit, and Holy Ghost.

Split—See Separation.

Stand aside—An action taken by an individual who has genuine reservations about a particular decision by the meeting, but who also recognizes that the decision is clearly supported by the weight of the meeting. The action of standing aside allows the meeting to reach unity.

Stand in the Light—To expose oneself to God's searching Light, which may reveal both the good and the bad within one. To place oneself in the Light that both reveals and heals.

Stand in the way—A position taken by someone not in unity with a proposed action, and who is not willing to stand aside. When this happens, it is the responsibility of the meeting to discern whether the Friend is acting from a Spirit-led place. The meeting then decides whether to leave things as they are, to postpone the decision, or to override the dissenting member.

State of the meeting—An annual report of the spiritual condition of a monthly meeting sent to the regional meeting and from the regional meeting to the yearly meeting (or directly to the yearly meeting).

State of the society—A report of the spiritual condition of a yearly meeting or a summary of the reports from the individual meetings. Often encapsulated in the yearly meeting's epistle. See also State of the meeting.

Statistician—See Recorder.

Steeplehouse—See Church.

Step aside—When a clerk (or recording clerk, reading clerk, or assistant clerk) leaves the clerk's table to join the general body of the meeting. This is usually done because an item of business he or she is personally concerned with is before the meeting.

Stop or **Stop in the mind**—An expression Friends use to explain that they cannot follow a course of action or approve a decision. More of a gut feeling than something fully thought out, so the Friend is unable at the time to verbalize why he or she feels uncomfortable. The stop is understood to come from divine guidance.

Sufferings—(1) When a member's commitment to Quaker principles results in imprisonment or other form of hardship for themselves and/or their family. Traditionally when this happened, meetings named a Committee for Sufferings to serve as advisors and to make sure physical, emotional, and spiritual needs were met. This might mean taking on the care of a family, giving public support to the witness, or simply helping the individual to clarify priorities. (2) In Britain Yearly Meeting, Meeting for Sufferings has evolved over time into a standing representative body entrusted with the care of the business of the Yearly Meeting when it is not in session. It began as the first regular standing committee of London Yearly Meeting after the Meeting of Ministers and Elders.

Swarthmoor or **Swarthmore**—Swarthmoor Hall was the home of Judge and Margaret Fell in Ulverston, Lancashire, England, which was a center for early Friends. Quakers established Swarthmore College, named after the Fells' home, in 1869 near Philadelphia, Pennsylvania.

Tender—Caring, sensitive, earnestly seeking for truth, open to God's leading. In Fox's writing, the word "tender" was used with the connotation of being receptive to the Light and power of God.

Test—To bring both rational thought and the Spirit's guidance to bear on discerning whether a particular course of action is in line with the divine will.

Testimony—A guiding principle of conduct for Friends that is shared by members of the Society of Friends. There is no official list of Friends' current testimonies, but one widely-accepted list includes Simplicity, Peace, Integrity, Community, and Equality (SPICE).

That of God in everyone—An expression derived from a letter George Fox wrote to Friends from Launceston prison in 1656: "Be patterns, be examples in all countries, places, islands, nations, wherever you come; that your life and conduct may preach among all sorts of people, and to them. Then you will come to walk cheerfully over the world, answering that of God in every one; whereby in them ye may be a blessing, and make the witness of God in them to bless you: then to the Lord God you shall be a sweet savour, and a blessing."

Among Liberal Friends, the phrase is often taken out of its original context and turned into a statement: "there is that of God in everyone," which is often cited as a core Quaker belief. Friends expect to look for and appeal to that divine spark within another person. Some Friends take it to mean that people are inherently good. A better understanding is that "that of God within" makes communication with the divine possible, but many people never act on that possibility. See also Inner Light.

This Friend speaks my mind—A shorthand phrase signifying that one is in agreement with the Friend who just spoke to an item of business. Though quaint sounding, it is still used because it is useful during extended wrestling with an item of business to let the meeting know quickly and with a minimum of words that one is in agreement.

Threshing meeting, threshing session, or listening meeting—A meeting held to consider in depth a controversial issue. At such a meeting all points of view are heard, but no decision is made.

Travel minute or **traveling minute**—A statement of endorsement a meeting may give to a member who has a concern to visit other meetings and Friends groups. It establishes the good standing of the Friend and indicates the affectionate interest of the meeting in the various meetings being visited by the member. This is distinct from a letter of introduction.

Traveling in the ministry or **traveling ministry**—A visiting ministry. Throughout our history, Friends have recognized both women and men who felt called to travel and minister.

Truth—With a capital T, Truth is used among Friends to refer to the revealed will of God, which gives us ultimate truth insofar as humans can understand.

Unable to unite—The position taken by someone who feels strongly that the group is in error in its proposed action and does not feel clear to stand aside. When this happens, the meeting needs to discern whether to wait for the Friend, because it senses that the Friend has a truth it should hear, or if it senses that there is unity.

Unaffiliated—(1) A monthly meeting that is not affiliated with a yearly meeting. (2) In the U.S., a yearly meeting that is not affiliated with any of the three large umbrella organizations: FGC, FUM, and EFCI.

Under the care of—An activity, program, or event for which a meeting takes responsibility and to which it gives oversight, such as a marriage, a preparative meeting, or a school.

Under the weight of—A sense of burden associated with discerning and acting on the divine will. Often used in the context that one is "under the weight of a concern."

United meeting—See Reunification.

United Society of Friends Women International (USFWI)—An organization closely tied to FUM, founded in 1882 as the

Women's Missionary Union of Friends in America.

Unity—Synonymous with "sense of the meeting."

Unprogrammed meeting—A Quaker meeting in which worship is based on silent, expectant waiting for guidance from God. Individuals may be led to give vocal ministry.

Valiant Sixty—Fifty-four men and twelve women who went out to spread the Quaker message beginning about 1654. They actually numbered sixty-six. Most of them were young people.

Visitation—Formal visiting among Friends for any one of several purposes.

Visiting Friend—A Friend traveling in the ministry.

Vocal ministry—Words shared in a meeting for worship. Ideally, they come from the Spirit. Also called messages.

Wait upon the Lord—Actively seek and attend to God's will.

Waiting worship—Unprogrammed worship.

Way forward—Discerning a position around which a group can unite and proceed in faithfulness.

Wear it as long as thou canst—Legendary response of George Fox to William Penn when asked whether he should continue to wear his sword, a usual article of dress for gentlemen at the time. It implies that one should change one's behavior only when led by God, rather than from social pressure.

Weight—Spiritual maturity and experience that influences others.

Weighty Friend—An informal term for an influential or highly respected Friend whose life and understanding have proven valuable to the point where they are heard with keen attention.

Western Friend—The official publication of Pacific, North Pacific, and Intermountain Yearly Meetings in the U.S. Formerly *Friends Bulletin*.

Wilburites—In the early 1840s, Orthodox Friends in the U.S. split between evangelicals who stood with Joseph John Gurney, a Quaker evangelist from England, and those who stood with John Wilbur of Rhode Island, who wanted to maintain quietist Quakerism. Over the next several decades, a number of Wilburite-Gurneyite separations occurred. Today's Conservative Friends are considered to be Wilburite because they share common practices even where there are no historic ties to Wilburites.

William Penn House—A Quaker hospitality center on Capitol Hill in Washington, DC. It runs workshops and retreats, houses overnight guests, and offers communal housing.

Witness—(1) One who testifies to or gives evidence of religious beliefs and convictions. (2) The words or actions of a person so testifying. See Testimonies.

Women's meeting—The first Friends meetings for business were made up of men only, but by 1656 women's business meetings began to appear. In 1671, Fox urged all meetings to set up business meetings for women as well as for men. Eventually, women participated at all levels. For Friends to act on any matter of business or doctrine, the unity of both men's and women's meetings was required. Women's business meetings provided an opportunity for women to take on leadership roles. Men's and women's business meetings merged toward the end of the 19th century when it was felt that separate leadership opportunities for women were no longer needed. At the time of the feminist movement in North America in the 1960-70s, YFNA set up separate pre-business meetings for men and women as a way of keeping men from dominating the sessions. Eventually, a third "mixed" pre-business meeting was added for those who objected to the separate meetings.

Woodbrooke—A Quaker study and retreat center in Birmingham, England.

Woolman Hill—A Quaker retreat center in rural western Massachusetts.

Worldly—Having to do with non-spiritual values. Originally referred to non-Quaker values. In current use among Conservative Friends, but archaic elsewhere.

Worship group—A group convened to worship regularly after the manner of Friends but with no or only minimal responsibilities for business.

Worship on the basis of silence—See Silent worship.

Worship sharing—A small group exercise during which those present share their experiences or thoughts on a particular topic, hearing from all who wish to speak and focusing on listening deeply to one another without discussion.

Yearly meeting—(1) An association of monthly and regional meetings within a geographic region. The yearly meeting gathers once a year for worship and business. (2) A yearly meeting's annual sessions. (3) The body of Friends who make up a yearly meeting.

Young Adult Friend (YAF)—A young adult who is an active participant among Friends. The age range varies, but is usually around 18 to 30.

Young Friend—(1) Same as Young Adult Friend. (2) Sometimes refers to high school age young people.

Young Friends of North America (YFNA)—A vital movement by and for Friends under 30 years old that functioned between 1955 and 1984. It sponsored weeklong conferences, sporadic newsletters, and a number of "caravans" where young Friends traveled together in ministry to Quaker groups. It brought together young Friends from all the branches of Quakers in the U.S. and Canada. Although it is currently defunct, a reunion was held in 2007 in Barnesville, Ohio, and some individuals who are part of an emerging movement among young Friends look to the old YFNA for inspiration.

Organizations Commonly Referred to by their Acronyms

(also called the Quaker alphabet soup)

This list does not attempt to cover all Quaker organizations, but hopefully provides a short list of organizations commonly referred to by their acronyms. For an extensive list of Quaker organizations on the web, go to www.quaker.org and click on the link for Quaker organizations.

AFSC	American Friends Service Committee
AVP	Alternatives to Violence Project
CFSC	Canadian Friends Service Committee
EFCI, EFI, or EFA	Evangelical Friends Church International (formerly Evangelical Friends Internatioal, and before that Evangelical Friends Alliance)
FCNL	Friends Committee on National Legislation
FCUN	Friends Committee on Unity with Nature (now QEW)
FGC	Friends General Conference
FLGBTQC	Friends for Lesbian, Gay, Bisexual, Transgender, and Queer Concerns (formerly FLGC)
FOR	Fellowship of Reconciliation
FUM	Friends United Meeting
FWCC	Friends World Committee for Consultation
QEW	Quaker Earthcare Witness
QIC	Quaker Information Center

QUIP	Quakers United in Publications
RSOF	Religious Society Of Friends
RSWR	Right Sharing of World Resources
USFWI	United Society of Friends Women International
YFNA	Young Friends of North America (currently defunct)

Acronyms for Meetings

Every yearly meeting has its very own acronym. For instance:

NYYM	New York Yearly Meeting
PYM	Either Philadelphia Yearly Meeting or Pacific Yearly Meeting. Because of this ambiguity, Philadelphia YM is sometimes written as PHYM.
BYM	Baltimore Yearly Meeting; also Britain Yearly Meeting, but context usually makes clear which is meant.

Anything ending in **YM** is a yearly meeting.
Anything ending in **MM** is a monthly meeting.
Anything ending in **QM** is a quarterly meeting.
Anything ending in **PM** is a preparative meeting.
Anything ending in **WG** is a worship group.

Other Acronyms

FAP	Friendly Adult Presence
YAF	Young Adult Friend

Works Cited

Full bibliographic references for the books, articles, and web sites quoted or referred to, with some comments.

Books of Discipline (Faith and Practice)

A number of books of Discipline are available on the web. A directory can be found at www.quakerinfo.com/fandp.shtml (as of October 2010).

Baltimore Yearly Meeting: *Faith and Practice* of *Baltimore Yearly Meeting of the Religious Society of Friends*, 1988. 117 pages. Concise and well-written, it includes a set of extremely helpful appendices with sample letters as well as guidelines and queries for applying for membership and marriage. It also includes an index.

Britain Yearly Meeting: *Quaker Faith and Practice: The Book of Christian Discipline of the Yearly Meeting of the Religious Society of Friends (Quakers) in Britain*, 1994, third edition, with revisions and corrections approved 1995-2008.

Canadian Yearly Meeting: *Organization and Procedure, Canadian Yearly Meeting of The Religious Society of Friends*, 2004

Evangelical Friends Church Southwest: *Faith and Practice*, found on their website April, 2011 (www.friendschurchsw.org/faithpractice.html)

Freedom Friends Church: *Faith and Practice*, 2009. 67 pages. A fascinating, contemporary take from a Quaker church that describes itself as "Christ centered, Quaker, inclusive . . . semi-programmed, lightly pastoral, and socially progressive." Highly recommended.

Intermountain Yearly Meeting: *Faith and Practice of Intermountain Yearly Meeting*, 2006 version, found on the web at home.earthlink.net/~imym-faith-and-practice May 2008. They plan to revise it. Contains extensive sample forms.

Iowa Yearly Meeting of Friends (Conservative): *Discipline of Iowa Yearly Meeting of Friends (Conservative)*, 1974 version (currently being revised). Conservative Friends have kept many traditional Quaker business practices alive while they have been lost to many other unprogrammed Friends. Iowa's Discipline contains helpful descriptions and advice on a number of practices seldom addressed in other books of Faith and Practice.

New England Yearly Meeting: *Faith and Practice of New England Yearly Meeting of Friends*, 1985

New York Yearly Meeting *Faith and Practice: The Book of Discipline of New York Yearly Meeting*, 2001

North Carolina Yearly Meeting (Conservative): *Faith and Practice: Book of Discipline of the North Carolina Yearly Meeting (Conservative) of the Religious Society of Friends*, 1983

North Carolina Yearly Meeting (FUM): *Faith and Practice: Book of Discipline*, 2004

North Pacific Yearly Meeting: *Faith and Practice of North Pacific Yearly Meeting*, online version found at www.npym.org/2007/FnP/fnp_idx.htm March 2008, undergoing revision. Written in contemporary language, it contains much practical and wise advice.

Northwest Yearly Meeting (EFCI) *Faith and Practice*, 2003.

Ohio Yearly Meeting (Conservative): *The Book of Discipline of Ohio Yearly Meeting of the Religious Society of Friends*, 2001. Found on the web at ohioyearlymeeting.org/discipline.htm March 2008.

Ohio Valley Yearly Meeting: *Book of Discipline of the Ohio Valley Yearly Meeting: A Guide to Christian Faith and Practice*, 1978

Philadelphia Yearly Meeting: *Faith and Practice, Philadelphia Yearly Meeting of the Religious Society of Friends, A Book of Christian Discipline*, 2002

Southeastern Yearly Meeting: *Faith and Practice*, under revision, found online at www.seym.org/FandP.html, November 2009.

Western Yearly Meeting: *Faith and Practice of Western Yearly Meeting of Friends Church*, 2005

Wilmington Yearly Meeting: *Faith and Practice of Wilmington Yearly Meeting of the Religious Society of Friends (Book of Discipline)*, 2000

Other Books and Pamphlets

Abbott, Margery Post and Peggy Senger Parsons, ed., *Walk Worthy of Your Calling: Quakers and the Traveling Ministry*, Friends United Press, 2004. A collection of autobiographical stories of contemporary Quakers who have traveled in the ministry, understood broadly.

Australia Yearly Meeting, "Quaker Business Method: The Practice of Group Discernment," about 16 pages, found on the website for Australia Yearly Meeting (quakers.org.au) under "Publications/Pamphlets." For those with some experience of business meeting.

Barbour, Hugh, editor, *Margaret Fell Speaking*, Pendle Hill Pamphlet 206, 1976

Barbour, Hugh, *The Quakers in Puritan England*, New Haven, CT: Yale University Press, 1964

Benson, Lewis, "The Gospel Generates Moral and Fellowship Forming Power," published in *None Were So Clear*, ed. T.H. Wallace, 1996

Bieber, Nancy L., "The Spiritual Companions Group: A Design for Nurturing Small Groups for Spiritual Growth in Your Meeting," in *Companions along the Way: Spiritual Formation Within the Quaker Tradition*. Ed. Florence Ruth Kline with Marty Grundy. Philadelphia Yearly Meeting, 2000. 194 pp. The article is on the web at http://archive.pym.org/worship-and-care/s-f-program.htm as of July 2011.

Boyd, Arthur Meyer, "When Quakers Disagree," November 2010 *Friends Journal*, pp. 18-19

Brinton, Howard, *Guide to Quaker Practice*, Pendle Hill Pamphlet 20, 1955, 72 pages. Since its publication in 1943, this has been a standard guide for Liberal Quakers. With some revisions, it remains in print today.

Brown, Thomas S., *When Friends Attend to Business*, Philadelphia Yearly Meeting. Eight page pamphlet available through QuakerBooks. Also available online at pym.org/pm/comments.php?id=1121_0_178_0_C (or pym.org, Resources, Publications, Pamphlets Online).

Cazden, Elizabeth, *Fellowships, Conferences, and Associations: The Limits of the Liberal Quaker Reinvention of Meeting Polity*, Beacon Hill Friends House #1001, 2004, 36 pages. A critique of common practice among Liberal Friends from a historical perspective.

Claremont Friends, *Fellowship in Depth and Spiritual Renewal through "Creative Listening": Suggestions for Leaders of Group Dialogs Derived from the Experience of Claremont, California, Friends*, self-published by Claremont Friends Meeting, 16 pages.

"Community Nurture of Members' Faithfulness to the Leadings of the Spirit," presented to Central Philadelphia Meeting for Business September 2003 by an ad hoc committee

Cooper, Wilmer A., *A Living Faith: An Historical Study of Quaker Beliefs*, Friends United Press, 1990

Cronk, Sandra L., *Gospel Order: A Quaker Understanding of Faithful Church Community*, Pendle Hill Pamphlet #297, 1991. 48 pages.

Dorrance, Christopher A., ed., *Reflections from a Friends Education,* Friends Council on Education, 1982.

DuBois, Rachel Davis, *Deepening Quaker Faith and Practice through the Use of the Three-Session Quaker Dialog*, issued by Friends United Press and sponsored by New York Yearly Meeting committees, FGC, FUM, and FWCC in 1976.

"The Epistle from the Elders at Balby, 1656, as in the copy in the Lancashire Records Office at Preston, from the papers of Marsden Monthly Meeting." Quaker Heritage Press online texts, found on the web at qhpress.org/texts/balby.html, November 2009.

Farrington, Debra K., *Hearing with the Heart: A Gentle Guide to Discerning God's Will For Your Life*, Jossey-Bass, 2003. 247 pages. Much helpful guidance on a practical level from a writer and retreat leader familiar with Friends.

Fendall, Lon, Jan Wood, and Bruce Bishop, *Practicing Discernment Together: Finding God's Way Forward in Decision Making*, Barclay Press, 2007, 146 pages. An excellent book from three seasoned Friends from the Pastoral tradition. Includes a very detailed description of what should happen in a meeting for business, thoughtful discourse on discernment, some checklists, and a selected bibliography.

Fox, George, *Autobiography [Journal]*, Christian Classics Ethereal Library (online at ccel.org/ccel)

Fox, George, Epistle 149 (1657)

Gates, Thomas, *Members One of Another: The Dynamics of Membership in Quaker Meeting*, Pendle Hill Pamphlet 371, 2004. 40 pages. A thoughtful and thought-provoking discussion of the meaning of membership and stages of growing into being a Quaker.

Grace, Eden, "An Introduction to Quaker Business Practice." Four page paper written for the World Council of Churches in 2001. Found at wcc-coe.org/wcc/who/damascuspost-03-e.html (November 2009). A concise explanation for non-Friends.

Greene, Jan and Marty Walton, *Fostering Vital Friends Meetings: Part II*. FGC. A compilation of 184 different resource materials, organized by topic, to accompany the handbook; available in a 3-ring binder. Also available on the "Quaker Library" part of FGC's website as individual articles or one downloadable PDF file at fgcquaker.org/library/fosteringmeetings (October 2008).

Griswold, Robert, *Creeds and Quakers: What's Belief Got To Do With It?* Pendle Hill Pamphlet 377, 2005. 35 pages. An examination of the basis of Quaker faith in experience of the Divine rather than belief about the Divine, and the pitfalls Friends sometimes fall into.

Haines, Deborah, "A Practical Mystic's Guide to Committee Clerking." An article published in *FGConnections*, Spring 2004, and available on the FGC website.

Haines, Deborah, *When You're the Only Friend in Town: Starting a New Friends Meeting*, by the Advancement and Outreach Committee of FGC, Deborah Haines, clerk. Quaker Press of FGC, 2005. 40 pages. Expanded edition includes materials that are also available for download on the web as "A Quaker

Toolbox" on FGC's Advancement and Outreach Committee's pages.

Hamm, Thomas D., *The Quakers in America*. Columbia University Press, 2003. 293 pages including a chronology of Quaker history, a short glossary, notes, an excellent list of resources for further study, and an index. An even-handed and historically precise account of all flavors of contemporary U.S. Quakers with explanatory history on how we got to be this way. Written for non-Quakers as well as Quakers. Highly recommended.

Hoffman, Jan, "Clearness Committees and Their Use in Personal Discernment," Twelfth Month Press, 1996.

Hoffman, Jan, "Comments on Corporate Discernment," from the *Summary Report of the Friends Consultation on Discernment, 1985*, Earlham School of Religion. Quaker Hill Conference Center, Richmond, Indiana, 1985.

Hoffman, Jan, "Words on Practical Aspects of Meeting for Business," from *Friends Consultation on Discernment*, Earlham School of Religion. Quaker Hill Conference Center, Richmond, Indiana, 1985.

Human Relations Committee, Ohio Yearly Meeting (Conservative), *Growing in Marriage*, 1984. A pithy eight-page pamphlet that covers both things to consider when contemplating marriage and topics and advice on maintaining a marriage. Highly recommended.

Humphries, Debbie, "Four Pillars of Meeting for Business," *Friends Journal,* September 2009, p. 25.

Hutchinson, Dorothy H., "Friends and Service." 1996. One of the pamphlets in the "Friends And" series. On the web at fgcquaker.org/library/welcome/fa-service.html or in pamphlet form from QuakerBooks of FGC.

Ingle, H. Larry, *Quakers in Conflict: The Hicksite Reformation*, Pendle Hill, 1998.

Jacobsen, Katharine, "Eldering as a Spiritual Gift," *The Conservative Friend*, Eighth Month 2007.

Kelly, Arlene, "Conflict in the Life of Our Meeting: Friends Peace Testimony at Work?" in *Friends Journal*, July 2008

Lacey, Paul A., "Leading and Being Led," Pendle Hill Pamphlet

264, 1985

Lacey, Paul A., "Quakers and the Use of Power," Pendle Hill Pamphlet 241, 1982. A provocative call to Friends to claim the power of God's Truth.

Lacey, Paul A., "Some Thoughts on Quaker Process" in *Fostering Vital Friends Meetings: Part II*, a compilation of resource materials to accompany the handbook written by Jan Greene and Marty Walton (see Greene, above).

Lacey, Paul A. and Bill Taber, "The Purpose of Meetings for Worship and for Business" in *Fostering Vital Friends Meetings: Part II*, a compilation of resource materials to accompany the handbook written by Jan Greene and Marty Walton (see Greene, above).

Loring, Patricia, *Spiritual Responsibility in the Meeting for Business*. Quaker Press. Four-page pamphlet. An excellent brief exposition of the grounding needed for Quaker process to work.

Loring, Patricia, *Listening Spirituality, Volume II: Corporate Spiritual Practice Among Friends*, Openings Press, 1999

Morley, Barry, *Beyond Consensus: Salvaging Sense of the Meeting*. Pendle Hill Pamphlet 307, 1993. 32 pages. An excellent essay on what's at the core of Quaker decision making. Highly recommended.

Nevin, Bruce, "Trouble Comes to Meeting," *Friends Journal*, July 2008.

"A Quaker Path: A Spiritual Journey from Visitor to Attender to Member," Membership Brochure Working Group, Western Quarterly Meeting, Philadelphia Yearly Meeting, 2002. Pamphlet.

"Report of the Ad Hoc Committee on Recognizing and Supporting Ministries," Chestnut Hill Friends Meeting, approved November, 2004, found on Chestnut Hill Meeting's web site under "Chestnut Hill Meeting minute on Ministries (2004)" at quaker.org/chestnuthill/potpouri.htm, January 2011.

"Seasoned Friends: A Two Session Study Guide for the Friends General Conference Traveling Ministries Program Paper on Seasoned Friends," 6/01/04

Seaver, Madge, "On Minutes of Exercise," in *Friends Bulletin*,

April, 1985

Selleck, George A., *Principles of the Quaker Business Meeting.* Friends United Press, 1986. 14 pages. A pithy and deeply insightful pamphlet. Highly recommended.

Selleck, George A., *Quakers in Boston, 1656–1964: Three Centuries of Friends in Boston and Cambridge*, Friends Meeting at Cambridge, 1976. 349 pages.

Smith, John, in *Friends Understanding of the Word of God*, Ohio Yearly Meeting.

Smith, Susan, "Friends Business Meeting, as Conservative Friends Experience It," a presentation made on June 28, 2007, to QuakerCamp at Stillwater. Six pages. Copies are probably available directly from Susan Smith, who is a former clerk of Ohio Yearly Meeting. A concise and well-written description of how Conservative Friends do business.

Taber, Frances, "Applying and Adapting the Tradition of Eldering for Today," a paper given as part of Ohio Yearly Meeting's Gathering on Eldering held in June of 1996. Printed in *The Conservative Friend* (Fall 1996), pp. 3-5, and as part of a pamphlet, "So that You Come Behind in No Gift: Ohio Yearly Meeting's Gathering on Eldering 6/20–22/1996" that also contains an overview of eldering by Susan Smith and its history by John Brady; available from Ohio Yearly Meeting.

Taber, William, Jr., "Friends Consultation on Discernment" reprinted as "The Purpose of Meetings for Worship and for Business" in *Fostering Vital Friends Meetings: Part II*, a compilation of resource materials to accompany the handbook written by Jan Greene and Marty Walton (see Greene, above).

Thomas, Charles F., ed., *The Church in Quaker Thought and Practice,* Faith and Life Movement, 1979, distributed by FWCC.

Vogel-Borne, Jonathan, "Traveling in the Ministry," paper written for Friends Meeting at Cambridge, 1987. Found on the web at fgcquaker.org/library/ministry/travelingintheministry.html, November 2008.

Wajda, Michael, *Expectant Listening: Finding God's Thread of Guidance*, Pendle Hill Pamphlet 388, 2007

Walton, Marty, *The Meeting Experience: Practicing Quakerism in*

Community, Canadian Quaker Pamphlet Series No. 45, 1997. 48 pages. Often challenging and always thought-provoking essays on issues critical to Quakers from a seasoned Friend. Extraordinary.

Watson, Elizabeth, *Clearness for Marriage*, published by Family Relations Committee, Philadelphia Yearly Meeting, based on a talk given on Oct. 4, 1980. 27-page pamphlet.

Watson, William Braasch, *Before Business Begins: Notes for Friends Meeting Recording Clerks and Recorders*, Mosher Book and Tract Committee of New England Yearly Meeting, 1996. 59 pages. Contains sample minutes for a variety of routine items, advice on writing minutes, and guidelines for keeping the meeting's records.

Weening, Hans, *Meeting the Spirit: An Introduction to Quaker Beliefs and Practices*, 1997, distributed by FWCC. 34 pages. A concise introduction to Quakerism packed with useful information. Refreshing in its outlook on worldwide Quakerism; the author is a member of Netherlands Yearly Meeting.

Whitmire, Catherine, *Plain Living: A Quaker Path to Simplicity*, Sorin Books, 2001. 192 pages. A collection of quotes, organized into categories based on living a focused life.

Willcuts, Jack L., "One in the Spirit," *Evangelical Friend* 10, September 1976

Willcuts, Jack L., *The Sense of the Meeting*, Barclay Press, 1992. A collection of editorials compiled from 27 years of editorials published in the *Northwest Friend* and *Evangelical Friend* magazines. They cover a wide variety of topics with humor and clear insight.

Willcuts, Jack L., *Why Friends are Friends: Some Quaker Core Convictions*, Barclay Press, 1984, 98 pages. Written from the perspective of a Friends missionary, pastor, superintendent, and magazine editor in the Friends Evangelical tradition, this book is a call to Evangelical Friends to return to those Quaker traditions that are authentic expressions of the Spirit, including Spirit-led worship, pacifism, and traditional Quaker business practices.

Wilson, Lloyd Lee, *Essays on the Quaker Vision of Gospel Order*,

Pendle Hill Publications, 1993.

"Words on Practical Aspects of Meeting for Business," from *Friends Consultation on Discernment.* Earlham School of Religion. Quaker Hill Conference Center, Richmond, Indiana, 1985.

Yeats, Liz, "Spiritual Friendships," in *Fostering Vital Friends Meetings: Part II* by Jan Greene and Marty Walton (see Greene, above).

Materials Consulted in Compiling the Glossary

Abbott, Margery Post and Peggy Senger Parsons, ed., *Walk Worthy of Your Calling: Quakers and the Traveling Ministry.* Friends United Press, 2004. Glossary.

Fendall, Lon, Jan Wood, and Bruce Bishop. *Practicing Discernment Together: Finding God's Way Forward in Decision Making,* Barclay Press, 2007. Glossary.

Handbook of the Religious Society of Friends, FWCC, 1952. Glossary.

Intermountain Yearly Meeting: *Faith and Practice of Intermountain Yearly Meeting,* 2006 version, found on the web at home.earthlink.net/~imym-faith-and-practice, January 2008. Glossary.

Iowa Yearly Meeting of Friends (Conservative): *Discipline of Iowa Yearly Meeting of Friends (Conservative),* 1974 version (currently being revised). Glossary.

Kimball, Beatrice and Joyce Holden, *Dictionary of Friends Terms,* Friends Faith and Life Curriculum, Friends United Press, 1983.

New York Yearly Meeting: *Faith and Practice: The Book of Discipline of New York Yearly Meeting,* 1998 revision. Glossary.

North Pacific Yearly Meeting: *Faith and Practice of North Pacific Yearly Meeting,* online version found at npym.org/FnP/fnp_idx.htm, March 2008. Glossary.

Ohio Valley Yearly Meeting: *Book of Discipline of the Ohio Valley Yearly Meeting: A Guide to Christian Faith and Practice,* 1978. Glossary.

Ohio Yearly Meeting (Conservative): *The Book of Discipline of Ohio Yearly Meeting of the Religious Society of Friends*, 2001. Found on the web at ohioyearlymeeting.org/discipline.htm, November 2008.

Philadelphia Yearly Meeting: *Faith and Practice*, Philadelphia Yearly Meeting 1997. Glossary.

Additional Resources on Quaker Process and Clerking

Books and Other Printed Materials

In addition to many of the works cited above, the following materials specifically address Quaker business process.

Birkel, Michael, *Silence and Witness: The Quaker Tradition*, Orbis 2004. 144 pages. An excellent history of Quaker spirituality written for non-Quakers.

Heathfield, Margaret, *Being Together: our corporate life in the Religious Society of Friends*, Quaker Home Service, 1994, 121 pages

Hickey, Damon D., *Unforeseen Joy: Serving a Friends Meeting as Recording Clerk*, North Carolina Yearly Meeting, 1987. 35 pages.

Sharman, Cecil W., *Servant of the Meeting*, Quaker Home Service, 1983. 47 pages.

Sheeran, Michael J., *Beyond Majority Rule*, Philadelphia Yearly Meeting, 1983. 153 pages.

Stanfield, David O., *A Handbook for the Presiding Clerk*, North Carolina Yearly Meeting, 1989. 20 pages.

There are many other good things to read. The author has found the staff at QuakerBooks of FGC to be knowledgeable and helpful in suggesting readings in areas of interest to the inquirer. Lists of Quaker books can also be found on the web. From Quaker.org's home page, scroll down to "Introductory Items," then click on "Joel Gazis-Sax's book list." Or check out

FGC's website, especially under "Resources for Individuals" in the "Advancement and Outreach" section.

Workshops

There is an outline for a two-hour workshop, "A Consideration of Our Quaker Business Process" by Jan Greene in *Fostering Vital Friends Meetings: Part II* by Jan Greene and Marty Walton (see reference in Works Cited). It is designed to help a meeting consider how well it is using Quaker business process.

Index

bold—topic covered in depth
number in italics—glossary entry
f—footnote
S—Sample forms, letters, minutes, and reports on the web at friendsjournal.org/quakerprocess

A

B

C

D

E

F

G

H

I

J

L

M

N

P

Q

R

S

T

U

Y

CPSIA information can be obtained at www.ICGtesting.com
Printed in the USA
BVOW010739210512

290210BV00005BA/1/P